The Contradictions of Freedom

The Contradictions of Freedom

Philosophical Essays on Simone de Beauvoir's *The Mandarins*

Edited by

Sally J. Scholz
and
Shannon M. Mussett

State University of New York Press

Published by
State University of New York Press, Albany

Printed in the United States of America

Cover photo courtesy of the National Archives, photo no. 111-SC-193785.
WWII # 106.
"This girl pays the penalty for having had personal relations with the Germans. Here, in the Montelimar area, France, French civilians shave her head as punishment." Smith, August 29, 1944.

For information, address State University of New York Press,
194 Washington Avenue, Suite 305, Albany, NY 12210-2384

Production by Diane Ganeles
Marketing by Anne M. Valentine

Library of Congress Cataloging-in-Publication Data

The contradictions of freedom : philosophical essays on Simone de Beauvoir's The mandarins / edited by Sally J. Scholz and Shannon M. Mussett.
p. cm.
Includes bibliographical references and index.
ISBN 0-7914-6559-4 (hardcover : alk. paper)—ISBN 0-7914-6560-8 (pbk. : alk. paper)
1. Beauvoir, Simone de, 1908– 2. Beauvoir, Simone de, 1908– Les Mandarins. I. Scholz, Sally J. II. Mussett, Shannon M.

B2430.B344C66 2005
843'.914—dc22

2004027812

10 9 8 7 6 5 4 3 2 1

Contents

Acknowledgments

This collection owes its greatest debt to Simone de Beauvoir. The novel that sparked the philosophical essays collected here is as timely now as it was fifty years ago when it was published.

The editors wish to acknowledge the generous support and assistance provided by Villanova University and Utah Valley State College. Villanova provided a summer research grant that greatly facilitated the writing of the introduction and the final production of the volume. Numerous colleagues inspired and encouraged us in this project, and Beauvoir scholars around the world expressed their eagerness to have such a volume published. Their support has been truly sustaining.

We are grateful for the invaluable research assistance of Allison Ford, Mike Olson, Rebekah Siefert, Dera Sipe, and Adriel Trott, which was made possible by a Research Support Grant from Villanova University. We would also like to thank Bente Polites for her time and enthusiasm in helping us research the introduction to this volume and Theresa DiMartino for her expert secretarial work. Jane Bunker at State University of New York Press believed in this project and helped us bring it to completion. For her backing we are truly grateful.

Special thanks go to all of the contributors who shared our commitment to the philosophical importance of *The Mandarins*. And finally, our sincerest appreciation to our families, who have had to listen to our ideas, copyedit drafts, and endure our hours in front of the computer. They have shown enormous patience and love when it mattered most.

Cover photo courtesy of the National Archives 111-SC-193785.

Introduction

Sally J. Scholz and Shannon M. Mussett

> *Existence—others have said it and I have already repeated it more than once myself—cannot be reduced to ideas, it cannot be stated in words: it can only be evoked through the medium of an imaginary object; to achieve this, one must recapture the surge of backwash, and the contradictions of life itself.*
>
> —Simone de Beauvoir, *The Force of Circumstance*

"The contradictions of freedom." This poignant phrase, penned by Iris Murdoch, eloquently describes Simone de Beauvoir's monumental novel, *The Mandarins* (*Les mandarins*). In 1956, Murdoch reviewed Beauvoir's novel in the *Nation*, saying, "*The Mandarins* is a novel about loss of faith, about the contradictions of freedom, about the possibility of despair" (Murdoch 1956, 494). Aptly captured by Murdoch, Beauvoir's tumultuous epic about the personal and political lives of post–World War II French intellectuals inspires this study of the various contradictions of freedom. Although based in a specific historical, social, and cultural period, *The Mandarins* transcends the narrow confines of time and place to speak powerfully to audiences fifty years after its original publication.

This collection of philosophical works brings together some of the most respected scholars in the fields of existentialism, phenomenology, and feminism. Although there has been some attention devoted to the literary aspects of *The Mandarins*, the philosophical content remains a largely untapped treasure.[1] This edited volume aims to remedy that oversight.

Beauvoir's most acclaimed novel demonstrates her vision into world politics, interpersonal relationships, professional and private life, gender roles, and personal choice and responsibility. In this introduction, we provide a backdrop for the further exploration of these issues. We begin with a summary of the novel, followed by a history of Beauvoir's writing of the text, which draws upon her autobiographical accounts as well as her letters. Next, we offer a survey of the critical reception of the novel in France and around the world. The reviews of the novel after its initial publication reveal the various ways Beauvoir's text pushed the boundaries of acceptable literature while also recording a distressful period in history. Finally, we provide a brief summary of each of the essays collected in this volume.

Life and the Text

> *Henri found himself looking at the sky again—a clear, black crystal dome overhead. It was difficult for the mind to conceive of hundreds of planes shattering that black, crystalline silence! And suddenly, words began tumbling through his head with a joyous sound—the offensive was halted . . . the German collapse had begun . . . at last he would be able to leave.*
>
> —Simone de Beauvoir, *The Mandarins*

Paris fell early in World War II. From June 1940 to August 1944, the people of France lived under Nazi Occupation. Simone de Beauvoir and her companion, Jean-Paul Sartre, became political in that war. "The family," as Beauvoir called her close group of friends, felt the deprivations of war as well as the experience of loss when friends and acquaintances were killed by the Germans in concentration camps or while fighting in the Resistance. The Occupation was "a long fast" (Beauvoir 1956, 11), and the solidarity experienced during the Liberation held tremendous promise. But Beauvoir, like so many of her fellow citizens, soon discovered that freedom, too, is fraught with paralyzing contradictions.

In August 1944, still besieged by German troops, Paris became a model of unity as resistance movements with members having vastly different political viewpoints mounted a climatic struggle to retake their city.[2] Some of these were the *maquisards*, who went from being guerrilla fighters to fighters in more organized units, and others were citizens who bravely joined the battle. The insurrection became intense on August 18–19 with a call to mobilize against the Nazi occupiers (Chambard [1970] 1976, 201). By August 25, 1944, when the Second Armored Division entered Paris commanded by General Jacques Leclerc, all the German strongholds in the city were taken back. General von Choltitz, the German officer in charge of operations in Paris (who in spite of orders to destroy Paris's treasures had refused to do so) negotiated the surrender with General Leclerc and Colonel Rol-Tanguy. The American Fourth Infantry division entered Paris at this time and joined in the battle for liberation.

Historian Claude Chambard notes that the revenge against collaborationists began even before the surrender had been signed. He claims that the "hatred focused mainly on female 'collaborationists' or on women merely suspected of having collaborated—for many mistakes were made" (Chambard

[1970] 1976, 221). These "horizontal collaborationists" had their heads shaved and marked with swastikas. Other collaborationists were not as lucky; the vengeance became murderous.

General de Gaulle spoke the evening of August 25, asking for national unity, but it was not long before it was clear that various political factions would dispute France's future. By August 28, the liberation of Paris was complete.[3] The next four years were marked by dramatic events in France and around the world, not least of which was the bombing of Hiroshima on August 6, 1945. Clearly, a new era had begun. France and Britain, concentrating their postwar energies on reconstruction, found themselves forced into a position of choosing between the two great superpowers that emerged at the end of the war.

As post–World War II reconstruction pushed forward, the cold war between the United States and the Soviet Union intensified. As a result, a number of questions emerged regarding France's relations with both the US and the USSR. Bourgeois politics effectively trumped leftist politics in the years after the war. Accepting American aid during reconstruction essentially put France in opposition to the Soviet Union. But for many intellectuals, the Soviet Union held the promise of a liberated future. Beauvoir and her colleagues felt the antinomies involved in how to respond to such a situation as well as the responsibility of acting on behalf of the world's oppressed. Many of the bourgeois politicians gained their fame fighting in the Resistance alongside members of other diverse political parties, many left of center (Vinen 1995, 227). Reform minded leftists became increasingly split over the means to achieve European unification. The intellectuals in France were among the vanguard of leftist politics, and their disappointment with the Fourth Republic and its reconstruction alliances has been well documented.

In 1954, the prestigious Prix Goncourt went to an author whose novel was the first major literary attempt to capture this postwar period. Simone de Beauvoir's monumental novel *The Mandarins* examines France in the years immediately after liberation (1944–48) and records the aspirations of the Left as well as their disagreements and disappointments. In *The Prime of Life*, Beauvoir explains that the time following the liberation of France from Nazi Occupation was an emotionally chaotic period. Stating that her memories of this time were very confused, she elaborates, "I have often felt, since the restoration of peace, how difficult it was to speak of those days to anyone who had not lived through them" (1966, 601). *The Mandarins* is an attempt to speak of the difficult situation in which France in general and the French intelligentsia in particular tried to establish their roles after World War II. In other ways, Beauvoir's own struggle with the relationship between the political and the private permeates the novel. She tells us in rich detail that when she first began the novel, she wanted it to be an all-encompassing project:

> I wanted it to contain all of me—myself in relation to life, to death, to my times, to writing, to love, to friendship, to travel; I also wanted to depict other people and above all to tell the feverish and disappointing story of what happened after the war. . . . I had no lack of things to say; but how to set about it? This was to be no pot-boiler, oh no! I was high with excitement, but frightened. How long would it take, this new adventure? Three years? Four? A long time anyway. And where would it land me? (1992a, 193)

Beauvoir readily admits that *The Mandarins* was a profoundly personal and all-consuming work, and in many ways these are the very reasons for its tremendous success and longevity. It begins with a party on Christmas Eve 1944 when the liberation of Paris was still forefront on everyone's mind. The first lines of the novel (quoted in the epigraph of this section) illustrate the profound sense of freedom that liberation from the Nazis brought to the people of Paris. However, what should mark a period of calm after a long, tumultuous time, instead ushers in an era of personal and political tensions. Beauvoir uses two narrators to chronicle the excitement of liberation, the factions among left-wing intellectuals, the possibilities of love relations, and the dramatic disappointment with Stalin's regime. Truly, this was an age that marked generations of people the world over. But France faced many more specific problems given its place in Western Europe and its past status as a powerful nation. The post-war era brought with it an identity shift as the people of France had to rely on the new world powers: the United States, the Soviet Union, and, to a lesser extent, Britain. As Elizabeth Fallaize argues, Beauvoir's novel addresses a number of "political doubts" in this new situation: "[W]hy have the Americans not gone on to remove Franco and Salazar, after Hitler? How are the American liberators treating the inmates of the German camps? Is American aid not a form of colonization?" (Fallaize [1988] 1990, 102). Furthermore, how can the French maintain a relation with a country that drops the atomic bomb on Hiroshima, killing hundreds of thousands? Can the French continue to support Communism in light of the oppression of millions as subproletariat? But what other alternative is available? These are among the salient ethico-political questions Beauvoir's narrative addresses. Is it possible to remain neutral in such a world-historical situation?

The first narrator of the novel is Henri Perron: a writer in his mid-thirties whose first book made him famous. Henri edits a newspaper for the noncommunist Left, *L'Espoir*, a name loaded with political and personal meaning. It is the *hope* for a peaceful future, the *hope* for a united Europe, the *hope* for quality working conditions for workers all over the world, and the *hope* for time and solitude to pursue the innumerable personal pleasures denied during wartime. Henri's activities in the Resistance movement inspired him to see the potential of collective political action, but he longs to sink into a sort of political oblivion and merely concentrate on his next novel, which he hopes will be a "light novel." As the book opens, he has made plans to go to Portugal. Ostensibly it is to meet with political activists against the dictatorship there, but in his mind the trip to Portugal will be a well-deserved vacation. Henri desperately wishes to get away from politics, at least for a time.

Henri's mentor, Robert Dubreuilh, is in his early sixties and has distinguished himself as perhaps the most important thinker and writer of the age. As early as this opening scene, Dubreuilh is making plans for the next political movement. His aim is to unite the Left and the workers in a noncommunist party, the SRL. Dubreuilh's party mirrors the ill-fated RDR (Rassemblement Démocratique Révolutionnaire), a leftist movement founded by Jean-Paul Sartre, David Rousset, and Gerard Rosenthal in 1948 (Ritsch 1966, 175). Both the RDR and the fictional SRL were meant to be distinct from the French Communist Party and aimed at providing a new, powerful voice of the Left. Dubreuilh lobbies Henri not only to join his political cause but to make *L'Espoir* the organ of the SRL, thereby clearly defining "a position in relation to the Communist Party" (Beauvoir 1956, 124).

Anne Dubreuilh alternates with Henri as the narrator of the story, and unlike Henri, speaks in the first person. She is Robert's wife, twenty years his junior, and has made a name for herself as a psychoanalyst. At the opening party, Anne's primary concern is her teenage daughter, Nadine, whose lover died in a concentration camp during the war. As the story unfolds, Anne is confronted with personal choices and contradictions that mirror the political ones unfolding for Henri. Anne often provides an intimate analysis of the relationships in the book. Given the postwar situation, it is not surprising that Anne's analysis is tainted by death and its significance for those who survive.

Another major character is Paule, Henri's lover of ten years. Paule was once a successful singer, but she gave it all up in order to love Henri. Paule's story forms a backdrop of madness resulting from the failure to take responsibility for meaning in her life. Her single-minded focus on Henri has already alienated him from her as the novel begins. Given that Beauvoir had published her most famous work, *The Second Sex*, just prior to beginning *The Mandarins*, it is no surprise that her analysis of the situation of woman reappears here, reflected in the character of Paule. Paule has given up a potentially lucrative singing career because she believes she is absolutely necessary to Henri. Like the "woman in love" from Beauvoir's *The Second Sex*, Paule defines herself by her relation to Henri; she has "relinquish[ed] everything for the benefit of a master" (Beauvoir 1952, 642). As the novel progresses, the reader watches as Paule's self-denying narcissism turns to self-loathing and madness.

The Christmas Eve party during which we meet Paule, Anne, Robert, and Henri is presented from Henri's perspective and introduces most of the other characters and their political positions as well. At the outset, Beauvoir captures the tension between the various factions within the left intelligentsia regarding the direction of postwar France. But she also uses this party to illustrate tension in various love relationships, thus effectively blending public and private affairs to illustrate the interconnections of personal commitment and political choice. Henri and Paule, Robert and Anne, Nadine and Lambert, and others ruminate on their relationships and the ironies that almost of necessity emerge when one is committed to acting. Paule is the most obvious case, but each of the characters experiences the contradictions of freedom in his or her political and personal life.

As the story unfolds, we learn more about Nadine. Her lover, Diego, had been killed in a concentration camp, and Anne speculates that her current promiscuity is an attempt to hide from that and to avoid ever loving again. Nadine even gets Henri drunk and, after he wakes up in bed with her, explains that sleeping with people is a way of breaking the ice (Beauvoir 1956, 63). For her it is important that Henri like her because she wants him to take her to Portugal. Eventually, Henri agrees and then faces the task of telling Paule. It is noteworthy that Beauvoir herself traveled to Spain and Portugal in 1945. There she published a number of articles under the pseudonym Daniel Secrétan so as to protect her sister Hélène and her diplomat brother-in-law, Lionel de Roulet, with whom she stayed while in Portugal (Bair 1990, 300–1).

Beauvoir's fictional counterparts, Nadine and Henri, are struck by the contrast between Lisbon and Paris. At first they gorge themselves on delights and fill their luggage with presents for people back home. But they also tour the squalid parts of Lisbon, and the tyranny, poverty, and corruptness overshadow their joy at the plenty they had discovered. This trip to Portugal becomes a fitting symbol of the dilemmas encountered during postwar reconstruction. On the political level, the US policy not to intervene against the dictatorships of Franco and Salazar was a stark contrast to its willingness to participate in the ousting of Hitler. On the personal level, Nadine and Henri experience the guilt of plenty—in spite of their four years of deprivation under Nazi Occupation—in the face of the extreme privation suffered by so many in Portugal. In her real-life articles, entitled "Quatre jours à Madrid" (Four days in Madrid), published in *Combat* on April 14 and 15, 1945, and "Le Portugal sous le régime de Salazar" (Portugal under Salazar's Regime), published in *Combat* on April 23 and 24, 1945,[4] Beauvoir likewise exposes the political hypocrisy and grapples with the sharp contrasts between poverty and opulence, between the beauty of the region and the devastation of civil war, and between her own deprivation during the war and the unqualified hunger of the masses in Portugal.

Henri's trip to Portugal and the responsibility incumbent upon him as a writer to expose the injustice there make concrete the question of the power of literature. All of the central characters of the novel grapple with whether literature ought to be for its own sake or serve some other purpose. Henri desires to write "sincere books" (Beauvoir 1956, 57), while Anne and Robert wonder if it is possible to write sincere books and also be involved in politics. Involvement in politics has the potential to transform one's writing into scandal (45). Literature and the role of the intellectual functions as a driving concern throughout the novel and was clearly one of the issues with which Beauvoir and her cohorts wrestled.

Among the issues confronting postwar France, and its politically active intellectuals, was that of European unification. Prior to the war, a number of voices had spoken in favor of a "United States of Europe," perhaps most notably Edouard Herriot (Ritsch 1966, 3). After the war ended and as cold war tensions mounted, this idea was revived with Winston Churchill taking a leading role. The idea in uniting Western Europe was to create a third power that would oppose both the Soviet Union and the United States. After the war, a number of intellectuals dreamed of "an independent Europe federated under Socialism" (222). The Marshall Plan and the unification that followed served as an approximation to this aspiration but the dream of socialism met numerous obstacles. While the central concern of where France would stand in relation to the two developing super powers occupies a great deal of Beauvoir's novel, the issue of European unification is a bit more understated, lending to the setting of the story and providing a context for some of the relationships.

Framing these concerns is the question of whether accepting American money for reconstruction makes France a pawn to American policy as well. The Marshall Plan called for a united economic front in Western Europe that would be able to oppose Communism. Secretary of State George Marshall revealed the plan during a speech in June 1947. Clearly an underlying motive was to shore up US interests in Europe while also playing to the various leftist political parties' interest in unity. By 1948, however, "the non-Communist intellectuals and the French Communists appeared . . . to be converging on the theme of peace. . . . [T]he intellectuals were now convinced that neutralism was the only course for France and Western Europe to follow" (Ritsch 1966, 222). Dubreuilh's position follows this course in the book: his initial goals for a united socialist Europe transform into a humanism that aims to prevent war.

Victor Scriassine, an anti-Communist/pro-American Russian émigré, charges Dubreuilh with "dreaming of a united, autonomous, socialist Europe," adding "[I]f Europe refuses the protection of the United States, she'll inevitably fall in to the hands of Stalin" (Beauvoir 1956, 122). Dubreuilh brackets the European unity question by concentrating on the immediate situation in France: "[H]ere in France we have a clear-cut objective—to achieve a real popular front government. And for that, we need a non-Communist left that's able to hold its own" (122). The SRL is that popular front government, he hopes. Dubreuilh represents this position later as well when arguing with Anne and Henri about whether to publish information about the Soviet gulags and when he embraces politics again in a revived hope for a united leftist front at the end of the novel.

A clear tool for effecting a change in public opinion is the press. Dubreuilh mounts an intense campaign to convince Henri to dedicate *L'Espoir* to the SRL, but Henri resists, in part because he would like to remain neutral and in part because he believes that if he takes a clear stance he will lose the readership of the workers. The workers will abandon him because he'll be considered too much like the communist papers. But Henri does take a bold stand for the truth. He publishes his stories on Portugal and also criticizes American policy for not ridding the Mediterranean region of Franco and Salazar.[5] For Henri, this sort of truth-telling is the job of the journalist; he does not see it as "opening that campaign" (Beauvoir 1956, 139). When pushed to see that publishing certain facts might have unfortunate consequences, Henri declares his intent to give up journalism rather than suppress the truth. Henri confronts similar versions of this ethical dilemma again in his work at the paper as well as in his personal life.

Beauvoir explores the power of the media through Henri's decision of whether or not to make *L'Espoir* the organ of the SRL. Although Henri had viewed the paper as "a sort of toy," the politics entailed in this decision made him see that it was more of a "weapon," and that "people had the right to hold him to account for the way he used it" (Beauvoir 1956, 155). Joining forces with the SRL has the potential to factionalize the Left. Similarly, the planned SRL mass meeting would be viewed as an attack on the Communists. As the Communist Lachaume states, "[T]he moment [the SRL] annexes a newspaper, the moment it organizes a mass meeting, then the only conclusion to draw is that they mean to undermine us. In the beginning the Communist Party wanted an alliance. But when they come out against us, we have no other choice but to fight back" (158). The third chapter ends with Henri musing that "everyone had died in the war. . . . Act, unite, serve, obey Dubreuilh, smile at Samazelle"—that was all that was left (175). Henri resigns himself to giving the paper to the SRL.

Anne takes up the narration in the fourth chapter, and the reader gets a more intimate look at the relationships among the characters. Henri and Robert open the office of *Vigilance* and publish the first issue. *Vigilance*—like its real-life equivalent, *Les Temps Modernes*, which Sartre, Beauvoir, and others began in 1944—is a leftist literary and political magazine. Anne's personal story begins to take what will become quite a dramatic turn with an invitation to give a series of lectures in the United States. While she resolves not to go early on (ostensibly because she perceives Robert's frailty in the post-Liberation era), by the end of the chapter she has decided to go to New York and views this decision as an opportunity "to live again" (Beauvoir 1956, 234). Anne's postwar experience may be characterized as a preoccupation with death. Her psychoanalytic practice aims at helping others deal with the atrocities of the war, her relations with her daughter are haunted by the death of Diego, and even her marriage with Robert is tainted by the specter of death as she sees him becoming old. Her decision to travel, then, is really an existential choice—the choice to live.

While deciding whether or not to accept the invitation to the US, Anne visits Paule, which provides the reader with a different lens through which to examine the Henri/Paule affair. Paule explains that she and Henri are not distinct beings and that her life's work was creating Henri: "When I took him, at twenty-five, he thought only of literature. But I knew at once I could make him rise much higher than that. What I have taught him is that his life and his work should become a unit so completely realized, so pure, so absolute that it would serve as an example to all the world" (Beauvoir 1956, 194). Paule's attempt to take on Henri as her own life's work reveals nothing less than a maniacal obsession.

Although Anne and Henri have many things in common, including their affection for Dubreuilh, they rarely speak throughout the novel. One notable exception is when they are swept along by the crowd during the celebration of victory in Europe. This encounter blends the two perspectives momentarily as they discuss Paule and Robert in turn. More interesting, perhaps, is their discussion of their own lives and choices. But the conversation ends as quickly as it began with a silent walk to the subway and a return home.

L'Espoir undergoes a number of changes throughout the years covered by the novel. When its finances reach a critical low point, Henri and the editorial board are forced to consider the possibility of accepting private money to keep the paper afloat. Trarieux, a wealthy leftist, offers to provide the necessary funds but attaches the condition that Samazelle get a position on the board. Henri immediately suspects Robert of participating in what he views as blackmail and contemplates breaking with Dubreuilh. Ultimately, however, it is not the question of finances that causes the break between Robert and Henri. *L'Espoir* manages to stay afloat with money from Vincent, who extorts it (or steals it) from collaborators whom he single-mindedly pursues in order to punish. This raises the question of whether a paper can exist as a moral body in spite of its financial ties to an immoral action. Henri clearly disapproves, saying that by accepting the money the paper implicitly encourages Vincent to continue his murderous campaign against collaborators (Beauvoir 1956, 252). Lambert offers to buy into the paper as well, thereby allowing Henri to maintain the majority vote should Samazelle join the board. This serves as an adequate solution for a time, but the paper continues to be the site of tension because of its ambiguous relation to the Communist Party and the Right.

The reality of the intensifying cold war is brought into sharp relief during a holiday bicycle trip in August 1945. When the United States drops the atomic bomb on Hiroshima, the unbelievable destruction is contrasted with the setting of Vercors. Anne, Robert, and Henri cycle into Vercors in the midst of a funeral procession. While the hundreds of thousands dead in Hiroshima may seem remote, the lived experience of death in Vercors offers a concrete example of human suffering that illustrates the incredible misery humanity can inflict on humanity.

But the suffering is not reserved for wars between nations. In different ways, Paule and Henri cause each other to suffer. Paule's love for Henri, she says, is "with complete generosity, with an absolute respect for [Henri's] freedom" (Beauvoir 1956, 305). Precisely the opposite is the case, however. Paule tries to control Henri and even claims that the lucidity of her solitude makes her understand that Dubreuilh is destroying him. Paule tries desperately to preserve their past relationship while simultaneously claiming that she wants Henri to be free. For his part, Henri misleads Paule by masking his ambivalence toward her. Rather than make a clean break with Paule, Henri continues to reassure her of his love and dedication while also beginning a mutually instrumental romance with Josette Belhomme, a young actress/model who is given the lead in his play about the Occupation. He even depicts Paule and his future breakup with her in his new novel, but when she reads it, she refuses to recognize herself in the character.

Before the fifth chapter ends, two startling revelations are made: the existence of Stalin's work camps and Josette's Nazi lover. Scriassine accompanied George Peltov to Dubreuilh's house in the hopes that *L'Espoir* would expose the camps and the Soviet regime for what it is. Peltov had been the head of Tebriuka Agricultural Institute and offers evidence of an estimated 15 million in the camps:

> The program of the Soviet State requires surpluses which can only be furnished by excessively hard labor. But if the consumption of free workers falls below a certain level, their productivity drops accordingly. Therefore, the State resorted to the systematic creation of a subproletariat receiving only absolutely minimal sustenance in exchange for a maximum amount of labor. Such a system is possible only when concentration-camp methods are brought into play. (Beauvoir 1956, 319)

The revelation shatters the mirages of Soviet-style Communism and Henri's personal pleasure. His easy, playful romance with Josette is contrasted with the fact that "in every corner of the earth, men were being exploited, starved, murdered" (318). The existence of the camps meant that the hopes placed on the Soviet Union, the prospects of communism for "a thousand million subhumans slowly dying of hunger in China and India, the only hope for millions of workers enslaved to inhuman conditions," were utterly destroyed (322). Publishing this news would devastate the Communist Party in France, and yet if the camps really existed, not publishing the news would be complicity in their evil. The board of *L'Espoir* urged publication, but the SRL, with Dubreuilh in the lead, warned that publishing the news of the camps was an alignment with the Right against the Communists. Henri chooses to follow the board and precipitates a hostile break with the SRL and Dubreuilh himself. Anne agrees with Henri and questions Robert's hesitation in not publishing the information (356–59). While the circumstances of the break between Robert and Henri differ, the public airing of their differences mirrors the break between Sartre and Camus in 1952 (see McBride 1991, 91).

Beauvoir has taken some liberties in dating the revelation of the Soviet work camps. The "news of the existence of the Soviet labour camps . . . broke at the end of 1949" (Fallaize [1988] 1990, 91) but comes much earlier in the novel. However, her depiction of the effect on leftist movements within France is striking. The unity found during the Resistance had shown numerous cracks in the postwar years, but it shattered completely with the news about the Soviet Union. Nor did it help to have the United States, France's ally in war and prominent partner during reconstruction, preparing for war against the USSR.

The United States is painted in bold personal colors when Anne takes her journey there to attend a series of conferences and lectures. While in the US she begins a passionate affair with an American writer, Lewis Brogan. This aspect of the story is Beauvoir's mildly fictionalized version of her love affair with Nelson Algren, to whom *The Mandarins* is dedicated. In Lewis's arms, Anne describes her body coming to life again. Through Lewis's eyes, Anne sees America its seedy side as well as its self righteous side. The same United States that produces Lewis also threatens the world with its bombs and its aggressive form of capitalism.

By printing the articles about the Soviet labor camps, Henri loses his private life just as Anne is rediscovering hers. Wooed by the anti-communists and reviled by the Communists, Henri finds himself politically isolated and socially misplaced as he continues to live the bourgeois lifestyle with Josette. His attempts to break with Paule send her into a spiral of denial as she tries to convince him of the love that she thinks he demands. When she finally comes to grips with the break, she throws an insane dinner party for everyone involved in "the conspiracy." Anne eventually manages to have her taken to a hospital, where her "cure" will leave her a sort of empty shell that completely denies her relationship with Henri.

The contrast with Anne's love for Lewis and her commitment to Robert could not be more striking than at this point. However, Anne's hold on Lewis is also fleeting. She rejoins him in the US for a trip on the Mississippi followed by a holiday in Mexico, but they leave Mexico early for a meeting in New York in anticipation of the publication of Lewis's new book. When Anne discovers that Lewis deliberately cut their trip short, she confronts him. Lewis desires to marry Anne and accuses her of controlling their relationship. Clearly taken aback by this startling parallel to Paule, Anne, like Paule, tries to salvage their relationship by affirming his freedom. Before Anne departs again for her alternate life in France, Lewis admits that he had tried to love her less but was not able (Beauvoir 1956, 484).

In chapter 9, Lucie Belhomme reveals that her daughter, Josette, had been in love with a Nazi officer and was being blackmailed by an informer who was recently arrested. Lucie pleads with Henri, as a prominent former member of the Resistance, to testify that the informer was a double agent within the Resistance movement.

> He withdrew his hand and ran it over his face. Playing the part of the devil didn't suit him. He would give that false testimony because he couldn't do otherwise, that's all. "How did I ever come to this?" It seemed to him at the same time both completely logical and absolutely impossible. Never had he felt sadder. (Beauvoir 1956, 504)

Henri thus experiences the contradictions of freedom in his realization that his personal liaison and the loyalty it inspires is utterly contrary to his political stance as a Resistance fighter and intellectual on behalf of the oppressed. Henri's acquiescence in discounting the testimony of two concentration camp survivors underscores the irony of Beauvoir's title, *The Mandarins*. Like the Chinese mandarins who inspired the title of the novel, Henri's revolutionary spirit and his intellectual commitments have brought him to the critical moment wherein he discovers his own obsolescence.

Although Henri saves Josette's life, he cannot be with her any longer. Moreover, Sézenac and Lambert know that Henri has given false testimony, and Sézenac has become a police informer as well. Henri is left with little choice; he writes a letter of resignation from *L'Espoir*. Ironically, Henri's false testimony and resignation facilitate a reunion with Dubreuilh, who writes expressing his friendship. Henri has seemingly sold out the Resistance and his soul in one quick act to save a collaborator. Dubreuilh argues that the story proves "That personal morality just doesn't exist. . . . You can't lead a proper life in a society which isn't proper" (Beauvoir 1956, 518).

The reader's attention turns again to America when Anne makes another trip to visit Lewis. This time the couple plans to spend the summer in a house on Lake Michigan. Anne's anticipation for the trip is surpassed by her disappointment at finding that Lewis no longer loves her. Like the parallel relationship between Henri and Paule, and the leftist political relations in France, Lewis and Anne can find no hope of recovering the past. Anne's view of America subsequently shifts as well. No longer does she see the picturesque; this is the

America that dropped the bomb and is ever preparing for war in order to avoid having one.

Anne returns to France very much disheartened, but her granddaughter awaits her. This baby, Maria, is the daughter of Nadine and Henri, who had once again started to date. Nadine explains that she got herself pregnant out of a "maternal desire" for a baby, not to trick Henri into marrying her (Beauvoir 1956, 530). To his own surprise, however, Henri finds he similarly anticipates the pleasures of fatherhood and is astonished at having produced a daughter. The three take up domesticity but hesitate to devote real affection to each other. Henri wonders why he didn't really love Nadine, musing that she even "kept her distance" from her own baby:

> She sat down on a tree trunk, Maria in her arms. She gave the baby her bottle with authority, with patience; she made it a point of honor of being a competent mother, she had acquired both a solid background in child care and a lot of hygienic gadgets. But never had Henri caught a look of real affection in her eyes while she was tending Maria. Yes, that was what made it difficult to love her: even with her own baby she kept her distance; she still remained shut up in herself. (572)

Nonetheless, Henri and Nadine plan to move to Italy, where he will be able to write in peace, unperturbed by politics. It quickly becomes evident, however, that Henri is not cut out for solitary life. He agrees to write another article on Madagascar and rejoins Robert in an effort to revive leftist politics. The Madagascan affair was the last important thing he exposed while still editor of *L'Espoir*:

> One hundred thousand Madagascans massacred as against one hundred and fifty Europeans; terror reigned on the island; all the deputies had been arrested even though they had disavowed the rebellion; they were being subjected to tortures worthy of the Gestapo; an attempt had been made on their lawyers' life with a hand grenade; the trial was fixed in advance—and there was not a single newspaper to denounce the scandal. He took out his pen. (506–7)

Once again, then, Henri will attempt to live history by speaking out against injustice. His foolish plans to write a "light novel" with no political significance give way to his true feelings about the role of literature.

In the meantime, Sézenac, who has been exposed as a Nazi informer, arrives at the Dubreuilh's country house and admits his work with the Gestapo. The dilemma of how to deal with past betrayal reemerges. Vincent steps in to solve the problem by killing Sézenac while he sleeps. As he and Henri dispose of the body, Henri tries again to revive a sense of justice.

Anne has the final word of the novel. With her relationship to Lewis completely over, she wonders what there is left to live for. "Dead is the child who believed in paradise, dead the girl who thought immortal the books, the ideas, and the man she loved, dead the young woman who walked overwhelmed through the world promised to happiness, dead the woman in love who would wake up laughing in Lewis's arms" (Beauvoir 1956, 608). But, with Maria representing the future, Anne realizes that she does not own her death, others do. Hope revives again.

A chronicle of this important time in French history, *The Mandarins* is also something of a revelation of the tensions among intellectuals. In addition to recording the history of the immediate postwar period between 1944 and 1948, Beauvoir interweaves events that unfolded during the writing and polishing of the manuscript from 1949 to 1953, such as the founding and breakup of the RDR in 1948–49 and the revelation of the Soviet labor camps (see also Fallaize [1988] 1990, 90–92). Events in her own life from both periods find their place in the narrative flow. The most notable is Beauvoir's affair with Nelson Algren, which began during her lecture tour of 1947 and reached its climatic resolution in 1950 and 1951 during two visits to Lake Michigan. But Beauvoir does not wish her book to be viewed as a roman à clef, a point taken up in many of the reviews of the novel. Fallaize views Henri's description of his own novel as Beauvoir's presentation of *The Mandarins*. The novel is a "portrait of the times," a depiction of "present-day people, men and women who are in somewhat the same situation as ours" (Fallaize [1988] 1990, 98, citing Beauvoir, 586).

To many at the time, the richness of the novel was found in the way it portrayed the lives of real individuals such as Beauvoir, Jean-Paul Sartre, Nelson Algren, Albert Camus, and Arthur Koestler. Beauvoir acknowledges that some of the scenes and characters resemble real individuals with whom she associated.[6] In her autobiographies, Beauvoir claims that Henri is modeled both on Albert Camus (whose work in the Resistance and on *Combat* is well known) and on herself. Robert Dubreuilh resembles Jean-Paul Sartre, and his wife, Anne, is also like Beauvoir. Anne represents Beauvoir's personal love choices, while Henri represents her political dilemmas as a writer and intellectual in the face of post–World War II reconstruction. But these two characters also embody Beauvoir's character traits, traits that Fallaize argues are coded according to the male/positive female/negative structure. "Henri has her optimism, her appetites, her taste for activity—and, of course, the pen. Anne has fear and shame, and the 'negative aspects of my experience'" (Fallaize [1988] 1990, 115, citing Beauvoir 1992a, 280). Anne's preoccupation with death may also reflect Beauvoir's; in 1952 Beauvoir had a tumor removed, and although it was nonmalignant, it certainly made her confront personal mortality. Many of the other characters (such as Nadine, who shares traits with Beauvoir's former student Natalie Sorokine) are also reminiscent of Beauvoir's friends, peers, or acquaintances.

The most important parallel to Beauvoir's real-life relationships is found in Anne's American liaison. Nelson Algren, who reacted violently when he was finally encouraged to read the novel, finds his relationship with Beauvoir aired quite publicly through the character of Lewis Brogan (see also Beauvoir 1992a, 124). Algren found it faithful enough to actual events to warrant breaking with Beauvoir. In her biography of Beauvoir, Deirdre Bair relates that when Algren read the English translation of *The Mandarins* in 1956, "it made him furious and caused the second most serious rupture in their relationship. . . . He read the book, and after that she was never again his 'own Simone.' Everything about her was fair game for attack as far as he was concerned" (Bair 1990, 428).[7] For her part, Beauvoir felt that in telling the fictional story of Anne and Lewis, she was in fact offering her American lover the greatest testament of her affection. In letters to Algren she insists that this book is meant to be not only a book about her love for him, but is in fact to be *his* book. In a letter dated October 15, 1949, she writes to him, "I work steadily and lovingly about your book. I want it to be the best I ever wrote, to be a real good one, since it is a gift for you" (1997a, 290). In perhaps the most telling admission, she writes on October 13, 1952, "You ask about 'your' book, honey: It comes to an end, at last; it is a very thick novel and there is only a part of it about lovely you" (472). This part, however, was enough to cause an irreparable rift between her and the American writer.

Following its publication, Beauvoir expressed profound satisfaction with the book's reception by both the Right and the Left, as well as with the letters and visits she received from past and present friends and colleagues. Yet there is one point that irked Beauvoir about the novel's effect on the public:

> My only problems came from the legend, planted and nurtured by the critics, that I had written an exact and faithful chronicle; this legend turned my inventions into indiscretions or even into denunciations. Like dreams, novels are often prophetic simply because they deal with possibilities; thus Camus and Sartre quarreled with each other two years after I began to recount the avatars and the breakup of a friendship. Several women wanted to recognize Paule's story as their own. These coincidences finished off the process by which my fables became accepted as accredited truths. Did Camus or Sartre bear false witness as I described Henri doing? people have asked me. When did I practice psychoanalysis? In one sense, it pleased me that my story carried such conviction; but it upset me that people thought me so unscrupulous. (1992b, 37)

Thus, although Beauvoir willingly admits that her own experience of the post-Liberation period forms the framework of the story, she adamantly refuses to agree with those who claim that the book is nothing more than surreptitious autobiography. Throughout this epic tale, Beauvoir alludes to the various factions of the Resistance movement, the moral dilemmas that confronted individuals both during the war and subsequent to it, and the world-historical social and political questions that marked France immediately after the war. *The Mandarins* is perhaps the most personal of her novels, but it is also the most political.

History of the Text

In her memoirs and letters, Beauvoir depicts the writing of *The Mandarins* as a difficult, deeply personal, and protracted writing project. Undergoing a number of rewrites and corrections, the novel was begun in the fall of 1949 and finished in the fall of 1953 (with only minor corrections of proofs made in 1954). In many senses, the book began much earlier, as the events of the Second World War and its aftermath were its central themes. The journey of the actual book itself—its transformations and rewritings—show the difficulty of the task Beauvoir had set for herself, as well as the sense of personal connection that she had for her beloved story.

In her autobiography, Beauvoir claims that the first words she wrote were Anne's first monologue (1992a, 193) and in a letter to Algren, October 8, 1949, she tells him that the first page of her new novel carries the inscription: "'To Nelson'" (1997a, 287). She continues, "Now it is so brightly began, it will be easy to go on." In another letter to Algren dated November 22, 1949, Beauvoir recounts the fate of her initial work. She relates a story of how she had misplaced two months of writing in a taxicab. She elaborates: "In two months I had torn away most things I had written and chiefly worked in my head. Then I saw with great pleasure that I remembered really by heart the hundred first pages I had written (I mean hand-written pages, just of this shape) so I began copying feverishly out of my head. Your book is in no danger in the end, honey; it means just a week more, which is not much on three four years [*sic*]" (1997a, 302). So engrossed in her project, Beauvoir was able to reproduce the lost hundred pages from memory in a mere week.[8]

In *Force of Circumstance*, Beauvoir informs us that she had finished the first version of *The Mandarins* in June 1951 and had found it to be a peculiar experience: "[C]ontrary to my usual habit, I had so far shown none of it to Sartre; I found it painful to wrench it out of myself, and I could not have endured any other eyes, even his, to see those pages that were still warm" (1992a, 243). Beauvoir, accustomed to sharing her work with Sartre at most stages of its development, was unusually cautious with this novel. Unable to deal with any criticisms (which both Sartre and Beauvoir gave to each other without reservation in most cases) until she was ready, Beauvoir was very protective of *The Mandarins*. She does not take long to explain why she had been hesitant to show the manuscript to Sartre. When he did finally read it during their cruise to Norway in the summer, he assured her that although it was going to be her best novel, she still had a lot of work to do on it. According to Sartre's scathing assessment, "as it stood, the book was badly constructed and discouraged the reader" (249). Furthermore, he criticized the dialogue, the lack of suspense, the general incoherency of the plot, and the unbelievability of the characters. Following his analysis, a dejected Beauvoir decided to keep part of it, "But for the rest, I decided to rework the whole thing" (249). Even after she had completely redrafted the book from beginning to end, Sartre was still unsatisfied with it after his second read-through in the late fall of 1952 (1992b, 9).

Despite the good intentions of her partner and his honest critique, Beauvoir felt disheartened by her progress. Even though Sartre encouraged her to continue, she didn't feel up to the task and decided simply to shelve the project. In the spring of 1953, Beauvoir showed the text to Lanzmann. She writes, "It was actually Bost and Lanzmann who convinced me to keep going; they were reading it for the first time, and they were more affected by its positive value than by its weaknesses. So I went back to work" (Beauvoir 1992b, 9). Her work paid off, and in the fall of the same year she completed the book with much relief and gaiety. The only thing remaining for her to do was to find an appropriate title. She was dissatisfied with the candidate, *The Survivors* ("after all, life hadn't actually stopped in 1944") as well as with *The Suspects* (as the word had "already been used a few years earlier by Darbon"). Sartre suggested *The Griots* ("we rather liked comparing ourselves to those blacksmiths-cum-witchdoctors-cum-poets whom certain African societies honor, fear and despise all at the same time; but it was too esoteric") (Beauvoir 1992b, 20). It was Lanzmann who, in the end, suggested *The Mandarins*, and Beauvoir was immediately enamored with the title.[9] After correcting the first galleys of the book, she wrote to Algren on July 12, 1954: "I don't know how you call in English this [*sic*] Chinese intellectuals among whom some revolutionary leaders were picked, but who looked a little out of date, first: Mandarines? It makes a nice title in French" (1997a, 502). Capturing the ideas of revolution, the weight of the past, and the richness of Parisian intellectual and political life, *The Mandarins* was indeed the perfect title for the book.

As one of the first books to portray the Reconstruction, the novel went to press in October 1954 and exploded onto the French literary scene. Even though Beauvoir was extremely anxious about the book's reception because of her intimate connection with it and years of labor on it, she was soon relieved and even elated by the book's instant success. In fact, she found that she had written a book that was accessible and relevant to many different political and social factions. She recounts,

> Was I going to be greeted with approval from all sides? On the whole, yes. Reversing my expectations, it was the bourgeois critics who found that my novel had a pleasing odor of anti-Communism, while the Communists took it, quite rightly, as an expression of sympathy for them. As for the non-Communist left wing, it was in its name that I had been attempting to speak. Only a few Socialists and the extreme Right attacked me with any venom. Forty thousand copies were sold in the first month. (1992b, 35)

Having completed an enormous undertaking that had consumed four years of her life (not to mention the years of thought that had preceded the moment of taking pen to paper), Beauvoir was able to experience success and satisfaction immediately.

Bair tells us that the publication date of *The Mandarins* had been set for October "to launch the novel at exactly the most fortuitous moment to be a candidate for the prestigious Prix Goncourt. A massive publicity campaign was launched, and Beauvoir cooperated with everything her publisher asked her to do" (Bair 1990, 427–28). The Prix Goncourt is widely held to be the most distinguished literary award in France and is given annually to a generally young and unknown author. The Prix Goncourt, which was first awarded in 1903, was meant to provide fresh talent with a monetary award that would free them from financial worries so that they could write their second book. Among the earlier recipients were such authors as Marcel Proust (1919) and André Malraux (1933). The publicity campaign, coupled with the wide appeal of the book, won Beauvoir the Goncourt in January 1955. As evidenced by her supporters and critics, many believed that she unquestioningly deserved the award and others complained that she was too old and too established to have been deserving. *The Mandarins* was, after all, her fourth novel, and she had already established worldwide fame as the author of *The Second Sex*. Regardless, the award brought greater fame and wealth (both from the prize money and the ensuing increase in sales of the book itself). In fact, with the money Beauvoir was able to purchase a Parisian apartment for the first time in her life and nicknamed her new domicile "the place that Goncourt bought" (quoted in Bair 1990, 453).

Despite the book's success, Beauvoir gave only one interview (namely, to *Humanité-Dimanche*), and did so to make clear "that my novel was not hostile to the Communists and that it had not aroused their enmity" (Beauvoir 1992b, 36). She avoided public appearances, because she found it repugnant to exhibit herself. Whereas she admits that ten years earlier she would have enjoyed the attention, at the time *The Mandarins* received the award and all of its consequent accolades, Beauvoir declares plainly, "I have neither braggadocio nor indifference enough to offer myself as willing fodder for the curious" (36). She had made the decision to let the book stand on its own merits and with a modicum of interference by the author.

Not everyone was thrilled with *The Mandarins*, however. As Beauvoir had learned with *The Second Sex*, there are plenty of people who are not receptive to women authors at all, and certainly not to ones who freely discuss social, political and intimate issues that are far from uncontroversial. The Catholic Church placed both *The Second Sex* and *The Mandarins* on the index of prohibited books—both books for which Beauvoir felt tremendous affinity.[10] Castigating the two books for their portrayals of "free love" and their critiques of marriage and motherhood, the ban actually had the effect of increasing, rather than harming, their sales (Bair 1990, 456–57). Barbara Klaw explains how even the American edition of *The Mandarins* mitigated more offensive language and deleted two scenes depicting oral sex (Klaw 1995, 197, 205). Beauvoir was not unaware of the editing practices of American publishers; she had experienced it with H. M. Parshley's translation of *The Second Sex* (Simons [1983] 1999). Beauvoir recounts that when discussing the translation of *The Mandarins* with her publisher, he apologized for "having had to make a few cuts here and there, just a few lines. 'In the States it's all right to talk about sex in a book,' he explained, 'but not about perversion'" (1992b, 70).

Despite the small roar from the socially and religiously fastidious, the book was translated into numerous foreign languages (even Braille) within the first few years of publication. In the end, Beauvoir considered it to be one of her greatest achievements and her favorite novel (Fallaize [1988] 1990, 88). Its success is due to the clarity of vision and inspiration of its author and to the wealth of themes and issues that it fearlessly tackles. Because of its constellation of characters and situations, *The Mandarins* was interpreted by many different critics to hold a diversity of meanings and themes. With this, we turn to the critical reception of the novel.

Critical Reception of *The Mandarins* at Home and Abroad

As Beauvoir notes in *The Force of Circumstance*: "A book is a collective object. Readers contribute as much as the author to its creation" (1992a, 38). The idea that a book is formed through a collaborative effort between readers and author is certainly vindicated by the wide array of reactions from reviewers of *The Mandarins*. Beauvoir's novel managed to create a stir—both positive and negative—with many different critics.

The high praise for the novel added to its resounding success. Arguing against those who criticized the choice of Beauvoir for the Prix Goncourt, Maurice

Chavardès writes in *La Vie Intellectuelle* that regardless of her age or the number of books she had published, *The Mandarins* is "representative of the epoch, probably the best book of the year" (Chavardès 1955, 134). In fact, Chavardès asks, what does it matter if there are similarities between actual people and characters in the novel? How else can one faithfully recreate the post-Liberation era? (134). In an interview with Alexandre Arnoux in *Le Figaro Litteraire*, Arnoux compares Beauvoir to Balzac and remarks frankly that the prejudice against the book is a result of Beauvoir's notoriety and in no way reflective of the story's merits (Guth 1954, 4).

Some critics, taking note of an aspect of the story that many miss, commend the book for its humor. Dominique Aury's review of *The Mandarins* in *La Nouvelle Revue Française* argues that humor, often forgotten in women's writing, is a central strength of Beauvoir's novel (Aury 1954, 1080). In the American publication *The Reporter*, Madeleine Chapsal highlights the irony of the title by pointing out that the mandarins are themselves intellectual figures who live separated from the masses. She continues, "It is with humor that Simone de Beauvoir, who is one of them, describes the tormented adventures of writers and thinkers—these overexcited, irritable, unstable characters who are always questioning the wisdom, the usefulness, and the purpose of each of their actions" (Chapsal 1955, 46). But far from being a scathing lampoon of these French figures, Chapsal finds that Beauvoir has instead "written the most humane novel that has appeared in France in recent years" (46). Highlighting the wide appeal of the book beyond France's borders, *London Magazine*'s Erik de Mauny finds that the novel delves "into the always vital issues of freedom and compromise in modern society, of personal loyalty and political commitment. It so happens that the small brightly-lit stage of Left Bank politics throws these issues into glaring contrast, but the shadows stretch far beyond the Seine" (Mauny 1957, 73).

Of course, there are those critics who, while trying to compliment Beauvoir, actually do so in backhanded fashion. For example, Yves Gandon in *Livres de France* artfully argues against the characterization of *The Mandarins* as a roman à clef and says that its chief merit lies in the fact that it is a reflection of actual events that transpired. However, sandwiched around a photograph of Sartre and Beauvoir with the former titled "the master" and the latter "the disciple," Gandon writes that the Goncourt Academy, having missed awarding Sartre the prize for *Nausea*, instead gave it to Beauvoir. This action was "an honor to the master through the disciple" (Gandon 1955, 13). Sexism toward Beauvoir and her work was nothing new. Often considered to be nothing but a disciple of Sartre, her work was scrutinized by both men and women in a harsher light than was the work of her male existentialist counterparts.

Having undergone the tribulations of publishing *The Second Sex* in 1949, Beauvoir was somewhat prepared for the acrimonious criticisms that inevitably result from a woman writing frankly and with a sense for great detail (no matter how shocking) about important and often silenced issues. Anticipating the arrival of *The Mandarins* in the bookstores in October 1954, Beauvoir recalls, "*The Second Sex* had taught me a lesson; I could almost hear all the unpleasant gossip in advance. I had put so much of myself into this book that there were moments when my cheeks burned at the idea of indifferent or hostile eyes moving across its pages" (1992b, 35). And indeed, there were certainly those critics who lambasted Beauvoir for any number of offenses: indecency, verboseness, age (regarding her winning of the Prix Goncourt), mimicry (of Sartre), and, of course, for transposing her personal life into what many claimed to be a thinly veiled roman à clef. As with all great works, the harshest of critics also reveal layers of depth and insights into the work that would be lacking were we to only focus on the high praise. With this in mind, it is helpful and sometimes even amusing to turn to a few of the most severe reviews.

Critical of the Academy for awarding the Prix Goncourt to a well-known author, Isolde Farrell writes in *America* that the skeleton of the story is "dry and brittle" and that "The flesh with which she covers it, in introducing us to her heroes' private lives, is frankly malodorous" (Farrell 1955, 594). Given that *America* is in fact the *National Catholic Weekly Review*, such criticism is hardly surprising.[11] Also finding fault with the Academy for its choice of Beauvoir, Italian critic Anna Banti writes in *Paragone* that Beauvoir's novel (what she calls "an 'essay' that is novelized") serves to show the "profound distance" between French and Italian literature (Banti 1955, 110).[12] In a caustic attack on Beauvoir for what she finds to be a sloppy mixture of personal experience, moral and political reasoning, and fictional intrigues, Banti concludes that the Goncourt Academy had no business giving Beauvoir the award. In so doing, they had to forgive her for "the long reportage and journalistic dialogues, the innumerable martinis and whiskies and *couchages all'americana*"[13] (111). In the German publication *der Monat*, François Bondy goes so far as to claim that the novel is almost entirely autobiographical and should be read as a complement to her memoirs rather than purely as a work of fiction. He also argues that her descriptions of sociopolitical events are somewhat touristy and superficial: "[S]he can mourn about her close friends, but the remaining people are either 'masses'—like Castro's five hundred thousand listeners, such that we are left to think how politics for Madame de Beauvoir was a bit of tourism and aesthetic travel experiences—or supporters of false ideas" (Bondy 1964, 29).

The criticism of the novel as mere reportage of actual people and events often took on unabashedly harsh overtones. The *New Yorker*'s Norman Podhoretz writes that *The Mandarins* "may very well be the most relentlessly thoroughgoing *roman à clef* since the eighteenth century. Indeed, virtually nothing in the book but the names of the characters appears to derive from her imagination" (Podhoretz 1956, 156). In his review, there is the distinct flavor of a typically American attitude toward French thinkers who were left leaning and critical of American actions. And Podhoretz was not alone in dismissing the novel because of its implicit and explicit critiques of American capitalism and international policies. Donald Malcolm's review in the *New Republic*, entitled "Simone Go Home," expresses great umbrage at Beauvoir's choice of the Soviet Union over America (Malcolm 1956, 19). The effrontery at the perceived anti-Americanism in the text reaches what can only be called comical pitches in Frank Getlein's attack in *Commonweal.* Claiming that the West is a "dirty word" for Beauvoir, Getlein recounts the story in condescending words, calling it "very dull and very flat" and filled with long and pointless love scenes (Getlein 1956, 279). In fact, Getlein writes priggishly, "The only narrative question raised by the constant cohabitation in *The Mandarins* is, Will they ever get out of that bed so we can get on with the story?" (279). Brushing aside Beauvoir as a writer, Getlein chides, "Thus the Goncourt Mandarins passed the palm to La Grande Sartreuse as one praises a three-year-old violinist: not that she writes so well, but that she writes at all" (279).

Time's anonymous review of *The Mandarins* is an extreme example of how the attitude toward Beauvoir as a person easily turned the book review into little more than an ad hominem attack. Completely unaware of the irony, the review opens with the claim, "Like many of her sisters in what she bitterly refers to as the Second Sex, France's Simone de Beauvoir would rather talk than eat" (Time 67 1956, 104). Not clarifying exactly what that might *mean*, the review proceeds to critique what it considers to be a detailed account of the Beauvoir-Algren affair (interestingly, the very next book reviewed is Algren's *Walk on the Wild Side*) and then gives a description of Beauvoir as a "handsome woman" who is involved in an unmarried "liaison" with Sartre. To determine why she is so unhappy and her philosophy so "bleak," her upbringing and social life are dissected long before the review returns to actually talking about the book—which it does quickly and insufficiently.

Many of the reviews, however, attempted a much more even-handed treatment of the novel. In these cases, the reviewers found the exceptional qualities of the book most noteworthy and also added their opinions about what could stand improvement. In this spirit of balance, Paul Engle argues in the *Chicago Sunday Tribune* that the book is complex and philosophically relevant. He adds, with humor, that "it contains what must be certainly the longest, if indeed not the only, sustained love affair between a Frenchwoman and an American man in Chicago" (Engle 1956, 3). And when Engle points to what he sees as anti-Americanism, his criticisms are astute and levelheaded: "What hurts us is that all of those men and women, while accusing the United States of trying to make them conform and while defending the soviet union, would be the first to be stamped into conformity if the soviet way ever took over in France" (3). Virgilia Peterson's review in the *New York Herald Tribune Weekly Book Review* claims that although some of the scenes are "needlessly vulgar;

some have a surprising capacity to touch"; and the failures of the text are often in the translation, not in the writing (Peterson 1956, 3). In fact, *The Mandarins* is, in her opinion, "by far Simone de Beauvoir's most impressive book" (3).

Perhaps the most sensitive and respectful review comes from Iris Murdoch. Murdoch shows us the value to be garnered by one author reviewing another. Noting the philosophical complexity of the book, Murdoch lauds it for having "the nerve to be intensely contemporary" (Murdoch 1956, 493). She pinpoints the keen political and psychological analysis Beauvoir employs in the development of the story and mentions some of the most fundamental themes amplified by Beauvoir: the tragic nature of action, the betrayal of the dead, the weight of the past, and the conflict between the sexes. Even though she finds that "too much of the book lies at one remove from reality" and that the characters live in a "far more denuded world" than the world of ordinary customs and virtues, Murdoch's criticisms are couched more in terms of admiration than condemnation (493). Respectful of the enormous accomplishment, sensitive to its philosophical and literary achievements, critical of its shortcomings, Murdoch shows us that the best way to approach *The Mandarins* is as part of the story, rather than as outside observers. Full of curiosity and questions, we too should approach this book like one of the mandarins who must come to terms with what it means to be a thinker and an actor, a citizen and a critic, an individual and a member of the collective. And we should always remember that Beauvoir herself considered her work to be a collective object. It is our task to contribute our part to it.

The Contradictions of Freedom

The pieces in this collection, taken from a broad spectrum of scholars and interpretative strategies, attest to the vividness of Simone de Beauvoir's ideas concerning politics, professional life, relationships, responsibility, choice, and the various contradictions that result when these areas of human experience come into conflict.

The political climate of post–World War II France is beautifully captured by Beauvoir. It is fitting that fifty years later a collection of philosophical pieces on the novel would begin with a chapter that scrutinizes this early cold war atmosphere. William L. McBride's "The Conflict of Ideologies in *The Mandarins*: Communism and Democracy, Then and Now" shows how Beauvoir used the intellectuals portrayed in her story to reflect on the cold war's two opposing ideologies and the political philosophies underlying them. McBride analyzes Beauvoir's assessment of communism and democracy by understanding the latter as overcoming domination and subordination worldwide. To be a communist was to believe in a long-term project that required a personal commitment to the

Party's current political judgment; the Soviet regime represented the promise of liberation for workers the world over. Contrasting sharply to this assessment is the assessment of the United States with its project of world capitalism, or neo-imperialism. He concludes with a salient social critique through the eyes of Beauvoir's mandarins fifty years later. As McBride demonstrates, if we look back at the political, ideological, and social rifts of the late 1940s and early 1950s in light of new and remaining tensions, then Beauvoir appears prophetic. Her insight into the political climate of her era through the experience of the intellectuals makes her a critic for our era as well.

Politics, as McBride's chapter illustrates, is about political positions as much as it is about political parties. Taking a stance against domination constitutes perhaps the most prominent political position within *The Mandarins.* Rarely does one act alone in movements for social change of this sort. Sally J. Scholz sees *The Mandarins* as a text addressing the solidarity of individuals within social and political movements for liberation in her chapter "Sustained Praxis: The Challenge of Solidarity in *The Mandarins* and Beyond." Scholz argues that Beauvoir's ethics and politics reveal three basic levels of solidary relations. She uses *The Mandarins* to illustrate the varying obligations that emerge in each of the levels characterized by situation, reciprocity, and commitment. Henri's experiences in Portugal, like his decisions to unite *L'Espoir* to SRL and give false testimony to save Josette, expand the bounds of solidarity and revise the aims of group praxis. For any political movement, one of the key questions is how to stay relevant and active. According to Scholz, Beauvoir offers some insights into this question of group praxis while also emphasizing the unique contribution of individuals.

Sonia Kruks's "Living on Rails: Freedom, Constraint, and Political Judgment in Beauvoir's 'Moral' Essays and *The Mandarins*" develops the theme of individual action in political struggle. Beauvoir, Kruks argues, emphasizes individual responsibility for decisions. Whereas Beauvoir's early essays remain abstract, *The Second Sex* and *The Mandarins* illustrate the importance of situation in any understanding of the individual's freedom. Even more telling is the way *The Mandarins* demonstrates that political judgment itself is action informed by situation. Henri's decision to make *L'Espoir* an organ of the SRL demonstrates how the numerous aspects of one's situation permeate decision-making processes. Far from being a resignation, Henri's judgment results from the shifts in his own existence and his own situation. Kruks's phenomenology of political judgment expands contemporary discussions of Beauvoir's political philosophy by deepening the importance of "situation."

Whereas an analysis of situation illuminates *how* an individual makes a political judgment, an analysis of the individual's responsibility to history and the Other helps to explain *why*. In "Testimony, *Historicité*, and the Intellectual in Simone de Beauvoir's *The Mandarins*," Ursula Tidd argues that a dominant problematic in Simone de Beauvoir's novel is the political and ethical implications of truth-telling and the intellectual's responsibility to history. Tidd seeks to analyze the notions of testimony and truth production at work in *The Mandarins*, that is, to show how speech or testimony is political action. She argues that Beauvoir's earlier fiction, especially *The Blood of Others* and *All Men are Mortal*, similarly focus on action but distinguish it from speech in personal and political relations. *The Mandarins*, according to Tidd, politicizes speech and literature, thereby highlighting the intellectual's role in social change. She reflects on the ethico-political responsibility of the committed intellectual, especially in light of the Holocaust, postwar reconstruction, and cold war tensions.

Karen Vintges's article "The Return of Commitment: Simone de Beauvoir's *The Mandarins* Revisited" furthers the theme of the commitment of intellectuals, arguing that Beauvoir's novel offers insight into taking a position in ethics and politics while avoiding the pitfalls of dogmatism. Vintges sees *The Mandarins* as developing an ethical "art of living" or "mode of life" that helps to inform political commitment while keeping that commitment from taking on an existence of its own over and against the individual. The key is to avoid the absolutism of Truth but not to sacrifice political struggle. Vintges uses Foucault to push the existentialists' view of freedom into a more nuanced understanding of culture and multiculturalism. However, she also uses Beauvoir to challenge the insufficiency of Foucault's "specific intellectual" as the model of the committed intellectual.

But this raises something of a dilemma for the intellectual. As Gail Weiss argues, the individual is faced with the problem of how to engage in politics but also be true to his or her own projects and values. Her chapter "'Politics Is a Living Thing': The Intellectual's Dilemma in Beauvoir's *The Mandarins*" illustrates that political commitment must be individualized; responsibility for one's past and present entails participation in political engagement for a liberated future. Moreover, as Anne's experiences reveal, passion plays an important role in commitment. Anne's passion brought her back to life after the realization that her love affair was over, but it also suffuses the relationships and decisions of Lambert, Henri, Nadine, and Robert. Philosophy, as Weiss concludes, is not the passionless, abstract activity it is often purported to be. Beauvoir's position requires philosophy, and indeed all intellectual activity, to be politically engaged while recognizing the political import of personal decisions.

Shannon M. Mussett's "Personal Choice and the Seduction of the Absolute in *The Mandarins*" takes up the theme of the personal dimension in decision-making by exploring Beauvoir's critique of absolutism in relation to her depiction of the character of Anne Dubreuilh. Mussett begins with a detailed discussion of Beauvoir's critical analysis of absolute values in her ethical works and proceeds to show how Beauvoir uses the character of Anne as the site where the struggle against absolutism plays itself out most clearly in the novel.

Anne is an illustration of the complex conflict the existent must face in moving from dependence upon external values and authority to the assertion of freedom as the only ethical absolute. Following a discussion of absolutism and seriousness in *Pyrrhus et Cinéas* and *The Ethics of Ambiguity*, Mussett develops Beauvoir's rejection of the Heideggerian being-toward-death as the ultimate absolute in favor of a being toward freedom. As Mussett contends, Beauvoir's philosophical critique of absolutism is portrayed in Anne's arduous journey away from her dependence upon external ideas and existents (such as God, her husband, and her American lover). Crucial to her journey, Anne must confront the figure of Paule Mareuil, who both mirrors and apes Anne's love choices. Illustrating the final break from dependency on external absolutes, Mussett focuses on Anne's truly free decision not end her own life.

Further exploring the dynamics of interpersonal conflicts and relationships, Jen McWeeny argues that Beauvoir develops a trialectical theory that challenges the Hegelian dialectic. In "Love, Theory, and Politics: Critical Trinities in Simone de Beauvoir's *The Mandarins*" McWeeny discusses a number of Beauvoir's "critical trinities" and argues that this structure allows Beauvoir to diagnose cases of oppression and to more successfully seek ways to overcome them. When these trinities are interpreted in light of Beauvoir's idea, espoused in *The Second Sex*, that woman stands outside of Hegel's master-slave dialectic, they offer a description of an alternative theory of personal and historical relationships. Whereas Hegel's dialectic is focused on the relationship of opposition, McWeeny finds that Beauvoir's alternative triadic theory centrally involves gifts and recognitions of absolute separateness. To bring this discovery to light, McWeeny focuses on third parties that are positioned outside of various dialectics (e.g., woman, intellectuals, socialists, and the French people) who assert themselves through the choice of whether to be complicit with or revolt against the systems that they are observing. McWeeny concludes by arguing that Beauvoir's trialectical theory points us beyond oppression by opening up the possibility of relationships based not on oppressive practices and exclusionary eclipses, but instead on gifts, withdrawals, and solitude.

Approaching Beauvoir in a dialogue with her existentialist contemporaries, Thomas W. Busch studies the relationship between Beauvoir and her fiction in "Simone de Beauvoir on Achieving Subjectivity." Busch emphasizes Beauvoir's success in writing a novel about characters in complex social and historical situations, rather than portraying characters as thinly veiled philosophical ideas. Busch contends that in their relationships to their situations and to one another and in their choices and their identity development, the characters in *The Mandarins* reflect neither the dichotomies of Sartre's ontology as expressed in *Being and Nothingness* nor the alternative lifestyles outlined there of bad faith and authenticity. These features of her philosophical outlook show, Busch argues, a similarity to the views of Merleau-Ponty and to Sartre's later (dialectical) work. Since Merleau-Ponty stressed, against Sartre, a concrete social/historical account of subjectivity, the question of the relationship to and possible influences between Beauvoir and Merleau-Ponty arises. Despite what postmodern critics of phenomenology (and of Beauvoir and Merleau-Ponty) have spoken about the contamination of phenomenological accounts of subjectivity by Cartesianism, Busch argues that it is possible to see both Beauvoir and Merleau-Ponty as exorcising the Cartesian contamination with their concrete notion of achieving subjectivity, a view of subjectivity that shares features with postmodernism.

Eleanore Holveck also focuses on the dynamics of relationships and the Beauvoirian critique of the Hegelian dialectic in "When a Woman Loves a Man: Ownness and Otherness in *The Mandarins*." Opening with the work of Milan Kundera, who depicts sexuality as a private, immediate relationship between a man and a woman, Holveck contrasts this view with Beauvoir's depiction of the relationship between Anne Dubreuilh and Lewis Brogan in *The Mandarins*. Holveck argues that Beauvoir's phenomenological existentialism emphasizes that one's freedom always exists in a world that is grounded at the same time in the freedom of others. Holveck claims that the love between Anne and Lewis exemplifies Beauvoir's reinterpretation of the sphere of ownness and its relation to otherness in Edmund Husserl's theory of intersubjectivity in the Fifth Cartesian Meditation. Holveck compares Beauvoir's analysis to that of Milan Kundera's *Slowness* and Nelson Algren's *Never Come Morning*. Tracing the maturation of the relationship between Anne and Lewis in stages, Holveck shows how at the peak of their relationship, the lovers achieve a merging of intentional temporality, only to have it fall apart when the differences of their past histories and lives come to the surface. Despite the eventual breakup between the lovers, Beauvoir, of all the authors discussed, alone successfully describes free sensuous communication between one free existent and the other. As Holveck shows, it is through her reading of Husserl that Beauvoir is capable of moving beyond Hegelian configurations built upon conflict to show us the possibility of a shared intersubjectivity.

Peg Brand argues in "Salon-Haunters: The Impasse Facing French Intellectuals" that Beauvoir maintains a unified theory of aesthetics throughout her ethics, feminism, and fiction. Brand notes that there are two possibilities for the work of art—either it functions ethically to encourage freedom and the general well-being of humanity, or it functions to glorify the artist and lead others to engage in unethical activities. Brand locates the impasse facing the artist in the two main figures of Henri and Robert (seen through the eyes of Anne, Robert's wife), who are constantly torn between their humanistic political goals and a personal desire to live the aesthetic lifestyle. Through their stories, Beauvoir portrays the conundrum that every artist faces—an impasse that sets action against inaction, politics against culture. Brand discovers that Beauvoir's theory of art in *The Mandarins*, aided by an analysis of women's oppression in *The Second Sex*, advocates the view that art keeps past events alive in the present and in so doing can change even the tragic into the life affirming. She concludes by returning to the idea of Beauvoir's compromise theory of art to show how even those who want to better the world through artistic creation are still plagued by doubt as to the eventual outcome of their activities. However, as Brand points out, Beauvoir's compromise theory advocates that the artist continue to engage in artistic endeavors in the face of such doubt in order to maintain an ethical relationship to the rest of humanity.

The Importance of *The Mandarins* Today

The Mandarins raises compelling philosophical questions regarding the individual's responsibility in state-sponsored violence, the possibility of attaining human solidarity in the face of poverty and inequality, the parameters of collective decision-making, the impact of the historical situation on the individual, the ambiguity of the artist's project, and the vicissitudes of love and personal choice. In line with the very premise of *The Mandarins*, the various essays in this collection address these issues and highlight the important role of the intellectual in shaping personal and political life.

Beauvoir's novel continues to speak to us in myriad and significant ways. The same questions that haunted the political scene of postwar Europe remain at the forefront of the contemporary world. Beauvoir often acknowledges her use of literature as a vehicle for exploring philosophical ideas, and the characters that populate this novel reveal the difficulties of living an intellectual or aesthetic life. *The Mandarins* also confronts head-on the obligations of intellectuals within political movements, while simultaneously drawing attention to the paradoxes and impossibilities of such participation. Since the student riots of 1960s, the academy has fought to remain connected and relevant; indeed, many would argue that the academy's role is not to comment on culture and politics but to be the vanguard of change. A fresh look at the moral implications of the "intellectual as activist" issue, sparked by Beauvoir's insightful articulation of it, lends an important new perspective to the current discussion. Additionally, the questions of responsibility for dictatorships, the unification of Europe into a common political and economic block, the struggle between capitalism and socialism in public policy, and, of course, the relationship between Europe and the United States all remain considerable issues. In particular, it is fascinating to see the current tensions between France and the United States, as the same paternalistic and condescending attitude remains alive and well in the latter's treatment of the former. The ever-present threat and reality of war hangs over the international community in many of the same ways that Beauvoir chronicles in her novel, and we would do well to heed her warnings about the consequences of war not only while it is waged, but also in its long-term effects on the survivors.

What Beauvoir offers us in *The Mandarins* is an opportunity to reflect on the political contradictions that result from war, occupation, and the clash of cultures, as well as the personal toll that these political realities take on individuals. The interpersonal relationships of the characters relay the complexities of love and choice, and the often treacherous results of our attempts to find meaning in the face of an objectively meaningless reality. Refusing to separate the two from each other, Beauvoir presents the readers with an extremely relevant testimony on lived experience in the modern age. We are called upon to pay close attention to Beauvoir's often painful and frightening descriptions of death, love, war, and politics. As she repeats throughout her philosophical and literary corpus, without constant vigilance to the past we are depopulating our future and annihilating our present. Perhaps we can read *The Mandarins* with minds willing to face past atrocities so as to prevent their present and future repetitions.

Notes

1. Prime examples of the literary studies include Ascher 1981, Brosman 1991, Fallaize [1988] 1990, Holveck 2002, Keefe 1983, and Keefe 1998.

2. In 1944, Beauvoir, ghost-writing under Sartre's name for the journal *Combat*, wrote "Un promeneur dans Paris insurgé" [A Walk in Insurgent Paris] about the street skirmishes experienced during the Liberation (Bair 1990, 293).

3. See Claude Chambard [1970] 1976 for a detailed account of the Resistance movement.

4. Some of the latter also appeared in the journal *Volenté.*

5. Just as Beauvoir herself did in her April 1945 articles for *Combat.*

6. For example, in a letter to Algren she writes, "I put a lot of things in it, travels, drunken evenings, young and mature people, some of Koestler, Camus and Sartre, and myself, indeed" (1997a, 472).

7. Bair tells us that although he was angry at the publication of *The Mandarins*, Algren's rage was "nothing compared to his fury over what she wrote about him in the memoirs" (Bair 1990, 500).

8. Bair tells us that Beauvoir blamed the absentmindedness of leaving the manuscript in the taxi on her preoccupation with Algren. She also recounts that Beauvoir recovered the lost manuscript in the lost-and-found ten days later (after she had rewritten the greater part of it from memory) (Bair 1990, 417).

9. Beauvoir credits Lanzmann with suggesting the title *Les Mandarins* (1992b, 20). However, Bair recounts that it was Bost, not Lanzmann, whom Beauvoir credits with the title (1990, 427).

10. Beauvoir writes, "I see myself reflected no less in *The Second Sex* than in *The Mandarins*, and vice versa. If I have used two different modes of self-expression, it was because such diversity was for me a necessity" (1992b, 41).

11. *Catholic World* is also critical of the "scenes of illicit love" (Hughes 1956, 230).

12. The editors would like to express gratitude to Lucio Privitello for translating Banti's text.

13. Perhaps best translated as "the American style of sleeping around."

Works Cited

Ascher, Carol. 1981. *Simone de Beauvoir: A life of freedom*. Boston: Beacon Press.

Aury, Dominique. 1954. Les romans: Personne ne triche. Review of *The mandarins*, by Simone de Beauvoir. *La Nouvelle Revue Française* 24 (December): 1080–85.

Bair, Deirdre. 1990. *Simone de Beauvoir: A biography*. New York: Summit Books.

Banti, Anna. 1955. Simone de Beauvoir. Review of *The mandarins*, by Simone de Beauvoir. *Paragone* 6, no. 64 (April): 110–12.

Beauvoir, Simone de [Daniel Secrétan, pseud.]. 1945. Quatre jours à Madrid. Combat, April 14 and 15.

———. 1952. *The second sex*. Translated by H. M. Parshley. New York: Bantam Books. (An English translation of *La deuxième sexe, vols. 1 and* 2, originally published in French by Gallimard in 1949.)

———. 1954. *Les mandarins*. Paris: Gallimard.

———. 1956. *The mandarins*. Translated by Leonard M. Friedman. New York: World Publishing Company. (The work was reprinted by W.W. Norton & Company in 1999.)

———. [1963] 1986. *Memoirs of a dutiful daughter*. Translated by James Kirkup. Middlesex, England: Penguin Books. (An English translation of *Memoirs d'une jeune fille rangée*, originally published in French by Gallimard in 1958.)

———. 1966. *The prime of life*. Translated by Peter Green. New York: Lancer Books. (An English translation of *La force de l'âge*, originally published in French by Gallimard in 1960.)

———. 1992a. *The force of circumstance*. Vol. 1, *After the War, 1944–1952*. Translated by Richard Howard. New York: Paragon House. (An English translation of *La force des choses*, originally published in French by Gallimard in 1963.)

———. 1992b. *The force of circumstance*. Vol. 2, *Hard Times, 1952–1962*. Translated by Richard Howard. New York: Paragon House. (An English translation of *La force des choses*, originally published in French by Gallimard in 1963.)

———. 1997a. *A translatlantic love affair: Letters to Nelson Algren*. Compiled and annotated by Sylvie le Bon de Beauvoir. New York: New Press.

——— [Daniel Secrétan, pseud.]. 1997b. Le Portugal sous le régime de Salazar. In *Les Écrits de Simone de Beauvoir*, edited by Claude Francis and Fernande Gontier, 317–23. Paris: Gallimard.

Bondy, François. 1964. Die Großmandarine—Rückansicht: Zum abschluß der memoiren Simone de Beauvoirs. Review of *The mandarins*, by Simone de Beauvoir. *Der Monat* 16, no. 192 (September): 24–29.

Brosman, Catherine Savage. 1991. *Simone de Beauvoir revisited.* Boston: Twayne Publishers.

Chambard, Claude. [1970] 1976. *The maquis: A history of the French Resistance Movement.* Translated by Elaine P. Halperin. New York: Bobbs-Merrill.

Chapsal, Madeleine. 1955. A prize-winning novel by Simone de Beauvoir. Review of *The mandarins*, by Simone de Beauvoir. *The Reporter* 12, no. 2 (January 27): 46–47.

Chavardès, Maurice. 1955. Les mandarins. Review of *The mandarins*, by Simone de Beauvoir. *La Vie Intellectuelle*, January, 133–37.

Engle, Paul. 1956. Long, furious novel explains postwar Paris intellectuals. Review of *The mandarins*, by Simone de Beauvoir. *Chicago Sunday Tribune*, May 27, 3.

Fallaize, Elizabeth. [1988] 1990. *The novels of Simone de Beauvoir.* London: Routledge.

Farrell, Isolde. 1955. Paris letter. Review of *The mandarins*, by Simone de Beauvoir. *America*, March 5, 593–94.

Gandon, Yves. 1955. Les mandarins par Simone de Beauvoir. Review of *The mandarins*, by Simone de Beauvoir. *Livres de France* 6, no. 1 (January): 13–14.

Getlein, Frank. 1956. Review of *The mandarins*, by Simone de Beauvoir. *Commonweal*, June 15, 279–80.

Guth, Paul. 1954. Review of *The mandarins*, by Simone de Beauvoir. *Le Figaro Litteraire*, November 27.

Holveck, Eleanore. 2002. *The philosophy of lived experience.* Lanham, Md.: Rowman and Littlefield.

Hughes, Riley. 1956. Review of *The mandarins*, by Simone de Beauvoir. *Catholic World* 183 (June): 230.

Keefe, Terry. 1983. *Simone de Beauvoir: A study of her writings.* London: Harrap.

———. 1998. *Simone de Beauvoir.* New York: St. Martin's Press.

Klaw, Barbara. 1995. Sexuality in Beauvoir's *Les mandarins.* In *Feminist interpretations of Simone de Beauvoir*, edited by Margaret A. Simons. University Park: Pennsylvania State University Press.

Malcolm, Donald. 1956. Simone go home. Review of *The mandarins*, by Simone de Beauvoir. *New Republic* 134 (June 18): 18–19.

Mauny, Erik de. 1957. Review of *The mandarins*, by Simone de Beauvoir. *London Magazine* 4, no. 6:73–75.

McBride, William L. 1991. *Sartre's political theory.* Indianapolis: Indiana University Press.

Murdoch, Iris. 1956. At one remove from tragedy. Review of *The mandarins*, by Simone de Beauvoir. *Nation* 182, (June 9): 493–94.

Peterson, Virgilia. 1956. Post-liberation Paris in Simone de Beauvoir's novel. Review of *The mandarins*, by Simone de Beauvoir. *New York Herald Tribune Weekly*, May 27.

Podhoretz, Norman. 1956. Experience of our time. Review of *The mandarins*, by Simone de Beauvoir. *New Yorker*, September 15, 156–63.

Ritsch, Frederick. 1966. *The French Left and the European idea, 1947–1949*. New York: Pageant.

Sartre, Jean-Paul [Simone de Beauvoir]. 1944. Un promeneur dans Paris insurgé. *Combat*, August 28, 29, 30 and September 1, 2, 4.

Simons, Margaret. [1983] 1999. The silencing of Simone de Beauvoir: Guess what's missing from *The second sex*? In *Beauvoir and the second sex: Feminism, race and the origins of existentialism*. Lanham, Md.: Rowman and Littlefield.

Time 67. 1956. Review of *The mandarins*, by Simone de Beauvoir. *Time*, May 28, 104, 106.

Vinen, Richard. 1995. *Bourgeois politics in France, 1945–1951*. Cambridge: Cambridge University Press.

Chapter 1

The Conflict of Ideologies in *The Mandarins*

Communism and Democracy, Then and Now

William L. McBride

The Mandarins is, of course, a period piece—in the best sense of that term. It is redolent of the early years of the cold war, which, as it documents very well, began almost as soon as the Liberation of Paris had been achieved. Although it is still probably unnecessary to explain to any but the youngest students what the cold war was in the broadest terms—a decades-long global conflict between the Soviet and Western blocs, during which the threat of a new world war involving atomic weapons was always thought to exist, at certain times more than others—its actual "feel" and its details are certainly in the process of being forgotten. Fifty years after the original publication date of *The Mandarins* is also fifteen years past the time of the dramatic changes in Eastern Europe that marked the dissolution of the Soviet Bloc. So to reread *The Mandarins* is above all to be reminded of other times, is it not?

Well, yes and no. For there are eerily deep similarities between then and now that the perceptive contemporary reader cannot help but note. Gone today, it is true, are most Communist Parties (China being the major exception) and communist ideology (China being no exception in this regard). But the sense of political conflict and of deep foreboding concerning the world's future that pervades *The Mandarins* is also very characteristic of the present time. And the fear of global American hegemony, which was still offset by a counterbalancing fear of Soviet imperialist aspirations in 1954, has become a major preoccupation once again in France, and indeed in most of the rest of the world, to a far greater extent than perhaps in any decade since the 1950s. As I shall attempt to show in this article, Simone de Beauvoir's vision in *The Mandarins* was in many ways prophetic.

But what was her "vision"? On the positive side, with respect to her vision of a possible better future, even her *Ethics of Ambiguity* yields no simple label for her ideal, and *The Mandarins* is even less yielding in this respect. "Socialism and freedom," the label (based on the name of a Resistance group to which he belonged) that I have suggested elsewhere for Sartre's ideal, is no doubt also applicable to hers, but it requires a great deal of explanation, especially in order to distinguish the envisaged form of socialism from the Soviet model (which is one of the constant tasks of most of the principal characters in *The Mandarins*) (McBride 1991, 10–11). The word "ambiguity" describes the *reality* of ethical practice, so beautifully illustrated by the dilemmas into which Robert Dubreuilh is plunged in that work, but is not itself an *ideal*. In the title of this paper, I have therefore utilized the word "democracy" as a contrast term, ambiguous and vague as it is, to "communism," because "communism *versus* democracy" was a standard *cliché* of the cold war period.[1] Beauvoir did not like to indulge in clichés, and the word "democracy" may not even appear more than once or twice in the entire book, but if properly understood as the overcoming, in a global context, of relations of dominance and subordination, it does not seem to me too wide of her mark.

What *would be* wide of her mark, and this brings us to the negative side of her vision of the future, would be to identify "democracy" as an ideal with the kinds of regimes with which it was usually identified in the Western camp during the cold war, notably the United States and, later, Gaullist France. *The Mandarins* is filled with fears (justified, in the event) of a Gaullist rise to power; as for the United States, the following passage is typical: "Maintenant l'Amérique, ça signifiait bombe atomique, menaces de guerre, fascisme naissant" (Beauvoir 1954, 515).[2] On the other hand, as the book's central political drama concerning the revelation of the extent and importance of the Soviet labor camps makes very clear, the USSR as it existed was horrendous, as well, although it still continued to point, but only in principle and in an ever-receding distant future, to a better world. In this article, I shall consider first Beauvoir's treatment of communism, then her portrayal of "the West" with the United States as its epitome, and finally the contemporaneity of the atmosphere depicted in *The Mandarins*.

Communism

Western philosophers sympathetic to Marx have long attempted to distinguish between his theory and Communist practice, despite his own insistence on the unity of the two. Although in *The Second Sex* Beauvoir devoted an entire early chapter to "the point of view of historical materialism," focusing primarily on Engels's *The Origin of the Family, Private Property, and the State* rather than on Marx himself, *The Mandarins* contains no, or virtually no, discussion of Marxism as a theory apart from its "official" standard-bearer of the time, the Communist Party. What was most salient about the internal structure of that party in all countries in which it flourished, and certainly in France, was its insistence on strict discipline, that is, on adherence to the "line" that had been decided upon by the leadership—which meant ultimately, at least in important matters, the leadership in Moscow. (This was the heritage of Lenin's notion of "democratic centralism," among other things.) The prewar turnaround in the "line," shocking as it had been to members and nonmembers alike, following the announcement of the Stalin-Hitler pact was still a relatively recent memory for Beauvoir's generation, though of course Germany's subsequent invasion of Russia and the terrible sufferings of so many Russians followed by the ultimate victory of the Allies had to some extent assuaged or even obliterated it. But it showed very well how active Communist Party members might be asked, on penalty of expulsion or sometimes worse, to say that black was no longer black but, rather, white if the leadership should happen at some time to deem it expedient. Beauvoir's character Lachaume, whom she portrays with some sympathy, embodies this attitude. When Henri asks Vincent, who has seen Lachaume recently, whether Lachaume isn't embarrassed by the revelations concerning the Soviet camps, Vincent summarizes Lachaume's thinking as: "Que ça n'existe pas; que c'est une excellente institution; que ça disparaîtra de soi-même" (Beauvoir 1954, 382).[3] In other words, this fairly intelligent and decent individual manages to maintain several completely contradictory opinions about them at once, while single-mindedly devoting himself, as we learn a few pages later, to writing a thoroughly scurrilous article about his former friend, Henri, because the latter had made the damaging disclosures public in his revue.

What, then, was the attraction of the Communist Party, especially for intellectuals, especially in a country like France where, unlike the countries of the Soviet Bloc in which it was the ruling and sole party, membership necessitated, at least in the short run, a high degree of altruism and could not be purely opportunistic? For many, no doubt, the belief that "history was on their side" in the *long* run played a part. In order to believe this, one needed also to have had to believe that Marx's (or "the Marxist") analysis of the capitalist system involved a demonstrable proof of its relatively imminent, and not indefinitely postponable, demise (a conclusion that has never seemed to me justified by the texts, but let that pass here)—in short, to believe that the main tenets of Marxism embodied "the truth" about the sociohistorical world. In addition, however, to be a Party activist required a strong element of personal commitment, for which belief in the ultimate correctness of the Party's political judgments (though it was admitted that temporary mistakes might occur now and again) was a necessary but not a sufficient condition. The further factor was acceptance of the idea that an eventual classless society, to be won through struggle by the Party working in the interests of the lower class, the proletariat, would be vastly superior to the existing state of affairs. In short, despite the official dogma's rejection of "ethics" as an idealistic, and therefore illusionary, approach to social problems, a highly normative vision underlay the typical Communist Party member's worldview.

Beauvoir brings this out very well throughout *The Mandarins*, but she portrays it in a particularly poignant way, late in the novel, when her two principal male characters, Henri and Robert, discuss the latter's attitude, at least at that moment, of being a Communist "wannabe" and his conviction that he is just too old to join the Party. As Robert says:

> — Je me rends bien compte que beaucoup de choses auxquelles j'ai tenu ne sont plus de mise; je suis amené à vouloir un avenir très différent de celui que j'imaginais; seulement je ne peux pas me changer: alors cet avenir je n'y vois pas de place pour moi.
> — [Henri] Autrement dit, vous souhaitez le triomphe du communisme, tout en sachant que vous ne pourriez pas vivre dans un monde communiste?
> — C'est à peu près ça. (Beauvoir 1954, 409)[4]

In both Henri's remarks here and in the larger text in which they are situated, there is an interesting conflation, which seems quite natural to the characters themselves, between "the Communists"—that is, the Party, which is not capitalized in the French as I am capitalizing it here—and a future "communist world." (In the English translation, there is also a conflation, but of the opposite kind: "Communist" and "Communism" are capitalized throughout. As the Communists used to say, "This is not by accident.") In other words, at that time in France, unlike the United States except for its by then very small group of Communist Party members, the Party had to a great extent cornered the market, so to speak, in the imaginations of a large part of the general public concerning a better future world. This helps to explain the statistical fact that up to a quarter of the electorate, most of whom, of course, were not Party activists, regularly voted "*PC*."

Ignorance and naïveté on the part of voters concerning actual conditions in the USSR no doubt played a role in maintaining this level of support. In fact, ignorance and naïveté play a large role in *any* so-called democratic voting situation in the modern world. But in the case of the Communist Party at the beginning of the 1950s, after the Soviet camps had become the object of widespread public discussion (including the important editorial in *Les Temps*

Modernes, "Les jours de notre vie,"[5] a close actual counterpart to Henri's fictional article about the camps in *L'Espoir* that achieves the rupture between *L'Espoir* and the party called the SRL in *The Mandarins*), its support level in the general public remained that of an extremely significant minority. This can only be explained by the widespread attitude, excellently portrayed by Beauvoir throughout her book and in my opinion highly realistic and accurate in terms of the actual situation of the time, that there were no serious political alternatives other than the Communist Party: the collapse of the RDR, the "real-life" counterpart of the SRL (though the circumstances of its collapse were rather different from those depicted in *The Mandarins*), seemed to demonstrate this. In other words, the Soviet reality that the French Communist Party endorsed and lauded, lamentable as it was in many ways, was all there was. Anticipating with remarkable precision the slogan that was to be widely disseminated by supporters of the Soviet Bloc especially in the 1980s, "really existing socialism" (that is, you intellectuals may prefer an ideal form of socialism, but the (self-styled) "socialist countries" of the bloc are the only ones that really exist), Beauvoir puts the following words into Dubreuilh's mouth, late in the novel:

> L'U.R.S.S. telle qu'elle devrait être, la révolution sans larmes, tout ça sont de pures idées, c'est-à-dire zéro. Évidemment, comparée à l'idée la réalité a toujours tort; dès que l'idée s'incarne, elle se déforme; seulement la supériorité de l'U.R.S.S. sur tous les socialismes possibles, c'est qu'elle existe." (Beauvoir 1954, 554)[6]

I have written, above, "no serious political alternatives." Alternatives to what? The answer to this question, as we find it in *The Mandarins* and as it was widely conceived in France at the time, is quite simple: to France's (and Europe's, etc.) succumbing to American hegemony, or more generally to the perpetuation of Western bourgeois dominance ad infinitum. Let us now look more closely at what that was thought to mean.

False Democracy

If "democracy" as I have defined it—to wit, a (global) society in which relationships of dominance and subordination have been largely overcome—is a not inapt name for the goal desired by Beauvoir's "mandarins," the non-Communist Left, then a good counterpart expression for the society that they detested, even while being enmeshed in it in so many ways, might be "false democracy." It is true that, frequently enough in *The Mandarins* as in so much French literature of the period, the opposing camp in the political struggle is identified as "the bourgeoisie." Since, like Simone de Beauvoir herself, so many of the characters in the book come from bourgeois backgrounds and have at least partially bourgeois lifestyles, they experience a sense of internal contradiction that is well depicted at the beginning of the book, where Henri is reflecting on his recent involvement with Resistance comrades from nonbourgeois backgrounds; he had sensed in them a class hatred, previously unknown to him, which he had managed to overcome in the common struggle. He says to himself,

> [S]i jamais il redevenait un bourgeois indifférent, [cette haine] renaîtrait et à bon droit. A moins qu'il ne fasse la preuve du contraire, il était un ennemi pour des centaines de millions d'hommes, un ennemi de l'humanité. (Beauvoir 1954, 15)[7]

The bourgeoisie, however, was able to retain the power and wealth that made it the object of this worldwide hatred. It was able to do so because of the existing political structures that reinforced it. Those who controlled the structures called them "democratic"—after all, it was possible for ordinary French people to vote for parties of the Left, the facts spoke for themselves, did they not?—but in reality the decks were stacked in their favor. Nominally democratic voting mechanisms concealed a deeply undemocratic division of resources and forces.

A major reason why this state of affairs was able to endure and perhaps even be strengthened in the period depicted in *The Mandarins* was the increasing hegemony of the bourgeois country par excellence, where almost everyone, so it seemed, lived in the apolitical situation of ignorance concerning the hatred felt by the others, the underprivileged of the world, the situation that had been Henri's (and Beauvoir's, as well as Sartre's): the United States. The United States, where a sizable portion of the action of the book takes place because of the visits made there by Beauvoir's principal female character and fictional narrator of half the novel, Anne, engendered deep concern and fear in a number of more specific domains in addition to the general animosity toward it that was due to its role as upholder of worldwide capitalism. Among these domains were the political, the cultural, and the military.

In the character of Preston, an American who plays a minor role in *The Mandarins*, we see the face of United States *policy*: manipulative, self-righteous, and deeply hypocritical. He makes it quite clear, for example, that his government has no intention of withdrawing support from the fascist dictatorships of Franco in Spain and Salazar in Portugal, because it serves perceived American interests to continue that support. At the same time, he offers to arrange to furnish more scarce paper to *L'Espoir* in return for its giving more favorable treatment to American foreign policy, and then acts shocked when Henri accuses him of attempted censorship. The most prominent right-wing character in the book, Scriassine, who precipitates the book's major crisis when he presents

Henri and his colleagues with documentation concerning the Soviet camps, is very much involved with American diplomats and goes so far as to urge French and European acceptance of American "hegemony"—a word that, I believe, is more frequently used in this context today than it was when Beauvoir employed it fifty years ago. To be sure, he is motivated, as Beauvoir makes abundantly clear, by his past experiences as an East European who hates Soviet Communism; but the actual reasoning with which she supplies him for favoring American hegemony seems rather weak:

> Je n'aime pas l'Amérique; je ne crois pas à la civilisation atlantique; mais je souhaite l'hégémonie américaine parce que la question qui se pose aujourd'hui, c'est celle de l'abondance: et seule l'Amérique peut nous la donner. (Beauvoir 1954, 111)[8]

Of course, the France of the time in question was a country impoverished by the war and far from the affluence that it enjoys today, as Beauvoir's reference to the paper shortage underscores; this is one of the most evident "period piece" aspects of *The Mandarins*, since it is highly unlikely that any French person today, however enamored of the United States he or she might be, would offer Scriassine's rationale. But the manipulation by American interests, both in foreign affairs and in domestic politics, that Scriassine embodies was already a very salient reality by then. It was quite evident, for example, in the subventions given by the American labor union organizations, the AFL and the CIO, to David Rousset, the guiding force of the real life "SRL," the RDR; it has since become clear that these funds were given with long strings attached and were apparently supported sub rosa by Washington.

American hegemony in the *cultural* domain was felt as particularly menacing by Beauvoir's mandarins, and again with good reason. The pointed question that Beauvoir puts in the mouth of Scriassine early in the book, at a time when Paris had been liberated but combat was still going on in central Europe, is: "Quelle portée gardera le message des écrivains français le jour où l'hégémonie du monde appartiendra à l'U.R.S.S. ou aux U.S.A.? Personne ne les comprendra plus; on ne parlera même plus leur langage."[9] When Anne replies that he seems to find this a pleasant prospect, he accuses her of being, as a typical woman, incapable of speaking objectively; she responds that, objectively speaking, it is not demonstrably true that the world will become either American or Russian in the future (Beauvoir 1954, 35). Beauvoir herself is clearly not the sort of critic who automatically rejects everything connected with American culture; on the contrary, she has much that is positive to say about it in Anne's descriptions of her travels to the United States (as Beauvoir herself does in *L'Amérique au jour le jour*), she has Anne ridicule the uninformed and cliché-driven questions about America that some people ask her upon her return, and of course she actually fell in love with the real-life counterpart of Anne's Lewis, the American writer Nelson Algren, to whom she dedicated *The Mandarins*. Lewis, like Algren himself, is an interesting case, inasmuch as he is a popular writer, given to long periods of moroseness during which he has very little to say, who hates intellectual theories; is he supposed to represent the best of American culture? On the other hand, we do find some recognition—most notably in Preston's question to Henri as to whether he knows the work of John Dewey and his subsequent expression of regret, when Henri says he does not, that "on nous connaît mal en France" (Beauvoir 1954, 127)[10]—of the fact that American culture also has a place for serious theoretical endeavor, the type of enterprise on which the mandarins thrive. On the whole, it seems to me, Beauvoir presents herself as being (and in fact *was*) considerably more positive and open toward many aspects of American culture than are her major characters. They, for their part, experience a constant temptation to succumb to feelings of impotence and irrelevance both personally and with respect to French culture in light of the cold war realities, and they have the feeling that Scriassine's right-wing attitudes may indeed be prophetic in certain respects and that that culture may be swallowed up in an American-style society of material abundance.

It is, however, in the *military* domain, the domain of hot wars into which the cold war was constantly threatening to metamorphose, that the suspicion of American hegemony is perhaps deepest and most corrosive in the world of *The Mandarins*. Fears of an imminent war precipitated by the United States grow ever stronger as the book proceeds. News of the atomic bombing of Hiroshima plunges its principal characters, who are on vacation, into deep depression, as they are led to contemplate a worldwide conflagration that could even bring about the end of humanity. It is in this context that Anne's previously mentioned bitter reflections, as she walks the streets of Chicago, take on much more significance than the mere frettings of a Frenchwoman whose love affair with an American man is turning sour: America was *indeed* the atomic bomb, threats of war, and incipient fascism. To be sure, that was far from *all* that it was, and for a "résistentialiste" (Beauvoir 1954, 392) believer in human freedom the future is never absolutely determined, unless and until all of humanity will have ceased to exist—as Anne's retort to Scriassine's sexist remark about her lack of "objectivity" clearly shows. But the sense in which, given its militarism as well as all of its internal domestic problems, postwar America's self-assurance about its supposed democratic purity was a falsehood and a charade—in its own way just as ideological, in the most pejorative sense of that word, as the official Communist Party's pretensions of the epoch—is manifested and demonstrated in a magisterial way throughout Beauvoir's work. America and France were both, indeed, *false* democracies.

Rereading *The Mandarins* Today

Fifty years is quite a significant period of time, especially in an age in which, as everyone living in it seems to agree, change is so rapid and pervasive. It is, then, quite astonishing to reread *The Mandarins* today and to see how thoroughly contemporary it is with regard to most of the issues that have concerned me here in this article. Of course, as I mentioned at the outset, the lacuna created by the demise of the Communist Party and movement, which played such a significant role in the mandarins' world, poses a huge problem for anyone who would try to pretend that "*nothing* has changed." The major historical development of the past half-century has been, in fact, the realization of one of the future possibilities envisaged by a number of the book's characters, namely, the triumph of American hegemony. In virtually all of them except Scriassine—he who stated, in an unnuanced way that would have seemed inappropriate in the mouths of most of the other characters, "I don't like America" even while expressing his wish for that triumph—this prospect occasioned deep gloom and foreboding. They were justified in feeling that way.

They are not depicted by their creator as having foreseen some other major sociohistorical developments, such as the ruinous French war in Algeria (the insurgency there actually began in earnest in 1954, which was also the year of France's final defeat in Indochina), the great influx of North Africans into the Metropole, the rise of Islamic fundamentalism, the creation of the European Union, and so forth. Likewise, some of the symbolism surrounding consumerist aspects of American hegemony—Coca-Cola, "Macdo" (as French slang denominates McDonald's), and so on—was not yet in place: in their world, "les cocos" meant the Communists. (The pathetic little Schlitz beer sign at the building where Lewis Brogan lived might, however, be regarded as a small intimation of what was to come.) Nevertheless, if they were somehow to be brought to life and deposited in Paris right now, they would feel very much at home. They would hear everyone talking about American imperialism; they would hear references to the announced prospect of an endless war; and if they were to read newspaper articles about the United States they would see that creeping fascism in the form of increased police state tactics (suppression of rights, vast augmentation of surveillance procedures, a "criminal justice" system that houses one-quarter of the world's prisoners drawn from less than 5 percent of its population, etc.), effective control of major media outlets by right-wing forces, strong encouragement of "patriotic" nationalism, and so on, were the order of the day in that country. They would also learn, soon enough, that the United States government had never agreed to renounce the first use of nuclear weapons, that it was in fact in the process of mass-producing a new, generally "smaller-scale" generation of such weapons, and that at the same time it was intensifying its efforts to prevent, by very unsubtle threats, other governments from acquiring the capacity to produce them. While our revivified mandarins would not be at all accustomed to hearing so many of their fellow citizens speak English, and fairly good English at that, they would soon enough realize that Scriassine's prediction with respect to the French language was gradually being fulfilled. And they would quickly enough learn the statistics showing that, while many shops, offices, and hotels in the City of Light now exhibit a degree of affluence that would have been difficult to imagine in the early 1950s, the structures of global capitalism have succeeded in creating an ever-expanding resource gap between the rich and the poor of the world.

They would even find that the domestic problems generated by the German Occupation and the large number of French collaborators with it, problems which figured so prominently at the time about which Beauvoir was writing, were still (or perhaps I should say "again," because there were interim years during which this was less the case) preoccupying people a great deal. Questions continue to be raised, for example, about the moral wisdom of Sartre's having had *Les mouches* (*The Flies*) and *Huis clos* (*No Exit*) produced on stage during the Occupation period. And ex-collaborationist octogenarians continue, from time to time, to be identified and sometimes put on trial. Even the issue of perjury, which Beauvoir raises in the form of Henri's giving false testimony in order to exculpate his young actress friend, Josette, has been resurrected quite recently in the case of the late Belgian collaborator, Paul DeMan, the revelation of whose perjured concealment of an earlier marriage in official documents filed in his adopted homeland (as we all call it now), the United States, occasioned anguish in his erstwhile friend and defender, Jacques Derrida.

Finally, the resurrected mandarins would once again witness many of the old, hand-wringing feelings of frustration, among French intellectuals and their overseas counterparts alike, about the decline of the Left and its impotence. Although they would no doubt take some pleasure in the recent attempt by a conservative French president, perhaps enjoying greater freedom of action than his Socialist Party predecessor, and supported by massive popular demonstrations, to oppose the American government's preemptive attack on Iraq, they would not be surprised that it had been unsuccessful and that the attack had been followed by a propaganda campaign designed to celebrate "victory" and to condemn opponents of the belligerency as having been, well, just *wrong*. In the realm of propaganda they would probably not be astonished, either, to learn about the now global reach of a few transnational media and publishing corporations, such as the Murdoch and Berlusconi empires; as Robert said at one point, commenting on Henri's experience, "[L]a presse libre: encore un joli bobard!" (Beauvoir 1954, 139).[11] They would thoroughly understand my personal experience, at the very moment at which I was completing the writing of this article, of being invited to contribute an essay to an issue on the United States that was being prepared by an international revue published in Paris, but being told when I cautiously inquired as to whether there would be any problem with my expressing criticism of US government policy in such an essay that of course that would be unacceptable. (The editors are *not* the ones to blame, nota bene.) In short, the mandarins' greatest surprise would be just how familiar the world of the first years of the twenty-first century would seem to them, a world still, or perhaps more than ever, filled with hypocritical cant about the glories of democracy and freedom together with tireless efforts to suppress democracy and freedom for all but the most privileged.

In rereading *The Mandarins* I was more impressed than on earlier occasions by the depth of the real depression about the world's future that it evinces. Although it contains remarks to the effect that pessimism and optimism are irrelevant to ongoing decisions about what course of action to take, and the final scene in which Anne decides against suicide at the last moment reinforces this point of view, it is of course very significant that the revue that Henri strives mightily, but ultimately without success, to keep afloat had as its title *L'Espoir.*[12] *L'Espoir* went under, but *Les Temps Modernes* still survives. The times of Simone de Beauvoir, Sartre, Merleau-Ponty, and Charlie Chaplin (whose film title was the inspiration of the founders of *Les Temps Modernes*), and also our times: essentially the same times. But at least today we are no longer subjected to patently unjustifiable "orthodox" Communist ideological self-promotion about "the radiant future of mankind" (Zinoviev 1981); its erstwhile counterpoint, pseudodemocratic ideological propaganda, goes virtually uncontested.

Notes

1. "Communism, Fascism, and Democracy" was the title given to college courses, intended to reinforce "American values," that received special funding from conservative interests and were offered in a number of institutions throughout the United States. It was also the title of a book by a philosopher, Carl Cohen: *Communism, Fascism, and Democracy: The Theoretical Foundations* (New York: Random House, 1962). (Cohen, incidentally, is the self-proclaimed civil libertarian who was the effective instigator of the important recent lawsuit brought against his university, the University of Michigan, to overturn its affirmative action policies.)

2. "Now, America meant the atom bomb, war threats, incipient fascism." (This and all subsequent translations from *Les mandarins* are my own.) Anne is walking through the Chicago Loop by herself after a very negative conversation with Lewis, thinking these thoughts and conceiving of most of the other pedestrians she is passing as enemies.

3. "That they don't exist; that they're an excellent institution; that they'll disappear by themselves."

4. "I'm well aware that many things that were important to me are no longer suitable; I'm led to wish for a very different future from the one I imagined; only I can't change myself; so I see no place for me in that future."

[Henri]: "In other words, you wish for the victory of communism, while knowing that you couldn't live in a communist world."

"That's about right."

5. See "Les jours de notre vie," first published in *Les Temps Modernes* in January 1950 above the joint signatures of Merleau-Ponty and Sartre, but in fact entirely written by Merleau-Ponty, and reprinted under the new title "U.R.S.S. et les camps" in the latter's *Signes* (Paris: Gallimard, 1960), pp. 330–43. Merleau-Ponty's "Essai sur le problème communiste," in *Humanism and Terror*, published in 1947, is of course very important background reading for *The Mandarins*, probably more important than any single publication by Sartre up to 1954.

6. "The USSR as it should be, the revolution without tears, all of that is pure ideas, in other words, nothing. Obviously, compared with the idea the reality is always wrong; as soon as the idea is embodied, it is distorted; only, the superiority of the USSR over all possible socialisms is that it exists."

7. "[I]f ever he were to turn back into an indifferent bourgeois, [that hatred] would be rekindled, and with good reason. Unless he should offer proof to the contrary, he was an enemy for hundreds of millions of men, an enemy of humanity."

8. "I don't like America; I don't believe in an Atlantic civilization; but I wish for American hegemony because the issue that arises today is that of affluence; and only America can give it to us." The translator substitutes a verb, "predominates," for the more dramatic and accurate "hegemony," and substitutes the word "community," a sociopolitical concept, for "civilization," which is cultural and is, I think, meant by Beauvoir to reflect, among other things, Scriassine's East European suspicions and concerns. Thus, a great deal has been lost, to coin a phrase, in this translation—a good illustration of my reasons for preferring, when possible, to cite original texts even in the case of Simone de Beauvoir. Although her very straightforward prose is less susceptible to serious distortion by translators than the writings of many other authors, she has nevertheless been badly served—especially by the translator of *The Second Sex*, as has been well documented.

9. "What significance will the message of French writers retain on the day when world hegemony belongs to the USSR or the USA? No one will understand them; no one will even speak their language any more."

10. "We are not well known in France." The translator "helpfully" (for uncultured American readers unable to identify Dewey, perhaps?) renders Beauvoir's simple "nous" as "we pragmatists," a specific reference that does not seem to me to have been her intention.

11. "The free press: one more pretty lie!"

12. Quite ironically, the title given to three interviews with Sartre by his secretary, Benny Lévy, no friend of Beauvoir's, the publication of which in *Le Nouvel Observateur* just days before Sartre's death caused her such anguish (for a number of reasons having

little or nothing to do with her or Sartre's evaluation of contemporary politics), was *L'espoir, maintenant.* In them, Sartre expresses an ongoing commitment to hope while at the same time giving a number of solid reasons for regarding the existing world situation as hopeless. *Plus ça change . . .*

Works Cited

Beauvoir, Simone de. 1954. *Les mandarins.* Paris: Gallimard.

McBride, William. 1991. *Sartre's political theory.* Bloomington: Indiana University Press.

Zinoviev, Aleksandr. 1981. *The radiant future.* London: Bodley Head.

CHAPTER 2

Sustained Praxis

The Challenge of Solidarity in The Mandarins *and Beyond*

Sally J. Scholz

Fifty years after Simone de Beauvoir's impressive novel about post–World War II France, we continue to grapple with many of the same political dilemmas she chronicles in the book. While *The Mandarins* may focus on the dilemmas of reconstruction in the emerging cold war era, today we face the dilemmas of globalization as the world becomes increasingly split between the rich and the poor. Both sets of circumstances question the morality of accepting support from countries or multinational aid agencies and the political strings that may be attached. Both demonstrate the interconnections between various personal and political actions. In numerous ways, the striking similarity in global politics during 1954 and 2004 force us to examine the structure and efficacy of social movements. Beauvoir began such an exploration in *The Mandarins* and refined what I call an ethics of solidarity. She addressed many of the same questions advocates for social change confront on a daily basis: To what extent are we united as individuals, as nationals, or even as human beings? What forms the basis of that unity? When we take a collective stance against injustice—whether it be Nazi Occupation, political tyranny, colonization, imperialism, or warism—what are our collective and personal obligations? How do we sustain praxis—collective action—once the injustice that bound us together in the first place ceases?

Simone de Beauvoir's political philosophy, found in both her essays and her literature, addresses these questions and, as I will argue, reveals three basic levels of solidary relations with different connections and obligations between individual members of the groups. I begin by drawing on some of her better-known concepts—situation and reciprocity—to articulate a political solidarity that focuses on relations of oppression. The first level of solidarity defines the relation according to *situation* in that similarly situated individuals are grouped together according to their relation to the One or Absolute. But it becomes clear that situation alone is unsatisfactory for political solidarity according to Beauvoir. She remarks in the introduction of *The Second Sex* that women lack solidarity (1952, xix). If situation were an adequate marker for group solidarity, women would surely be a prime example.

Reciprocity enters to help delineate the second level of relations of solidarity. Reciprocity is a mutuality of recognition; one consciousness recognizes another consciousness and in that moment of recognition understands that the other has projects. When individuals see their projects mingling with the actions of others for similar ends, reciprocity results and a relationship of solidarity is formed (Matarrese 2001, 44). It is a mutual understanding that in our individual freedom we are working for the same project. The French Resistance movement is a very good example of this mutuality. In resisting Nazi Occupation, individuals saw themselves as forming a social movement capable of bringing about liberation. That choice bound individuals together into groups engaged in praxis. It is well known how this experience of resistance affected the philosophical thought of Jean-Paul Sartre;[1] Beauvoir's reaction is less well known but nonetheless profound. *The Mandarins* is her account of that time and, through the lives of the characters, she demonstrates the development of her political philosophy.

In the third level of relationships of solidarity, we see Beauvoir moving from reciprocity to commitment as the binding force in group relations (though, of course, reciprocity is not abandoned). *The Mandarins* is the key text in this study, as it is that novel wherein Beauvoir offers her most developed discussion of commitment and its various facets in political solidarity. I begin by looking at the earlier essays because they offer a theoretical discussion of solidarity that serves as a backdrop for the literary presentation in *The Mandarins.* I then analyze four events in the novel to illustrate some of the nuances of Beauvoir's thinking as it is informed by her postwar experience.

An Early Account of Solidarity Ethics: *Pyrrhus et Cinéas* and *The Ethics of Ambiguity*

The first level of a relation of solidarity, based on situation, might be called passive solidarity in that individuals are bound together by a shared situation or resembling attribute. One need not actually engage with others in order to be grouped with them. In *Pyrrhus et Cinéas*, for instance, Beauvoir clearly appeals to this sort of passive solidarity whereby Flaubert is united with others of his class simply by existing at the same time with them: "Flaubert believes to have rejoined the universal when he writes in substance: 'Why interest myself in the proletariat of today rather than the slaves of antiquity?'; but he evades neither his epoch nor his class; he constitutes himself, on the contrary, like a nineteenth-century bourgeois whose fortune, leisures, and vanities mask his solidarity with his time" (Beauvoir 1944, 35).[2]

Similarly, in the section on humanity, Beauvoir critiques "the myth of solidarity" [le mythe de la solidarité] saying that when we speak of *one* humanity [*une* humanité] we necessarily refer to a unity of objects considered from exteriority (1944, 45–46). Individuals would be nothing more than passive, predetermined entities occupying a place "like the parts of an organism" [commes les parties d'un organisme] (46). Such a passive solidarity ignores the freedom of the existent. In both the Flaubert example and the case of solidarity among humanity, unity between individuals is accomplished by chance circumstances, such as proximity, class, or shared attributes. In later work, the term "situation" comes in part to stand in for these arbitrary characteristics. The shared situation of oppressed peoples creates a sort of unity but, like the solidarity of humanity, it is a unity considered from the exterior until or unless individual freedom is affirmed.

"Freedom is interiority," and thus an active solidarity requires that each individual act: "He will take a place by throwing himself into the world, he exists among others by his own project" (Beauvoir 1944, 46).[3] The individual's project allows him or her to *take* his or her place in the world. One "*throws* oneself into the world," thereby acting on freedom. By so acting on one's freedom, Beauvoir argues, one "situates others around oneself" (48). This is how solidarity is created, but it is impossible, she adds, to create a solidarity with every human person because "they do not chose the same goals because their choices are free" (49).[4]

By including this element of choice Beauvoir implicitly appeals to the second level of solidarity. Individuals who choose similar goals join in an active solidarity based on freedom and reciprocity. To understand the role of freedom and reciprocity in Beauvoir's ethics we must turn to *The Ethics of Ambiguity*. Although this essay is often read as an individualist ethics (or an ethics for individuals), she argues that an existentialist ethics requires a reciprocal recognition of the freedom of others. Reciprocity ensures that the other similarly recognize one's own freedom. This component allows Beauvoir to avoid the charge of solipsism while also making existentialist ethics more applicable to politics. In fact, one might plausibly argue that it is the very fact that Beauvoir is concerned with relations with others that marks her ethics as distinct and, I would add, as a solidarity ethic. *The Ethics of Ambiguity*, after all, opens with the question of solidarity, that is, "How could men, originally separated, get together?" (Beauvoir [1947] 1948, 18).

Her answer at this stage in her writings consists in two main elements—or two sides of the same coin. The first is that an individual's projects are meaningful only in relation to the projects of others; the interference with the projects of others defines an individual's project, which also must disclose freedom, opening up the future. The freedom of others keeps each of us from resting in facticity: "Man [*sic*] can find a justification of his own existence only in the existence of other men" (Beauvoir [1947] 1948, 72). One's own freedom is bound up with that of others such that "To will oneself free is to will others free" (73).

In addition to the importance of the individual's projects, Beauvoir includes the specific aim of action as the alleviation of oppression. This second element to active solidarity based on reciprocity means that liberation is the ultimate end of every authentically chosen project. Beauvoir argues that each individual must open the possibilities of the oppressed or remain a tyrant. Each individual participates in the collective project of liberation insofar as he or she discloses the world, embracing freedom in an authentic way. Liberation is the collective project in part because each project undertaken in a morally authentic manner turns back to freedom in an effort to disclose freedom for oneself and others. Liberation is also the collective project because oppression cuts off the possibility for transcendence not only for those directly affected by it but also for others whose projects obtain meaning through interaction with the projects of others. Failure to engage freedom in this way makes one culpable for oppression even if one is not directly responsible for the tyranny. As Beauvoir says, "Abstention is complicity" ([1947] 1948, 87). Mystification complicates matters by keeping individuals from desiring liberation (if one is oppressed), from recognizing one's role in the maintenance of oppression (if one is merely not participating in the liberation struggle or acting in a morally authentic manner), or from recognizing one's actions as tyrannical (if one is an oppressor). Combating the mystification, then, is one aspect of liberation struggles.

The universality of the struggle for liberation entails something of an epistemological and perhaps even moral privilege for the oppressed while also affirming the role of every person: "In any case, we can assert that the oppressed is more totally engaged in the struggle than those who, though at one with him in rejecting his servitude, do not experience it; but also that, on the other hand, every man is affected by this struggle in so essential a way that he cannot fulfill himself morally without taking part in it" (Beauvoir [1947] 1948, 88–89). Unlike the first level of solidarity (based on situation) wherein only those affected by an oppressive condition might be considered members of the solidary group, at this level sympathetic others may also join in the collective action of solidarity.

Liberation struggles, however, are complicated because oppression has more than one aspect. All suppression and oppression must be abolished by adopting the tactic of opportunity and efficiency. Each person's individual situation guides his or her participation. Nevertheless, in any liberation struggle, Beauvoir argues, one may experience any number of antinomies. In order to fight for the liberation of some, we inevitably do disservice to others either by our inattention to their plight or more directly by further entrenching oppressive practices while we seek liberation (see also Beauvoir 1944, 113). Many social movements provide troubling examples of such antinomies. The nineteenth-century woman's movement, led by bourgeois white women in the US, for instance, sacrificed the personhood of black women in an effort to advance the cause for "all" (read "white, educated, middle-class") women. Similarly, efforts to obtain remuneration for women who regularly perform housework simultaneously function to cement gendered divisions of labor. Rather than avoid these sorts of paradoxes, however, Beauvoir warns that we must continue to act but be ever cognizant of the potentially hazardous outcomes of our actions.

The oppressor inevitably raises the objection that he or she is being oppressed and deprived of freedom because he or she cannot continue oppressive practices. Beauvoir's response turns back again to freedom's interplay among existents: "For a freedom wills itself genuinely only by willing itself as an indefinite movement through the freedom of others; as soon as it withdraws into itself, it denies itself on behalf of some object which it prefers to itself" ([1947] 1948, 90). The oppressor's freedom, which manifests itself by denying the freedom of others, is a false freedom that inevitably results in the denial of the oppressor's own freedom as well. The two elements described here work together: "A freedom which is interested only in denying freedom must be denied; . . . to be free is not to have the power to do anything you like; it is to be able to surpass the given toward an open future; the existence of others as a freedom defines my situation and is even the condition of my own freedom" (91; see also Beauvoir 1944, 112–14).

Throughout her development of these connections between people, Beauvoir maintains individuality for each existent. This is summarized nicely in her response to utilitarianism. An individual's freedom presumes solidarity with others. She says, "[I]t is true that each is bound to all; but that is precisely the ambiguity of his condition: in his surpassing toward others, each one exists absolutely as for himself; each is interested in the liberation of all, but as a separate existence engaged in his own projects" ([1947] 1948, 112). Beauvoir's solidarity ethics arises from an existentialism founded on the individual and yet, as she argued, that individualism is precisely its strength. Each existent is recognized as unique; the unity of all is a unity of each to every other. Each individual is irreplaceable to the whole (108).

Kristana Arp points out that Beauvoir's essay "Existentialism and the Wisdom of Nations" makes the strong claim that "it is only in human relations that each individual can find the foundation and accomplishment of his being"

(Beauvoir 1948, 37, quoted in Arp 2001, 36). *The Blood of Others* (1945) explores this theme, drawing on activities of the Resistance movement. The epigraph of that novel, "Each of us is responsible for everything and to every human being," from Dostoevsky, highlights the delicate balance between individual uniqueness, an obligation, and the collective action. Similarly, in *The Mandarins* we see Henri defending the position that "each individual is affected by collective history" (Beauvoir 1956, 147). He rejects a focus solely on the individual because, in truth, the individual cannot be considered "as separate and single" (147). Individuals do not disappear but are rather considered in relation to concrete others. When those others form a collective through reciprocal relations and dedication to a particular goal from their varied project positions, they may be said to be in solidarity.

Most of Beauvoir's discussions of solidarity in *The Second Sex* revolve around the themes of opposition and oppression. In these cases, she uses the term "solidarity" to mark the unity of a group that is set up against the prevailing norms of society. The first and second levels (based on situation and reciprocity, respectively) may be obscured in these discussions. Moreover, individuals who do not experience the oppression and opposition seem to be excluded from the solidarity relation in these discussions. Consider her description of the solidarity among prostitutes:

> Because their relations with one half of humanity are of a commercial kind and because society as a whole treats them as pariahs, prostitutes have a close solidarity among themselves; they may happen to be rivals, to feel jealous, to hurl insults at one another, to fight; but they profoundly need one another in order to form a counter-universe in which they regain their human dignity. The comrade is the preferred confidante and witness; it is she who will appreciate the dress and the coiffure intended for man's seduction but which seem like ends in themselves under the envious or admiring gaze of other women. (1952, 530)

Their situation marks them as different and creates a "close solidarity," but it is the reciprocity within this "counter-universe" that allows them to "regain their human dignity."[5] She also claims in the introduction to *The Second Sex* that whereas workers, Jews, and Negroes experience solidarity in part because of their shared history and/or shared space, women are often more closely united to men of their social class than to other women, that is, women do not have any solidarity. Beauvoir here means that women do not participate in an active solidarity based in reciprocity. They do, however, share a passive solidarity based in situation but that merely marks their situation as oppressive.

Later in *The Second Sex*, she makes the distinction between mechanical solidarity and organic solidarity. This distinction likely draws on the work of sociologist Emile Durkheim.[6] According to Durkheim, mechanical solidarity is grounded on a notion of group cohesion resulting from resemblances. There is a low level of individuality within the group and a high level of shared consciousness. Altruism develops because of shared consciousness. Organic solidarity, on the other hand, is based on the function or role of individual members that leads to an intricate interdependent community. Altruism in this case arises because of the division of labor. According to Durkheim, it is only when individual consciences intermingle and yet remain unique that organic solidarity forms. Beauvoir's use of the terms "mechanical solidarity" and "organic solidarity" may vary slightly, but the spirit is preserved:

> Sometimes the "feminine world" is contrasted with the masculine universe, but we must insist again that women have never constituted a closed and independent society; they form an integral part of the group, which is governed by males and in which they have a subordinate place. They are united only in a mechanical solidarity from the mere fact of their similarity, but they lack that organic solidarity on which every unified community is based; they are always compelled . . . to band together in order to establish a counter-universe, but they always set it up within the frame of the masculine universe. (Beauvoir 1952, 562)

According to this quotation, then, the unity of women amounts to very little because it is merely a shared resemblance. For women to enjoy an interdependent community, they would have to form a bond based on actions. Beauvoir would also add that the action must be undertaken in freedom. Notice the use of "counter-universe" in both the description of the condition of women and the conditions of the prostitute. Beauvoir emphasizes the oppositional nature of solidarity; it arises because of exclusion from the social norm or another form of oppression. Individuals who recognize an injustice to which they themselves are not subject are not considered as part of the solidary group in these "counter-universes" based on shared situation.[7]

Beauvoir's ethics of solidarity relies on political freedom aimed at social movements. Beauvoir's discussion of workers in "Moral Idealism and Political Realism" explores the motivations for group struggle. Consistent with *The Ethics of Ambiguity*, Beauvoir sees the aim of political action as not just the particularity of the situation but the opening up of future possibilities. The project should always turn back on freedom and open up the future (Beauvoir [1947] 1948; see also Arp 2001, 34). But how can the solidary group sustain praxis? Or, to use the language of *The Ethics of Ambiguity*, how do we keep the activity of freedom in its collective aspect from turning into the serious, especially after the social and political oppression or injustice has ceased?

Beauvoir's answer to this question in the *Ethics* appeals to a sort of universal humanism. Insofar as anyone is oppressed, the individual's freedom is constrained. This, however, risks slipping into a sort of mechanical solidarity. That is, her argument might be obscured or transformed into an argument for solidarity based on some inherent human nature or, like the myth of solidarity discussed earlier, refer only to exteriority. In defense, Beauvoir would reaffirm the interconnection between one's own projects and those of others, noting that the individual's morally authentic project ought never to be subsumed by group endeavor. Sustaining praxis must then be an individual as much as a group project. The struggle continues as a "surpassing of the past" [elle est dépassement du passé] (Beauvoir 1944, 111). But there is always the risk that the collective praxis will devolve into the serious, that the cause will take on a life of its own and stand over against the individual participants.

This leads to the third level of relations of solidarity. Sandra Bartky's description of existentialist ethics aptly captures the third level of solidarity: "My obligation obliges because I choose to be obligated by it" (2002, 126). In solidarity, then, I *choose* to be part of a collective movement engaged in praxis. Arp similarly argues that Beauvoir's existentialist ethics is characterized by the fact that individuals might choose to be bound together in meaningful ways (2001, 36). Choice—or, more accurately, commitment—holds the key to the question of sustaining praxis. Commitment is an individual's formal or informal pledge or promise to a collective cause. Commitment subsumes reciprocity in that it transforms the reciprocal other into the entire group, each individual makes the commitment to the group out of their particularity. The group does not thus take on a separate existence but exists through individual commitment (see also Matarrese 2001). It is commitment that will maintain the solidary relation after the initial cause that brought the group together has been accomplished. *The Mandarins* presents compelling examples of the movement from reciprocity to commitment and explores the many problems of sustaining collective praxis.

The Mandarins

At the end of *Pyrrhus et Cinéas*, Beauvoir notes that one project is surpassed only through the realization of another project (1944, 121–22). This also may be read in light of the praxis of solidary groups. In order to sustain praxis, the group must, in surpassing one project, realize another. Kruks adds that it is through praxis that the very identity of the group exists; praxis "constitutes and reconstitutes social identities" (Kruks 2001, 119).[8] *The Mandarins* demonstrates this surpassing of one project and the subsequent reconstitution of the group as the Resistance transforms into a more organized political party, the SRL, and attempts to sustain the praxis and the solidarity felt during the Liberation. Beauvoir uses narrative to explore the crucial problems and possibilities of political solidarity. Both the solidarity and the nature of the group itself transform; a commitment and the duties it entails become the focal point of collective action. As the Resistance movement becomes the SRL, the individuals must commit to the group; reciprocity, too, becomes mediated through the group. As a study of solidarity, then, *The Mandarins* aims at uncovering what is required for a group to remain active and relevant.

I turn now to look at four different events in *The Mandarins* that illustrate aspects and refinements of political solidarity. Although the examples are drawn from key events in Henri's postwar life, he is merely a representative of the group, posing the central questions of praxis. His commitment is like the commitment of each of the members of the solidary group.

The Challenge of Portugal

Early in the novel, Henri and Nadine travel to Portugal. The trip is viewed as a holiday by Henri, who anxiously craves an escape from political involvement after the Liberation. Arranged by the French Propaganda Service, Henri is scheduled to give some lectures, but he is also going as a leftist journalist who will meet with members of the Left in Portugal. Once they arrive in Lisbon they are positively entranced by the riches they see on the surface of the city. Chocolate, leather, oranges, shoes of all kinds—these were the things they missed during the Occupation and now it seemed like Henri might rediscover the past here in Lisbon. But after a short walk on the "Hill of Grace" (Beauvoir 1956, 96–97) they realize that the "wealth of Lisbon" is a mirage: "[O]f seven million Portuguese, there are only seventy thousand who have enough to eat" (97). A party the next day at the French Consulate serves as both a sharp contrast to the reality of Lisbon and an opportunity for Henri to distance himself, to convince himself that the poverty of the Portuguese was of no concern to him.

The anti-Salazar "old revolutionaries" with whom Henri meets while in Portugal, however, hope that he will see the reality of the situation and convince people back in France to come to their aid in the overthrow of Salazar. In spite of relentless pursuit by the government, the revolutionaries "doggedly persisted."

> They wanted to believe that the destruction of Nazism would somehow bring to an end this hypocritical fascism, and they dreamed constantly of overthrowing Salazar and creating a National Front

> like the one which had been formed in France. But they knew they were alone: the English capitalists had large interests in Portugal and the Americans were negotiating with the government for the purchase of air bases in the Azores. "France is our only hope," they repeated over and over. "Tell the people of France the truth," they begged. "They do not know; if they knew they would come to our rescue." (1956, 98)

Henri promises to "get the facts to the people" but his experience of Portugal remains somewhat detached; he has "the feeling of being a completely important witness to a totally foreign disaster" (109). For Nadine, by contrast, the twinkling lights of the city are a mirage that cannot quite hide the filth behind them. Her reaction is one of disgust and hatred, a passionate response that paralyzes her ability to respond otherwise to the situation. Henri's response is one of detached commitment to "wage a campaign in the press" (98). One might argue that Nadine's reaction might motivate a second-level solidary relation in that her indignation forces her to see concrete individuals with whom she shares a reciprocal recognition of misery.

Henri's reaction, while potentially giving cause not to act at all, might, on the contrary, compel him to commit to a deeper solidarity that encloses all oppressed peoples in its folds. Henri's reactions actually mark a shift in his thinking regarding political solidarity. His experience in Portugal challenges what may be hailed as the Resistance movement's impassioned solidarity by expanding the borders of the group and transforming the individual's membership into a commitment. Reciprocity between two existents whose projects coalesce gives way to collective commitment as the primary bond of solidarity. The counteruniverse created among the French during Nazi Occupation is replaced by a different sort of relation marked by a much more abstract commitment to a cause. No longer is Henri directly affected by the injustice, but he recognizes its connection to his own freedom:

> Henri has experienced a sense of solidarity in the War which he needs to feel he can go on earning. On his trip to Portugal in the third chapter he is abruptly faced with the opposition between this duty—the need—and literature: the novel celebrating the pleasures of peace and the beauties of the world which he had planned to write seems impossible in the face of the poverty and the hardships which he meets. (Fallaize 1988, 93)

The original solidary group expands to include not just French Resistance fighters but liberation seekers of all sorts. Nadine provides a mediating voice that challenges the aim or goal of the social movement. For instance, when talking to Henri prior to the trip, Nadine questions the so-called revolutionary era. Although Henri presses her saying that everything changed in August (referring to the Liberation of Paris), her retort is the very point that he must learn in Portugal: "As I remember it, in August there was a lot of talk about *everything* changing. And it's just the same as ever. It's still the ones who work the most who eat the least, and everyone goes right on thinking that's just great" (Beauvoir 1956, 22, emphasis in original). The solidarity Henri experienced during the Resistance had an immediacy to it in the reciprocal relations among the Resistance fighters. But Nadine's point is that liberation is not a one-time event. Liberation continues until freedom-limiting oppression disappears.

The reality of Lisbon expands the borders of what constituted the solidary group. Henri realizes that the struggle for liberation does not cease once one's own experience of oppression ceases. This is why praxis requires a commitment at this stage of solidary relations. Passion or indignation will not be enough to sustain the solidary activity. The individual commitment ensures an ongoing participation in collective action; it ensures the collective. This is further emphasized during a conversation Henri has with a novice reporter, Marie-Ange, shortly after his return from Portugal. He tells her about a childhood memory of his parents discussing the imminent revolution and all the "horrible monsters who were going to swallow up all of humanity" (Beauvoir 1956, 113). Once he realized that "'no matter what happens, the winners will still be men,'" he was pacified. As he says, "[E]ver since then I've been hunting down monsters." While the monsters ("red peril, the yellow peril, barbarism, decadence, revolution, bolshevism") change, Henri sees his task as a sort of humanism. Revolution continues until no one is oppressed, until the future is opened to all. To a certain extent, this task requires the very distancing that Henri experiences in Portugal in order to avoid the despair that might overwhelm.[9]

Commitment to the SRL

In her insightful analysis of *The Mandarins*, Elizabeth Fallaize argues that "preference" is "the key value around which the text is organized" (1988, 89). Fallaize cites Robert's declaration that "Commitment is nothing other than a choice, love is nothing other than a preference. If you wait until you meet absolute perfection before committing yourself, you'll never love anyone and never achieve anything" (1988, 89, citing Beauvoir 1956, 729).

Henri confronts the importance of commitment not only in his stance against tyranny in Portugal but also in the decision of whether or not to join the SRL and the subsequent decision of whether to make *L'Espoir* the official newspaper of the organization. The SRL, spearheaded by Robert Dubreuilh, was a non-communist, leftist political party. The aim was to create a united leftist front. While some saw this as "throwing support to the Communists," Dubreuilh insisted on the SRL's independence while standing up for the working class. Henri reluctantly joins Dubreuilh's movement but tries to limit his participation.

Before joining with the SRL, *L'Espoir* was the "only non-communist paper in France that reache[d] the proletariat" (Beauvoir 1956, 26). Henri's reluctance to connect it with the SRL stemmed from his belief that, should the paper take a class stand, it would either be repeating what the communist paper says or opposing it. In both cases, he would lose the subscriptions of the workers. Dubreuilh attacks Henri's attempt at a neutral stance, saying that without a position, the paper "simply makes for pleasant reading, like a local sheet" (124). Moreover, Dubreuilh adds that in taking a position in relation to the Communist Party, *L'Espoir*, shares in the goals—if not the methods—of the SRL, thereby showing that the connection may be mutually beneficial.

Joining the SRL and putting the force of the paper behind it (however reluctantly), demonstrates the nature of commitment in a social movement. The discussions between Henri and Robert regarding the SRL reveal Henri attempting a halfhearted commitment. So too, Henri makes a valiant attempt to keep the paper neutral. While we may read these two cases as merely instances of Henri's selfish desires to protect his time and the financial viability of his paper, we can also see that both attempts are unsuccessful. Commitment cannot be halfhearted when it comes to liberation struggles. Beauvoir argues in *The Ethics of Ambiguity* that action always must turn toward freedom and consider the freedom of others in order for it to be morally authentic. It follows, then, that commitment cannot be partial, though of course it may take on many different manifestations as one works from within one's own situation and facticity.

But perhaps even more importantly, this particular example shows a shift in the nature of the solidary group. A much more organized group has replaced the "group in fusion" (to borrow a term from Sartre). Ultimately, of course, the SRL fails, and its members disperse to more established political parties. While there might be an indictment of organized groups in this, it is perhaps safer to simply note the variety of groups or relations of solidarity that emerge within Beauvoir's rich political philosophy.

Truth and Its Consequences

The quasi-utilitarian nature of Beauvoir's solidarity ethics comes into focus again with the question of the Soviet labor camps. In brief, Scriassine, a pro-American Russian émigré, brings a former Soviet functionary to a meeting with Henri and Robert. He reveals that an estimated fifteen million are interned in the camps, some with sentences of up to five years by administrative order and others with much longer sentences by trial. The camps ensure the functioning of the Communist regime: "The program of the Soviet state requires surpluses which can only be furnished by excessively hard labor" (Beauvoir 1956, 319). The crucial question for the novel and for our purposes here is whether to publish the information. For Henri and Dubreuilh, this becomes a question of loyalty to hundreds of millions of workers all over the world, but it is also a question of loyalty to the truth cast in a stance against injustice and tyranny wherever it occurs. In the end, Henri does publish the reports but is very careful not to condemn communism in the process. Nevertheless, the SRL drops him, the communists are infuriated, and he is left seemingly standing alone for justice.

Henri's commitment to truth compels him to publish news of the camps, even though he recognizes the hazards that might ensue for the Communist Party. Fifteen million in the camps suffer under the Soviet regime, but exposing this will dash the hopes of thousands of millions of people, most of them workers, who dream of a better life under communism. This example brings into sharp relief the variety of commitments one makes in solidarity. At times the commitment to a goal may conflict with a commitment to others with whom one has united in struggle. Henri sees his position as needing to be critical, not just siding with the communists at any price; Dubreuilh says he is interested in the results of his actions, not the moral considerations (Beauvoir 1956, 401). Beauvoir concludes that the goal of the social movement begins to temper the means used to attain it—that is, commitment to a particular goal in solidarity is also a commitment to maintain that goal through the methods used as well. As this example reveals, however, it is not always clear what the goal is or ought to be.

Whether from the perspective of the group as a whole or from Henri in particular, the conflict brings to light what Beauvoir referred to in *The Ethics of Ambiguity* as the "antinomies of action." In acting for a particular cause, one may simultaneously act against that same cause or another equally important cause. Ultimately, revealing the truth of the Soviet system of communism, with its subproletariat, does advance "the cause," although it may be a new project that emerges. Instead of communism triumphing over capitalism, Dubreuilh and Perron alter their collective project to a humanism that aims to prevent war and expose tyranny. The SRL has to pass away or be surpassed, in order for the new praxis to emerge.

In *The Ethics of Ambiguity*, Beauvoir appeals to a sort of utilitarian thinking to guide responses to the antinomies. Each case must be judged individually to decide on the route that best opens the future in freedom, but no decision should be taken lightly. Sacrifices will sometimes have to be made in order to promote freedom, but these sacrifices are not costless. Each case requires a confrontation between the values realized and the values aimed at as well as the meaning with the content of each act. "A choice will become possible in the light of the future, which is the meaning of tomorrow because the present appears as the facticity which must be transcended toward freedom" (Beauvoir [1947] 1948, 115). Unlike utilitarianism, the measure is not happiness or utility of any sort but freedom—transcending the present toward the future. Kristana Arp argues that in these "hard choices," the key is to ensure that the means used to advance a cause are consistent with that cause (Arp 2001, 131; see also Beauvoir [1947] 1948, 155). Henri's decision to offer false testimony on behalf of Josette might be seen as another example of the decision-making Beauvoir discusses in *The Ethics of Ambiguity.* While Henri continues to be engaged in the solidary group that began with the Resistance, his decision weighs the truth of the two concentration camp survivors against the life of a collaborator. In the end, he judges it futile to waste the life of Josette and her mother. We could argue that his decision is an attempt to realize freedom or open up the future for Josette. Paying debts for past injustice, even egregious examples of collaboration with oppressors, does not open the future for oneself or others to exercise freedom.

This tension between the past and the future is further emphasized toward the end of the novel when it is revealed that Sézénac worked for the Gestapo denouncing Jews. "Four years earlier, everything would have been simple. When action is a living reality, when you believe in certain objectives, the verdict is inevitable: A traitor is something you shoot down. But what to do with a traitor out of the past when you no longer have any hope?" (Beauvoir 1956, 590). The immediacy of second-level solidarity lends clarity to decisions precisely because of the limited bounds of the group. But once the immediacy disperses and we move to the third level of solidarity, decisions are no longer so clear-cut; one understands how actions may contribute to so many different, and at time opposing, causes. Henri muses: "There was a time when I would have been capable of killing him myself. . . . Today it would make no sense. And yet it is shameful to help someone like that to go on living" (591). Ultimately, of course, Sézénac does pay for his past treason, and Henri assists in the disposal of his body. But the pall of futility hangs heavily over his murder.

Sustaining collective praxis entails a commitment to the relationship between the means or actions used and the project aimed at. Nadine's comment, quoted earlier, that in spite of the revolution everything stayed the same not only expands the boundaries of the solidary group, as I argued earlier, but also challenges the revolutionaries themselves to see the revolution or liberatory struggle in all of their actions. Politics becomes a living reality when individual commitment transforms not just social structures but the life of the revolutionary as well.

Writing for the Revolution

Commitment may be measured, then, by the relationship between one's own projects and the projects of the group. The two coalesce in important ways such that the individual is never lost or subsumed in the group but the group nonetheless becomes something more than the collection of individuals. Falaize puts this point nicely while also emphasizing the relationship between an action's means and ends in her description of Henri: "How he feels about his own stance is thus valued just as highly as the effects of his actions" (1988, 96). The Madagascar affair and the general commitment to alleviate the plight of the worker illustrate this fruition of commitment by highlighting the individual's unique contribution to solidarity.

When writing his first article on Madagascar (shortly after giving false testimony), Henri sees his task as speaking for truth, but it is also clearly a revolutionary act: "He picked up his pen. He was going to speak of justice and truth, protest against murders, tortures. 'I've got to do it,' he said to himself emphatically. If he gave up doing what he had to, he became doubly guilty. Whatever opinion he might have of himself, there were those men there whom he had to try to save" (Beauvoir 1956, 508). In spite of recurring moments of doubt about his efficacy as well as lingering desires to concentrate on himself and his family, Henri's actions demonstrate commitment carried out through his writing. His second article on Madagascar was "written with intense emotion" and revealed the specific atrocities there, but "it wasn't just in Tananarive that those things were happening; it was right here, in France, as well. Everyone was guilty" (575). His commitment to speaking "justice and truth" keeps him from retiring to a pleasant writer's life in Italy. The Madagascan affair had become personal for him, and he was no longer satisfied with the bliss of country life. Henri opts to continue the project of the writer as a way to live history (Fallaize 1988, 96; see also Scholz 2001 and Keefe 1998, 108). This example also reveals the four elements of solidarity discussed in this section. The solidary group has expanded tremendously to encompass Madagascar; the means Henri employs are consistent with and calibrated against the desired ends; Henri's commitment is made explicit with his decision not to retire to Italy; and his contribution to the liberation struggle is intensely personal and unique—fulfilling his own project (writing) while also contributing to the cause.

The plight of the working class constitutes at least part of the commitment of most of the main characters in the novel and permeates the story. Anne and Lewis offer commentary on the class injustice in the United States; Henri and Robert (among many others) continually judge their actions against the effects on the working class. Both examples show that commitment, rather than subsuming the individual in the group, helps the individual complete his or her own project.

One might make the stronger claim that it is in working with others for a particular cause that one finds meaning in life. The character of Armand in Beauvoir's *All Men Are Mortal* demonstrates this by joining in solidarity with workers in 1848 (see Arp 2001, 43). Arp explains:

> In *All Men are Mortal* the bonds that humans can form are brought into relief because they are intuited by someone who, precisely because he lacks the limitations that define the human condition, can never form them himself. Only in *The Ethics of Ambiguity*, though, does this idea of the individual working with people to pursue common goals take center stage. There such activity becomes the hallmark of an authentic realization of freedom: moral freedom. (Arp 2001, 44)

Beauvoir's play *Les bouches inutiles* (*Useless Mouths*) presents this theme of the individual finding completion as part of the group or social movement. One of the central characters of the play resists involvement with others, but when the town leaders propose the horrific injustice of expelling the "useless mouths" (women, elderly, children) to be left to die or be killed, he recognizes his need to embrace a role within political solidarity (Beauvoir 1983). "Only if one is working with others in a joint project does one's sacrifice [of self] have meaning" (Arp 2001, 72).

As Beauvoir argued in *The Ethics of Ambiguity*, revolutionary action proceeds based on expediency. *The Mandarins* emphasizes this point by showing how each person acts according to his or her individual abilities. As a writer, Henri participates in the struggle for liberation in a different way, but a no less valued way, than those engaged in more direct combat.

Early in *The Mandarins*, Henri and Lambert discuss the relation between the individual and the collective. Lambert asks for a set of principles or an approach to life. But Henri is reluctant, because a set of principles entails a political attitude. Lambert counters, saying, "In politics, all you're concerned with are abstract things that don't exist—the future, masses of people. But what is really concrete is the actual present moment, and people as separate and single individuals." Henri responds, "But each individual is affected by collective history" (Beauvoir 1956, 147). The key point is that Beauvoir's politics refuses to allow political causes, social movements, or solidary groups to take on a life that erases the individual.

Conclusion

"Your crystal ball is no clearer than ours when it comes to predicting things that'll happen fifty years from now" (Beauvoir 1956, 121). Although predicting the future may be murky at best, recognizing the contributions of the past grows ever clearer. As I have sketched it here, Beauvoir's vision of solidarity lends a great deal to contemporary invocations of that term. In both her political essays and the novel *The Mandarins*, Beauvoir criticizes the sort of mechanical solidarity that presumes a connection between individuals based on shared situations that either erases the individuality of the members or obscures the individual obligations of members. It is a passive solidarity, a solidarity based on proximity or shared attributes, rejected because it is politically impotent. As a myth for humanity, it is often appealed to as a basis for morality (as in the Kantian notion of respect), but as a political principle, passive solidarity may simply be reduced to various forms of unity or commonality.

The active, committed solidarity Beauvoir supports, on the other hand, entails a group structure that necessarily acknowledges individual freedom while also mediating that freedom through projects limited by and interconnected with the projects of others. Reciprocity assures mutual recognition of freedom between existents. However, praxis within the solidary group is fraught with antinomies, as Henri's experience with truth-telling reveals. More challenging still is maintaining praxis once the initial reason for the group's existence no longer exists. Beauvoir does offer some clues that might prove helpful for sustaining praxis; commitment is the most important. Whether to an organized group or to a spontaneous cause, commitment challenges the individual to draw upon his or her uniqueness and contribute to the collective project. It demands, that is, a sort of life-choice in conjunction with the project of those in solidarity. In transforming social structures or society, then, the individual is also transformed.

In the years since Beauvoir's novel was published, the appeal of "solidarity" has gained strength.[10] The most notable is the Polish Solidarity movement that arose out of a protest against violations of human rights and citizen rights of workers, that is, economic conditions, increasing poverty, and exploitation of workers. Workers united in order to achieve certain goals such as free-trade unions, the right to strike, and freedom of expression. The basic values of this moral and economic protest, like Henri's basic project, were human dignity and the freedom of conscience, truth, and justice.

More recently, "solidarity" has replaced "fraternity" in the European Union's amendment of the French Revolution's ideals of liberty, equality, fraternity. The new slogan, "Security, Diversity, and Solidarity," issues some of the same challenges Beauvoir presented. Solidarity in this context—a civic solidarity—pertains to the state's obligation to the poor. It is the word used to mark the welfare state's redistribution of wealth within a state. "Solidarity" was "invented" by Pierre Leroux to counter "compassion" and "charity" (Bayertz 1999, 23), and while "justice" or "just distribution of wealth" might be more descriptive of an individual's claims against the state, "solidarity" emphasizes the state—and, perhaps more to the point, the community's responsibility to ensure that every member of the civil body has the adequate resources to pursue his or her projects in freedom (to use Beauvoir's terminology). Two related forms of civic solidarity pertain to health care and global policy. In the former, "solidarity" is used to mark universalized access to health care within a state. In the latter, civic solidarity indicates an obligation to aid distant peoples.

Beauvoir would endorse the shift in political morality that requires a focus on solidarity rather than individual interests or even national interests. Her evaluation of the social movements of her time reveals a complex understanding of the individual's role within collective action. Moreover, the optimism Beauvoir expresses for a liberated future continues to inspire generations of readers fifty years after her major novel, *The Mandarins*, first appeared. She stops short of world solidarity, however, noting that Henri's war experiences made him realize that the "immediate brotherhood of man" was a fiction. But solidarities do form, and their importance for politics, and for individual freedom, cannot be underestimated.

Notes

1. As William McBride notes, the solidarity of the Liberation served as an inspiration to Jean-Paul Sartre's later work (McBride 1991, 26–27). In the *Critique of Dialectical Reason*, Sartre describes four different types of groups as well as the process they undergo in folding into one another. Seriality denotes the group related by pure alterity; individuals are collected by their passive experience of habit. "Groups in fusion" have a clear project; an example of a group in fusion was the group amassed to storm the Bastille. Parts of the Resistance movement may also be cast in this vein, but branches of that movement also became more organized militias. Groups in fusion fold into pledge groups that are organized around clearly defined functions. Institutional groups take on a life of their own in that the projects end up opposing the self-actualization of the members of the group (Sartre 1991).

2. English translations are my own, unless otherwise specified. "Flaubert croit rejoindre l'universal quand il écrit en substance: 'Pourquoi m'intéresser au prolétariat d'aujourd'hui plutôt qu'aux esclaves antiques?"; mais il ne s'évade pas par là de son époque ni de sa classe; il se constitue au contraire comme un bourgeois du dix-neuvième à qui sa fortune, ses loisirs, sa vanité masquent sa solidarité avec son temps" (Beauvoir 1944, 35). When there is no published English translation of a text or when the English translation can be misleading, I include the original French.

3. "Il *prendra* place en se jetant dans le monde, en se faisant exister au milieu des autres hommes par son propre projet" (Beauvoir 1944, 46, emphasis in original).

4. "[I]ls ne choisissent pas tous les mêmes buts puisque leurs choix sont libres." I am grateful to Shannon Mussett for directing me to this passage.

5. See *Le deuxième sexe II* (Beauvoir 1976, 440). Beauvoir uses the expression "dignité humaine." She also encloses "contre-univers" in quotations.

6. Beauvoir does not cite Durkheim, although she appears to appeal to his very well known distinction.

7. Sonia Kruks notices a similar distinction between those who are oppressed and those who struggle for liberation in Sartre's discussion of "collectives" and "groups" in the *Critique of Dialectical Reason*. "Collectives" are individuals "serialized, atomized, isolated, and placed in competition with each other." "Groups," on the other hand, "involve organized and conscious nodes of resistance of various kinds (ranging from union activity, to spontaneous participation in brief acts of sabotage, to attempted revolution)" (Kruks 2001, 122). Beauvoir does not adhere to this terminology.

8. Kruks specifically addresses Sartre's notion of praxis in these quotations; she equates Beauvoir's conception with Sartre's.

9. Terry Keefe views Henri's decision as an instance of his "perverse or self-indulgent amoral mood" (Keefe 1998, 102). Eleanore Holveck argues that "Henri perjures himself for Josette, because he realizes that her lack of education and culture guarantees that she cannot make decisions freely and responsibly. . . . More importantly, Henri realizes how significantly he has contributed to Josette's oppression" (Holveck 2002, 137).

10. Beauvoir herself invokes it in the title of an essay from May 6, 1975, "Solidarity of Israel" (Francis and Gontier 1979, 522–32).

Works Cited

Arp, Kristana. 2001. *The bonds of freedom*. Chicago: Open Court Press.

Bartky, Sandra. 2002. *Sympathy and solidarity and other essays*. Lanham, Md.: Rowman and Littlefield.

Bayertz, Kurt. 1999. Four uses of "solidarity." In *Solidarity*, edited by Kurt Bayertz. Dordrecht, The Netherlands: Kluwer.

Beauvoir, Simone de. 1944. *Pyrrhus et Cinéas*. Paris: Gallimard.

———. [1947] 1948. *Ethics of ambiguity*. Translated by Bernard Frechtman. Secaucus, N.J.: Citadel Press.

———. 1948. *L'existentialisme et la sagesse des nations*. Paris: Nagel.

———. [1945] 1948 *The blood of others*. Translated by Roger Senhouse and Yvonne Moyse. New York: Bantam Books.

———. 1952. *The second sex*. New York: Alfred A. Knopf. (Orig. pub. 1949.)

———. 1956. *The mandarins*. Translated by Leonard M. Friedman. New York: World Publishing Company. (Reprinted in New York by W.W. Norton & Company, 1999. Orig. pub. 1954.)

———. 1986. *Le deuxiéme sexe II*. Paris: Gallimard.

———. 1983. *Who shall die?* Translated by Claude Francis and Fernande Gontier. Florrisant, Mo: River Press. (Orig. pub. 1945.)

———. 1992. *All men are mortal*. Translated by Leonard M. Friedman. New York: W.W. Norton. (Orig. pub. 1946.)

Fallaize, Elizabeth. 1988. *The novels of Simone de Beauvoir*. New York: Routledge.

Francis, Claude, and Fernande Gontier. 1979. *Les écrits de Simone de Beauvoir*. Paris: Gallimard.

Holveck, Eleanore. 2002. *Simone de Beauvoir's philosophy of lived experience*. Lanham, Md.: Rowman and Littlefield.

Keefe, Terry. 1998. *Simone de Beauvoir*. New York: St. Martin's Press.

Kruks, Sonia. 2001. *Retrieving experience: Subjectivity and recognition in feminist politics*. Ithaca, N.Y.: Cornell University Press.

Matarrese, Craig. 2001. Solidarity and fear: Hegel and Sartre on the mediations of reciprocity. *Philosophy Today* 45, no. 1:43–55.

McBride, William L. 1991. *Sartre's political theory*. Bloomington: Indiana University Press.

Sartre, Jean-Paul. 1991. *Critique of dialectical reason*. Translated by Alan Sheridan-Smith. New York: Verso. (Org. pub. 1960.)

Scholz, Sally. 2001. Writing for liberation: Simone de Beauvoir and woman's writing. *Philosophy Today* 45, no. 4/5:331–44.

Chapter 3

Living on Rails

Freedom, Constraint, and Political Judgment in Beauvoir's "Moral" Essays and The Mandarins

Sonia Kruks

> *When I was born, I was on rails . . . the little girl of three lived on, grown calmer, in the child of ten, that of the child in the young woman of twenty, and so on. Of course, circumstances led me to develop in many ways. But through all the changes I still see myself. . . . My life has been at once the fulfillment of an original project and the product and expression of the world in which it unfolded. This is why, in recounting it, I have been able to speak of many things besides myself.*
>
> —Simone de Beauvoir, *All Said and Done*

Among her numerous novels, Simone de Beauvoir thought most highly of *The Mandarins*; among her nonfiction works (which she usually referred to as her "essays") she most approved of *The Second Sex*. Beauvoir later remarked, when comparing her earlier novel *The Blood of Others* (completed 1943) with *The Mandarins* (completed 1953), that the former was not as successful because in it she reduced her characters to "mere ethical viewpoints," presenting "simple, unambiguous, and morally edifying" conclusions through them (1992a, 465).[1] Likewise, Beauvoir observes that in her first published novel, *She Came to Stay* (completed 1941), she used her characters above all as vehicles to make metaphysical points. Beauvoir came to regard what she called the "thesis-novel" [roman à thèse] as an unsatisfactory literary form, because it contradicts the actual intent of a novel: "[A] novel is about bringing existence to light in its ambiguities, in its contradictions" (1979b, 447). This is what *The Mandarins* does, and this is why she approves of it: "[T]hesis-novels always impose a certain truth that eclipses all others and calls a halt to the perpetual dance of conflicting points of view; whereas [in *The Mandarins*] I described certain ways of living after the war, without offering any solution to the problems that were troubling my main characters. . . . I showed some people at grips with doubts and hopes, groping in the dark; I cannot think I proved anything," (1992b, 270–71).

Among her nonfiction works, Beauvoir was most critical of the ethico-political essays from what she later disparagingly referred to as her "moral period" (1992a, 433). This period begins with *Pyrrhus et Cinéas* (written in 1943), includes a group of essays published in 1945 and 1946,[2] and culminates in *The Ethics of Ambiguity* (published in 1947). *The Blood of Others* and the "moral" essays were, of course, all written either during the war or in the turbulent immediate postwar period. Thus, it is perhaps not surprising that they bear a strong resemblance to each other, being marked by the same strongly moralizing tone. Beauvoir herself explains this tone as her way of responding to the dramatic collapse of her hitherto happy and stable world, and her ensuing sense of "chaos." Against this, she wrote, "I had as my only recourse this verbal exorcism: an abstract morality" (1992a, 433 TA; 1977, 626).

However, by the time *The Ethics of Ambiguity* was published, in 1947, Beauvoir was already at work on something very different: *The Second Sex*; and by the time volume 2 of *The Second Sex* was published, in November 1949, she was already busy with *The Mandarins*. Thus, the "essay" and the novel that Beauvoir regarded as most successful were written consecutively, and I argue that taken together they are indicative of a new period in her thinking. This period is marked by an increasingly profound acknowledgment of the weight of situations, of what she will call *la force des choses*. In this new period she stopped attempting to "exorcise" those elements of life that are beyond the control of the self. Instead she now accepted their presence as integral to her own existence and that of others. This new recognition profoundly informs her writings from the late 1940s onward.

A continuity of preoccupations—with questions of selfhood, freedom, responsibility, judgment, and resistance to oppression—runs throughout Beauvoir's entire oeuvre. But within this continuity an important change of emphasis and approach takes place. What is most striking, both in *The Second Sex* and *The Mandarins*, is Beauvoir's shift toward a notion of the self as one that does not only make its decisions "in situation" but is so thoroughly suffused by its situation that it is, to a significant degree, constituted by it. For example, when Beauvoir writes in *The Second Sex* that a woman's body "is her situation" (1989, 34), she does not of course mean that biology is a determining factor for a woman; biology does not irrevocably set down her entire life-course. However, she does mean that the facticity, or accident of birth, that requires that one grow to maturity and live one's life with a biologically female body will always be integral to one's selfhood and to one's projects.[3] Even though a female body (and likewise a male, white, black, healthy, disabled one, and so on) may be taken up and acted upon, or "assumed,"[4] in diverse fashions, it will always be integral to who one is, and so will indelibly color how one acts. Likewise, in *The Mandarins*, the main characters learn that the facticity of being "French" in the 1940s profoundly suffuses their possibilities for political action. "Freedom" here is doubly constrained. Freedom becomes not only a matter of acting within the small margins and many constraints of one's immediate situation, but also of making one's decisions as who one has already "become."

Famously, "one is not born a woman but becomes one" (1989, 267). But Beauvoir's statement, and her ensuing account of women's "lived experience," invokes two senses of the verb "to become": in becoming a gender, an ethnicity, a nationality, and so on, one "becomes" what one has been made by one's situation, and one also "becomes" what one has made of oneself as such a situated existent. Furthermore, depending on what one has become, one will be more likely to make certain kinds of choices in the future, and less likely to make other ones. For although what we have become may not *determine* our future actions, it does strongly *predispose* us to proceed along certain paths.

Although, for example, as Sartre insists in *Being and Nothingness*, I may in principle be free to overcome the inferiority complex with which I have lived for twenty years, Beauvoir's view of freedom is nearer to Merleau-Ponty's when he asserts (against Sartre) that such a transformation is not "probable." Probability, Merleau-Ponty points out, is not a fiction but a real phenomenon. For if I have made my inferiority "my abode" for the last twenty years, then "this past, though not a fate, has at least a specific weight and is . . . the atmosphere of my present." Thus, he continues, "our freedom does not destroy our situation, but gears itself to it" (1962, 442). Hence also Beauvoir's autobiographical comment about living "on rails" in the epigraph (taken from *All Said and Done*) with which I begin this paper.[5] Hence also Henri, a central character in *The Mandarins*, discovers that, having become a Resistance activist and a prominent left-wing intellectual during the war, he is now somebody who cannot cease to remain politically committed, even though he has ambitions to withdraw from politics in order to write.

Thus, in both *The Second Sex* and *The Mandarins*, Beauvoir moves away from what she later critically characterized as the "abstractness" of her early "moral period." She puts into question her earlier characterization of the self as always free to make its own choices within its situation. Instead, she develops an account in which selves make their choices not only as free affirmations of a future but also as expressions of their specific present situations—situations which are freighted by their past.[6] Thus, accompanying Beauvoir's greater focus on the weight of situations, in both *The Second Sex* and *The Mandarins* there is a greater attention given to the particularities of lived experience, and in both works Beauvoir turns more fully to the use of a phenomenological method.

Accordingly, in volume 2 of *The Second Sex* women are not characterized as one homogeneous group. Rather, Beauvoir offers a phenomenology of femininity as it is lived at different life-stages and by different kinds of women, (for example, heterosexual or lesbian, compliant or resistant). Likewise, as Beauvoir herself remarked, her quasi-fictional characters in *The Mandarins* cease to be above all the bearers of moral or metaphysical positions. Through the use of extensive internal monologue—a method that may be called phenomenological, since much of it is drawn from her own experiences and those of people close to her—she presents us with descriptions of the lived experience of a particular group of people: the politically engaged noncommunist Left in postwar France. However, through the evocation of the experiences of this particular group, Beauvoir illuminates for us aspects of political experience more generally. As such, without being a "thesis-novel," *The Mandarins* is a work that still speaks to concerns that persist well beyond the confines of its era. One key issue that pervades Beauvoir's early ethico-political writings, which she further addresses in *The Mandarins*, and which remains germane today, is the nature of political judgment. It is this topic which is the main focus of my paper.

◆◆◆

Consonant with Beauvoir's approach, I shall construe the term "judgment" widely here. Judgment refers to a synthetic movement—a "project"—that encompasses not only deliberating, making evaluations, and arriving at decisions, but also the accompanying upsurge of action in the world. For, as we shall see, Beauvoir's treatment suggests that "judgment" is seldom the detached and contemplative, or objective and impartial, process of deliberating and deciding that it is most often taken to be.

Contemporary normative approaches to judgment tend to remain predominantly neo-Kantian, usually positing an autonomous, rational agent of judgment: either one who dispassionately weighs and assesses the virtues of general principles or else one who, concerned with judging specific courses of action or events, evaluates these impartially against such general principles in order to decide what "ought" to be (or to have been) done. In her "moral period," as we shall see, Beauvoir's focus on political judgment still broadly remains within this tradition. She does already depart from a straightforward Kantianism, insofar as she insists that the self must decide "in situation," and often in situations that do not admit of a straightforward moral resolution through the application of principle. But she still attributes a strong autonomy, indeed an "infinite" freedom, to the self (1944, 86).[7] She argues that others' actions may impinge only on the "outside" [les dehors], and not on the ontological freedom of an individual (83, 86). Thus, she also argues, each of us must judge and act alone; consequently, we must also assume full moral responsibility for our individual actions. To deny this responsibility, it follows, is to attempt to flee one's freedom; it is to act in "bad faith."

In *The Mandarins*, however, Beauvoir puts into question these tenets of her earlier work. For what the novel reveals is that making political judgments is itself a form of situationally suffused *action*. "Judging," in this fuller sense, is an activity that we can very rarely undertake detached from the facticities of our own particular lives. For these facticities will color (even though they do not determine) how we view the world, and they will significantly inform what we decide and do. They will suffuse our freedom and shape our judgments in ways that Beauvoir does not admit of in her early essays, and which generally are not acknowledged in neo-Kantian conceptions of judgment.

◆◆◆

In *Pyrrhus et Cinéas*, the first essay from her "moral period" (1944; written 1943), Beauvoir initially follows the early Sartre in arguing that we are each an *ontologically* free and separate existent that, alone and through its own projects, constitutes the meaning of its own life. She makes a distinction between this ontological freedom, which she calls "liberté" and which she still insists "remains infinite" (1944, 86), and what she calls "puissance." The latter term refers to our concrete ability to act in the world, an ability I will refer to as our *effective* freedom. This, unlike *liberté*, is, she says, "finite," and so others "can augment or limit it from without [du dehors]" (86).

However, an ontological freedom which cannot realize itself in choosing effective projects, a freedom which cannot engage in meaningful action in the world, is doomed to consume itself uselessly. Thus, we can realize our *liberté* only insofar as we also possess *puissance*, or effective freedom—and this is not always the case.[8] For Beauvoir adds a highly significant caveat to her account of *puissance*, one that Sartre had not made in his treatment of freedom in *Being and Nothingness*. She argues that to enjoy effective freedom we must overcome our separation from others; we must both recognize and be recognized by them. Indeed, Beauvoir points out, to imagine myself alone in the world is truly horrifying. "A man alone in the world would be paralyzed by the self-evident vanity of all his goals; he undoubtedly could not bear to live" (1944, 65). Without reciprocal human recognition our lives lack the means to overcome our individual finitude. For it is only when others take up and prolong our projects that the import of our actions may travel on beyond us. Thus, through reciprocal relations of "generosity," we must seek to move beyond the conflictual relations of self and other, that Sartre had described in *Being and Nothingness*.[9] We must will for all others an enlarged capacity to act meaningfully in the actual world—that is, a greater degree of *effective* freedom.

Here is the claim that makes possible Beauvoir's move toward ethics, and that also integrally links her ethics to radical politics. In choosing my own freedom I must also choose to extend that of others. Not only must I (as far as is possible) recognize and respect the freedom of other individuals I encounter, but I also must act so as to maximize the realm of effective freedom of everyone. Because oppression, which negates effective freedom, is rife in the world, an ethically inspired political engagement follows from Beauvoir's account of human existence. I must endeavor "to create for all men situations which will enable them to accompany and surpass my transcendence . . . [men need] health, knowledge, well-being, leisure, so that their freedom does not consume itself in fighting sickness, misery, ignorance" (1944, 115).

However, as Beauvoir herself later comments, her arguments in *Pyrrhus et Cinéas* still remained too "enmeshed in individualism." She observes: "An individual, I thought, only receives a human dimension by recognizing the existence of others. Yet, in [*Pyrrhus et Cinéas*], coexistence appears as a sort of accident that each individual should somehow surmount; each should begin by hammering out his project in isolation, and only then ask the collectivity to validate it." She goes on to observe: "In truth, society invests me [m'investit] from the day of my birth; it is in the bosom of society, and in my own intimate relationship with it, that I decide who I am to be" (1992a, 435 TA; 1977, 628–29). For the later Beauvoir, then, our "coexistence" with others is no longer contingent but rather is integral to the self; and it thus follows that the self, even as a *liberté*, is always profoundly suffused by its social situation.

Because *Pyrrhus et Cinéas* still lacks such an account of the self the essay is also, as Beauvoir says more generally of her "moral period" essays, "abstract" (1992a, 433). In *Pyrrhus et Cinéas*, Beauvoir criticizes Kant, arguing that "respect for the human person is not generally sufficient to guide us" (1944, 91). An executioner and his victim are both full human beings, yet we cannot support both: we must decide whether to let the victim perish or kill the executioner (91). But how do we decide? Beauvoir argues, again against Kant, that we cannot decide "objectively," and that it is not possible adequately to evaluate such dilemmas from a dispassionate or "contemplative" attitude. For "if I am removed from all situations, all givens will seem equally indifferent to me" (92). Thus, we must make our judgments *in situation*.

But what does it mean to decide "in situation"? Beauvoir urges us to take up, or "assume," our freedom; we are told that we can and must choose, that we are responsible for our choices, and that we are in bad faith if we deny this. But in *Pyrrhus et Cinéas* she still operates at a level of abstraction that is too far removed from the actual world, from the concrete givens in which we make our specific judgments. Thus Beauvoir becomes mired in a problem analogous to the one she attributes to Kant. For, maxims such as "act so as to choose freedom for all" and "recognize that you alone are responsible for your acts" are, in themselves, as abstract as his categorical imperative. This becomes apparent in her subsequent "moral period" essays. For example, in "Moral Idealism and Political Realism," first published in 1945, Beauvoir sets out with only limited success to chart a course between an "idealism" that urges that we follow right principles irrespective of the consequences and a cynical "realism" that is concerned only with political efficacy.

Both the idealist's claim that one is bound to follow a preordained principle or duty and the realist's claim that objective necessity requires that we act in particular ways are forms of bad faith, Beauvoir argues. For they are both ways of evading responsibility for our own freedom and the anguish it evokes. Beauvoir agrees with Kant that "treating man as a means is committing violence against him; it means contradicting the idea of his absolute value" (1948, 98). However, in a world of oppression and conflict, it may be impossible to avoid doing violence to others. Thus, against Kant, Beauvoir also insists that it is not possible to act on behalf of "man" without sometimes treating certain men merely as means. In many situations, "whatever I may choose to do, I will be unfaithful to my profound desire to respect human life; and yet I am forced to choose; *no reality external to myself indicates my choice* [aucune réalité extérieure à moi-même ne m'indique pas mon choix]" (1948, 100; my emphasis). Neither pregiven ethical imperatives (which the Kantian autonomous self claims freely to follow), nor claims about the necessary course of history (beloved by certain mechanistic Marxists) may justify our decisions. Here, says Beauvoir, is the source of the anguish that so many flee in bad faith. For we are alone in our freedom and in our responsibility; we act in a world where nothing tells us what we should decide, and where we cannot avoid violence.[10]

Beauvoir takes as an example a choice that may have confronted leaders in the Resistance: one may have to decide whether or not to sacrifice the life of one man in order to save many—and either choice is a "scandal." Whichever one decides, she insists, the decision is mine alone. For "it is not reality that imposes a choice on me, it is only after I have made a choice that reality takes on any value" (1948, 99). But here we see the abstractness of Beauvoir's account. For if my decision whether or not to save the life of a particular man cannot be made by subsuming it under an ethical principle and is not the outcome of determining forces, how then *do* I decide? Assuming I do not just toss a coin, assuming that my decision is not wholly arbitrary, then what concretely enters into my decision-making process? Are there not factors that will predispose me to decide in a certain way?

In the passage I quoted with emphasis above, Beauvoir insists (paralleling Sartre in *Being and Nothingness*) that "no reality external to myself indicates my choice" (1948, 100). Certainly, no exterior reality *determines* my choice, in the strict sense of operating upon me with full causal necessity. Yet, as Beauvoir will later acknowledge, there still are many factors, some external, and some arising from how I have *already* assumed the world in which I find myself, that will strongly *predispose* me to decide in a certain way. These factors may include pressure from others, cultural norms, ethical considerations, my rational weighing up of other pros and cons, emotional responses such as anger or love, my habitual ways of responding to dilemmas, and so on. As Merleau-Ponty had argued against Sartre (1962, 442ff.), between determinism and the claim that my choice is not guided by *any* "external" factors lie many gradations. Beauvoir begins to explore some of these gradations in *The Second Sex*, when she considers the different degrees of complicity women have in their own oppression.[11] But it is in *The Mandarins* that Beauvoir explores yet more fully this in-between zone, in which our judgments are so often made.

If we presume that there are only two possible accounts of the way we arrive at a judgment, either through external determination or else through a choice made by a freedom that is "infinite," then by rejecting determinism we make of freedom a matter of choice that is so indeterminate that it becomes arbitrary. For if being free means only that we are not determined, then why, presented with a dilemma such as Beauvoir describes, should we not just toss a coin to decide? For no one outcome would matter more than another. Sartre's early work has sometimes been read as presenting us with such a nihilism.[12] But, irrespective of what one might say about Sartre's position (an issue I leave aside here), Beauvoir wishes to avoid such a conclusion.

It is true that in *The Ethics of Ambiguity*, Beauvoir does say of "political choice" that it is a "wager": one "bets on the chances and risks of the measures under consideration" (1967, 148). Yet political choice is also much more than a wager for her. But if, as Beauvoir argues, we must make our judgments in anguished awareness of our responsibility, then we need to give a fuller account of the ways we arrive at them than she is able to offer in her early essays. Between the bad faith claims (of idealists and realists alike) that our judgments and actions are imposed on us and Beauvoir's bald counteraffirmation, in "Moral Idealism and Political Realism" and other essays of her "moral period," that we decide alone and in our infinite freedom, we need an account that is more attentive to the experience of the self as one suffused by its situation. What Beauvoir still lacks in her early essays is a phenomenology that reveals the complex lived experience through which we arrive at political judgments.

Such a phenomenology will reveal our choices to be neither determined nor arbitrary. For, our freedom, to recall Merleau-Ponty's phrase again, "gears itself to our situation" (1962, 442). Since we are each a situated freedom, we will discover how the social milieu in which we live, with its normative and cultural practices, informs (even though it does not determine) our judgments. We will see how our prior decisions and actions shape (though, again, they do not determine) our future ones. We will learn, in short, that we do not only decide "in" situation, but that we decide as selves that are already strongly suffused by their situation. Here we need to turn to *The Mandarins*. For this is where we find Beauvoir developing such a phenomenological exploration of the making of political judgments. In *The Mandarins* we are shown how freedom and situation merge and meld, how our situation suffuses our "free" choices.

◆◆◆

Beauvoir insists that "contrary to what has been claimed, it is not true that *The Mandarins* is a *roman à clé*" (1992b, 267 TA; 1972, 366). Neither roman à clé nor thesis-novel, neither autobiography nor reportage, *The Mandarins* is described by Beauvoir as "an evocation" (1992b, 270). It is an evocation in which "fiction" is used as a tool to present complexities of life that mere reportage could not capture. I think Beauvoir must be taken at her word: *The Mandarins* is not a roman à clé. The fictitious characters do not align neatly with the actual dramatis personae of Beauvoir's circle, and although the novel treats of the impact of actual political events of the late 1940s, the chronology is not accurate. Yet, as an evocation, *The Mandarins* is also grounded in lived experience, and its "fictions" are in large measure woven from the autobiographical. Beauvoir says she put important elements of herself and of her own experiences in the postwar era into two different characters: Anne Dubreuilh and Henri Perron. It is above all through the character of Henri that Beauvoir explores the lived experience of political judgment. "Most of the time they are my own emotions and thoughts that inhabit him," she writes (1992b, 269), and in an interview given when she won the Prix Goncourt she says, "[I]t is with regard to Henri that I tried to pose the real problems [of practical politics]" (1979a, 359).

Henri Perron is a successful young novelist, Resistance activist, and editor of a leftist daily newspaper, *L'Espoir* [*Hope*], that he cofounded during the Resistance. He struggles throughout the novel to make sense of the shifting political currents and events of the postwar period, and to satisfy his diverse and conflicting desires. He wants to engage effectively and responsibly in a Left politics that navigates between the two great power blocs of the emerging cold war; to find the time to write a new novel; to disengage from a stifling affair with his long-standing mistress, Paula; to enjoy other liaisons; and to maintain his close friendship with Robert Dubreuilh, the older and highly charismatic intellectual who in 1935 had helped Henri to get his first novel published.

By following Henri through his dilemmas and decisions, we may begin to draw from Beauvoir's novel an account, one still absent from her "moral period" essays, of the lived experience of making political judgments. In the course of the novel, Henri has to reach a series of crucial decisions, each of which is at once personal and political, and each of which involves a freedom whose "choice" is, he discovers, profoundly suffused by its situation. These decisions include (among others): whether to join the SRL, the new "third way" Left political organization Robert Dubreuilh is founding[13]; whether (once having joined) to agree to make *L'Espoir* its official newspaper; whether to publish information that is emerging about forced labor camps in the Soviet Union; whether to perjure himself to protect his mistress, who had previously had an affair with a German officer during the Occupation; whether (at the very end of the novel) to exile himself to Italy to write or to stay in Paris and remain politically engaged.

I shall focus here on only one of these decisions: whether or not to turn *L'Espoir* into the official organ of the SRL. In this key exemplar, Beauvoir reveals judgment to be shaped by the convergence of multiple aspects of one's situated existence. She depicts structures, histories, and events that so strongly shape Henri's process of judgment as to put into question her earlier notion of *liberté*. Initially, we might believe that Henri is going to make a free choice of the kind Beauvoir had talked about in the "moral period" essays. His decision is not, strictly speaking, determined by exterior forces; nor is he able to decide what to do through the application of principles. It might appear that Henri must simply "wager" and, afterward, acknowledge his sole responsibility for what he chooses. But this is not the case. It becomes apparent that Henri's freedom is already profoundly suffused with the world in which he now finds himself situated, and that his choice is not random, but rather is constrained by who he has already become. Far from it being the case that nothing "external" to Henri "indicates" his choice, he discovers he is caught up in a set of strongly convergent force-lines that will significantly contribute to his decision.

◆◆◆

The Mandarins begins with an account of a joyous Christmas party, held in December 1944 in recently liberated Paris. Henri has devoted himself for four years to Resistance politics, above all to publishing *L'Espoir*, and is now aching to live life more fully again. He hungrily anticipates the end of the deprivations and drudgery of the Occupation years. He yearns to travel (he has an invitation that he intends to accept to give some lectures in Portugal) and, above all, he desires to write fiction again: "With no time for himself he had lost his taste for life and desire to write. He had become a machine . . . now he was determined to become a man again" (1972, 16). But even during this joyous Christmas celebration Robert Dubreuilh approaches Henri, and urges him to become involved with the political struggles looming in the new postwar era by participating in the SRL. In the Resistance, life had been straightforward, as had been running the paper. He knows that now "politics," in the sense of endless committees, conferences, meetings, maneuverings, and compromises, will consume his time and energies, and exasperate and bore him. However, when Dubreuilh approaches him he does not feel he has "the right to look for an out," and so he agrees to lend his name to the SRL and to "put in a few appearances" (18).

Already, the "impasse" is revealed. The trap is sprung. Henri wants to go back to being what he was and doing what he did before the war. But, as he discovers, he is no longer the "same" Henri; for now he is also the man he has become during the war. Moreover, he must act in a new national and international configuration not of his choosing, and which will to a significant degree define who he is and what his possibilities are. A leftist armchair intellectual in 1939, he now knows that he is obligated to be more politically active if he is to break away from the privileges of his class, if he is not to deserve the hatred of millions of oppressed people (17). However, if he gets sucked into politics, he will not have time to write. Another character, the emigré Scriassine, puts this dilemma into a wider context:

> French intellectuals are facing an impasse . . . their art, their philosophies [pensée] will continue to have meaning only if a certain kind of civilization manages to endure. And if they want to save that civilization, they'll have nothing left over to give to art or philosophy. . . . What weight will the message of French writers have when the earth is ruled by either Russia or the United States? No one will understand them any more; nobody will even speak their language any more. (1972, 43–45 TA; 2001, 54–56)[14]

The SRL stands for a "third way," for a democratic socialist France. This must be built by creating a space between the imperialism of US-dominated world capitalism and the deformed, expansionist socialism of the Soviet Union. Without an autonomous France there will no longer be a place for meaningful cultural expression by French intellectuals. Yet, even to keep such a possibility alive in the emerging cold war context will be an all-consuming struggle.[15] For Henri, and others in his circle, there is yet a further impasse within the "impasse." For their assessment is that, for all its deformations, the Soviet Union still remains the greatest force for progress. Moreover, the French Communist Party (PCF), which takes its line from Moscow, is still the party that enjoys mass working-class support in France, and which thus de facto represents socialist potential. The SRL must not alienate the PCF, but rather give it critical support. But if the SRL criticizes the Soviet Union and keeps its distance from the PCF, how then will it win the mass of people to its more democratic socialist agenda? It is within the context of these multiple dilemmas that Henri struggles over the decision whether or not to make *L'Espoir* the official organ of the SRL. Over time, and as various elements come to bear on him, he shifts from insisting that *L'Espoir* must remain independent to agreeing that it will become the organ of the SRL.

After this struggle is over, and when Henri has finally agreed that *L'Espoir* is formally to become the newspaper of the SRL, he has a conversation with Robert Dubreuilh's wife, Anne. Henri is resentful about the pressure Dubreuilh has put on him to give *L'Espoir* to the SRL. "But you did agree," says Anne. Yes, Henri says, he did agree. But, he adds, it is hard not to feel resentful when you are "pushed" into doing something "against your will [à contrecœur]" (1972, 254–55). But how does one come to make a "decision" that goes against one's will? One does not do so, Beauvoir's account suggests, only or even primarily through a process of clear reasoning and dispassionate judgment. For one is carried toward one's final judgment by the confluence of many aspects of one's situation that are not the object of one's rational deliberations.

This is not to say that Henri does not spend many hours trying to decide what is the most rational course of action, considering what appear to be the objective pros and cons of the matter. On the side of keeping *L'Espoir* independent of the SRL he can, most importantly, point to the need to go on maintaining full editorial independence if he is to keep trust with his readers and with his own commitments: "Now was the time to educate readers instead of cramming things down their throats. No more dictating opinions to them; rather teach them to judge for themselves" (1972, 28). He can also point to the financial risk of losing readers who may be displeased if *L'Espoir* ceases to be independent. But he hears conflicting arguments from different sides: the SRL will end up in bed with the Communists and so will *L'Espoir*, warns one. To the contrary, if the SRL has a newspaper of its own, it will become too strong a force for the PCF to accept, and it will be destroyed, warns another. On the side of giving the paper to the SRL the strongest argument is that Henri is already a prominent member of the SRL: if he supports this movement, then surely he should help it to grow by providing it with a daily paper. Moreover, in the postwar situation the paper itself now needs a clear program. Its "independence" threatens to become vacuous, a way of pleasing everyone by committing to nothing. The memory of the Resistance, the occasion of the paper's founding, no longer provides an adequate political program. Indeed, the Resistance is fast becoming a nostalgic myth, not an orientation to action.

But as he considers all of these arguments, Henri becomes aware of several things: one is that "concrete evidence" will never be a sufficient basis on which to arrive at a wise judgment. We never know enough to be sure that our decisions will have the desired outcome. Will the readership grow or shrink if he gives the paper to the SRL? Will the SRL grow or not as a result? On so many political matters, Henri reflects, you have to act without knowing. "First, you've got to speak, because the matter is urgent; afterwards events prove you right or wrong. 'And that's precisely what's known as bluffing,' he said unhappily to himself. 'Yes, even I bluff my readers'" (1972, 175). But if he is bluffing, if he fails to give his readers what he has promised them, then why defend the independence of the paper? Similarly, he tells the younger man, Lambert, one cannot defend the paper's independence on the grounds that one must be free to follow one's own conscience, for this too is to act from ignorance: "'[I]t's just a question of speaking as our consciences dictate!' Lambert said. 'Did you every stop to think what that means?' Henri asked. 'Every morning I tell a hundred thousand people how they ought to think. And what do I guide myself by? The voice of my conscience! . . . It's a gigantic swindle'" (177).

But if rational arguments, the "concrete evidence" we believe we possess, or our moral convictions are insufficient to justify our decisions, are we not after all in the realm of mere "wager"? Might Henri not as well toss a coin to make his decision? If he did so, however, it would turn out to be heavily weighted; it would be far more likely to come down one way than the other. For many aspects of his situation enter into how he decides. They include his personal "history," his present desires, fears, loves and friendships, his wider network of social connections, Paris, France, the international situation, and so on. It is Henri as the point of convergence and the totalizer of all of this who will "make" the decision.[16]

Although he does very seriously consider all the rational arguments, from the beginning Henri has what we might call a "gut" reaction against handing over *L'Espoir*. "No, he wouldn't give him [Dubreuilh] *L'Espoir*. That was so clear that it needed no justifying. Nevertheless, he wished he could find a few good reasons for his stand" (1972, 153). Why this gut reaction? Henri has created the paper and, in doing so, he has made being its editor vital to his own existence. The paper is his world. It is not only his project but also a place where he is profoundly at home. Beauvoir describes Henri entering the offices alone, late at night: "[H]e liked the familiar smell of stale dust and fresh ink. The offices were still empty, the basement silent. But soon a whole world would rise from this silence, a world that was his creation. 'No one will ever lay his hands on *L'Espoir*,' he repeated to himself. He sat down at his desk and stretched out" (1972, 166 TA; 2001, 207).

In addition, Henri's initial gut reaction against Dubreuilh's proposal is linked to his passionate desire to become again the "old" Henri, the creative and successful writer, the man with a zest for life. Putting *L'Espoir* into the hands of the SRL would mean being sucked further into the desiccating world of politics. Already he is "dry," and he will become more so. Then, writing will be impossible. There is also the matter of personal relationships, above all with Dubreuilh. Henri feels obligated to him, and his continued friendship with the older man who has been his mentor is important. But he also feels resentment and anger that Dubreuilh is making him feel guilty, and is using their friendship against him. There is also Samazelle, a powerful player in the SRL. Henri actively dislikes this man and distrusts his politics, and knows he will have to deal with him day after day if *L'Espoir* goes to the SRL.

Why then does Henri end by deciding to give *L'Espoir* to the SRL? It is not just that he chooses a rationally justifiable, or morally superior, course of action against the grain of his emotional preferences. Choosing against one's will here is not a matter of choosing reason over unreason, selflessness over self-interest. Rather, it has to do with a profound shift in Henri's own *experience* of self. It has to do with his realization that, for reasons both of his own making and beyond his control, his very existence has changed. "'It's funny,'" he remarks to himself, "'but whenever you do the decent thing, instead of giving you certain rights it only creates more obligations.' He had founded *L'Espoir*, and now that act was driving him to throw himself body and soul into the political madhouse" (1972, 190 TA; 2001, 237).

But the problem is not only one of being "forced" into politics. What Henri begins to realize—and to experience as a profound crisis—is that there is no going back to the prewar Henri. With regard to his desire to write, he begins to discover that the problem is not only one of lack of time—for actually he has nothing left to say! When he does sit down to work at his novel, he is blocked. The "impasse" is not merely a practical one. For now what should he say? And to whom? Who now will be his audience? His whole life lacks meaning, lacks flavor. He is "living like an engineer in a mechanical world," he has become "dry as a stone" (1972, 191). But that being the case, to refuse to get yet further involved in politics on the grounds that he needs time to write is a sham. Similarly, he comes to feel that his insistence on keeping control of *L'Espoir* is a sham, for he now realizes the paper cannot make much of a difference. In fact, he suddenly feels, he has been "playing" at being an editor. He has considered *L'Espoir* his toy, "a complete set of equipment for the little junior editor—life size. A magnificent plaything!" (190). He really doesn't believe in what he is doing anymore: if Dubreuilh and Samazelle still have hope that they can change the world, then they should have the paper.

In the end, Henri is overwhelmed with a sense of the futility of both his own life and of life in general. Massive structural changes in world power relations, apparently distant forces that are now being brought to bear on him locally, conjoin with other more particularistic elements of his own situation, and strongly predispose Henri toward his final "choice": the decision to give up *L'Espoir*, and so also to "choose" politics over writing. On the night that Henri finally arrives at the decision to give his paper to the SRL, he has an abrupt and terrible epiphany. He suddenly recognizes, not as a mere piece of intellectual information (for of course he "knew" this before), but as a profound shattering of his sense of his own existence, that geopolitics changes the meaning of our actions.[17] It is this devastating realization that precipitates his final decision.

Two things take place that night. One directly involves Henri, and the other seems more distant. Early in the evening, Henri has been to see Tournelle, a man whom he had known as a comrade in the Resistance and who is now a government minister. At the behest of the beleaguered old leftists he had met during his visit to Portugal early in 1945, Henri asks Tournelle for French government support of the Portuguese Left against Salazar's Fascist dictatorship. He already knows that, because of American influence on the government, the answer will be no, but he still feels morally obligated to try. "'You know the situation as well as I,'" says Tournelle. "'How can you expect France to do anything for Portugal, or for anyone else for that matter, when she can't do anything for herself!'" (1972, 204). Tournelle is trapped, bitter. Now he is not even sure that the Resistance had been worth all the bloodshed . . . and suddenly the realization hits Henri: in this new world France is no longer a world power, and what its citizens say, write, or do now simply makes no difference. "Suddenly he realized he was living in the moribund capital of a very small country. . . . Henri was nothing but an insignificant citizen of a fifth-rate power, and *L'Espoir* was a local sheet on the same level as a village weekly" (205). So what does it matter who controls *L'Espoir*? He may as well give it to the SRL!

But Henri still hesitates to do the deed. It is only later that night that he arrives finally at the tipping point, as his dreadful realization is reinforced from yet another direction. For this is also the night the triumphant Soviet army is entering Berlin. Nazism is definitively defeated—but there is no cause for celebration. *L'Espoir* is irrelevant in the new configuration, in which France, Europe, and indeed, the whole world is now the plaything of two great powers—and equally irrelevant is the project of being a writer.

> The Russians were sacking Berlin, the war was ending, or another one was beginning—how could one find pleasure in telling stories that never actually happened? . . . He was nowhere, had nothing, was nothing; there was nothing he could speak about. "Then I just have to shut up," he thought. "If I really come to terms with the inevitable, maybe I'll stop tearing myself to pieces, maybe I'll be able to bear with a lighter heart the drudgeries I'm forced to do." . . . He had believed that he lived in a very special part of the world from which every word echoed across the entire planet. But now he knew all his words died at his feet. (1972, 212–13 TA; 2001, 264–65)

And so Henri goes into a bar, gets drunk with an acquaintance, and "decides" he will give *L'Espoir* to the SRL. Moreover, drunk and maudlin, he declares to himself that he will abnegate his entire life to politics and simply follow orders: "[E]veryone had died in the war," including him. But "it's not upsetting being dead, if you give up pretending to be alive." So now, "act, act as a team, without worrying about yourself; sow, sow again, and never reap. Act, unite, serve, obey Dubreuilh, smile at Samazelle. He'd telephone them: 'the paper is yours.'" (1972, 215 TA; 2001, 267).

◆◆◆

What kind of "freedom" does Henri's decision entail? Is this an act of *liberté*, the choice of an ontological freedom that is untouched from the "outside" [les dehors]? Is this a choice that is in no way "indicated" by "an external reality"? And does Henri alone bear the responsibility for his final decision here? From the perspective of Beauvoir's "moral period," Henri is not only free, he is also profoundly in bad faith. He tells himself that because the world has changed he is no longer free to take responsibility for himself. Because the world has changed, he can no longer act meaningfully, and so instead he will commit to blind obedience. He will abstain from questioning or judging; he will just follow orders in the SRL.[18] Furthermore, he arrives at this moment of final decision drunk! He flees his anguish by diminishing his capacity to think and see clearly.

But Beauvoir does not invite her readers to sit in judgment on Henri. We are not asked to assess him in a dispassionate mode, or to evaluate his decision through a set of "abstract" criteria against which we will find him wanting. Rather, Beauvoir invites us to enter Henri's world and to discover that—from the perspective of lived experience—judgment, action, responsibility, and bad faith have become much more relative matters than she once had thought. Now, they admit of gradations and must be qualified by the fact that we so often act in an in-between zone, a place of neither *liberté* nor of determination *tout court*.[19]

When, after his final decision, Henri tells Anne that he has been "pushed" and that he has "agreed," but has done so "against his will," Beauvoir is offering us a very different account of our relations with the world than she had sketched in her early moral essays. Henri's "will," the freedom that Beauvoir had previously called *liberté*, is not impervious to its situation. On the contrary, it is thoroughly porous. Thus, the actions of others do not touch only the "outside" [les dehors] of our freedom—rather, they may radically alter it.

Through the person of Henri, Beauvoir "evokes" the realizations—emotional, intellectual, political—that she (and Sartre) made in the postwar period: freedom is not an "infinite" *liberté*, but rather a matter of acting within multiple constraints and as who one has already become. Thus, our judgments are not uniquely our own. Likewise, our responsibility for what we decide is not absolutely ours alone. For we come to make our choices suffused by our situation, enmeshed within and weighted by *la force des choses*. The insights

Beauvoir offers—about freedom, constraint, and political judgment—continue to illuminate the lives of all of us. For, to one degree or another, we all live our lives "on rails."

Notes

1. She is even more critical of this novel in another passage: "I wanted to speak directly to the reader, and indeed I thought I was doing so; but all the time my voice had been usurped by a sort of fatuous, didactic vampire. I was dealing with a genuine experience, yet I kept trotting out commonplace platitudes" (Beauvoir 1992a, 432).

References to works translated from the French are given to the English edition I cite, and the date of original French publication is also provided in the reference list. In some instances I have made a significant alteration to the English translation. In these cases, I have used the abbreviation TA (for "translation altered") and added the French page number from the edition I used in the text.

2. Most of these were originally published in *Les Temps Modernes*.

3. Toril Moi (1999, esp. 59–83) gives an excellent account of how Beauvoir can maintain "both that biology is extremely important to women's situation and that it is not a destiny" (62). Moi convincingly argues that Beauvoir espouses neither biological determinism nor a theory of the social construction of gender, but rather develops an account of a woman as a being "in situation" for whom the body "founds my experience of myself and the world" (63). For related arguments see also Kruks 1990; Kruks 2001; Heinämaa 1997; and Heinämaa 2003.

4. Beauvoir uses the French verb *assumer*. This has the sense of "taking up the responsibility for something." The English verb "to assume" may have a similar sense when one talks of "assuming" a burden of some kind, or of "assuming" a debt.

5. Indeed, in this work Beauvoir emphasizes, perhaps even more strongly than Merleau-Ponty, the continuity and stability of the self: "I have noted a great stability in what is called people's character—the entirety of their reactions in analogous circumstances . . . generally speaking, men and women, once they are settled into adulthood, remain consistent with themselves. Sometimes, indeed, they repeat their own conduct when they think they are being different" (Beauvoir 1993, 36 TA; 1978, 55–56).

6. Beauvoir's explicit pronouncements on the nature of time generally echo Sartre's in affirming that the present takes its meaning from one's future goals. However, from the late 1940s on she develops a more dialectical notion of time, in which the weight of the past, as well the openness of projects toward a future, shapes the meaning of the present.

7. "One may throw a man in prison, release him, cut off his arm, lend him wings; but in all cases his freedom [*liberté*] remains infinite" (Beauvoir 1944, 86).

8. Detmer, in discussing Sartre, renders this as the distinction between "ontological" and "practical" freedom (1986). However, I think my term "effective" freedom (see also Kruks 1990, 90ff.) better expresses what Beauvoir means when she uses the term

puissance. For *puissance* may be thought of as "power," in the sense of enablement, of having a capacity to do something, of being effective.

9. In *Being and Nothingness* Sartre still describes self-other relations as paradigmatically those of objectifying and being objectified. See especially 1956, 361–430. It is only later, notably in *Notebooks for an Ethics*, that he also begins to consider the possibility of generosity in self-other relations. For important discussions of the originality of Beauvoir's focus here, see Bergoffen 1997 and Bauer 2001.

10. Beauvoir expands further on these predicaments in *The Ethics of Ambiguity.* Even valid projects of emancipation may conflict, she notes. For example, "during the course of the last war, no [European] anti-fascist could have wanted the revolts of the natives in the British empire to be successful; on the contrary, these revolts were supported by the Fascist regimes; and yet, we cannot blame those who, considering their emancipation to be more urgent, took advantage of the situation to obtain it. Thus, it is possible, and often happens, that one finds oneself obliged to oppress and kill men who are pursuing goals whose validity one acknowledges oneself" (1967, 98–99).

11. For some women, oppression is so extreme that their compliance does not involve bad faith. See Beauvoir 1989, xxxv.

12. See, most recently, Nancy Bauer. She cites Sartre's infamous remarks from the end of *Being and Nothingness*: "[A]ll human activities are equivalent . . . it amounts to the same thing whether one gets drunk alone or is a leader of nations" (Bauer 2001, 142).

13. The model for the SRL is the Rassemblement Démocratique Révolutionnaire (RDR), with which Sartre and others in Beauvoir's circle were centrally involved. Founded early in 1948 as a nonaligned socialist organization, the RDR collapsed by the end of 1949.

14. In the novel, Anne Dubreuilh contests Scriassine's interpretation of the situation, but it becomes evident that there is more than a grain of truth to it.

15. With hindsight, it is apparent that a major theme of Beauvoir's novel is the crisis of French national identity precipitated by France's loss of status as a world power and intellectual center. Gaullism (to which Beauvoir was profoundly hostile) was, of course, also a response to this crisis.

16. In her portrayal of Henri (and others), Beauvoir arguably anticipates Sartre's later notion of the "universal singular." Of course, Beauvoir does not explicitly articulate the methods Sartre will later use, for example in presenting Flaubert as at once a unique individual and as the totalization of his era. Yet such methods are implicit in *The Mandarins.*

17. This is, of course, what, much earlier in the book, Scriassine had diagnosed as the "impasse" of French intellectuals.

18. In the event, Henri does not abnegate himself in this way for long, and he later chooses expulsion from the SRL rather than consent to remain silent about the use of forced labor camps in the Soviet Union. Which elements of his life predispose Henri to this latter choice is of course another interesting story, but one I do not have space to address here.

19. In her critique of my earlier work, I think Gail Linsenbard simply reasserts the dualism which Beauvoir has successfully overcome in *The Second Sex* and *The Mandarins.* Linsenbard says, "According to Beauvoir, in deciding the meaning of my situa-

tion, I thereby constitute it, I am thus never wholly passive with respect to my situation" (1999, 157–58). But the point is that we are neither fully the constitutors of our situation nor wholly its passive products. Rather, the significance of Beauvoir's account of Henri's decision is that it reveals the tensions and ambiguities of a freedom in situation. Beauvoir here discloses the dialectics of interiorization and exteriorization (to use Sartre's later terminology) through which our choices and projects are born. These dialectics profoundly confound distinctions between the constitutor and constituted which Linsenbard still wants to maintain.

Works Cited

Bauer, Nancy. 2001. *Simone de Beauvoir, philosophy, and feminism.* New York: Columbia University Press.

Beauvoir, Simone de. 1944. *Pyrrhus et Cinéas.* Paris: Gallimard.

———. 1948. Idéalisme moral et réalisme politique. Reprinted in *L'Existentialisme et la sagesse des nations*, 55–101. Paris: Editions Nagel. (Originally published in *Les Temps Modernes*, November 1945.)

———. 1967. *The ethics of ambiguity.* Translated by Bernard Frechtman. New York: Citadel Press. (First French edition: 1947.)

———. 1972. *The mandarins.* Translated by Leonard L. Friedman. London: Fontana Books. (Published in French as *Les mandarins*, vol. 1 by Gallimard in 2001; first French edition: 1954.)

———. 1979a. Interview de Simone de Beauvoir par J.-F. Rolland. Reprinted in *Les écrits de Simone de Beauvoir*, edited by Claude Francis and Fernande Gontier, 358–62. Paris: Gallimard. (The interview originally appeared in *L'Humanité Dimanche*, December 19, 1954.)

———. 1979b. Mon expérience d'écrivain (lecture given in Japan, October 11, 1966). In *Les écrits de Simone de Beauvoir*, edited by Claude Francis and Fernande Gontier, 439–57. Paris: Gallimard.

———. 1989. *The second sex.* Translated by H. M. Parshley. Introduction by Deirdre Bair. New York: Vintage Books. (First French edition: 1949.)

———. 1992a. *The prime of life.* Translated by Peter Green. New York: Paragon House. (Published in French as *La force de l'âge*, vol. 2 by Gallimard in 1977; first French edition: 1960.)

———. 1992b. *Force of circumstance.* Translated by Richard Howard. New introduction by Toril Moi. Vol. 1. New York: Paragon House. (Published in French as *La force des* chose, vol.1 by Gallimard in 1972; first French edition: 1963.)

———. 1993. *All said and done.* Translated by Patrick O'Brian. New introduction by Toril Moi. New York: Paragon. (Published in French as *Tout compte fait* by Gallimard in 1978; first French edition: 1972.)

Bergoffen, Debra. 1997. *The philosophy of Simone de Beauvoir: Gendered phenomenologies, erotic generosities.* Albany: State University of New York Press.

Detmer, David. 1986. *Freedom as a value: A critique of the ethical theory of Jean-Paul Sartre.* La Salle, Ill.: Open Court.

Heinämaa, Sara. 1997. "What is a woman?" Butler and Beauvoir on the foundations of sexual difference. *Hypatia: A Journal of Feminist Philosophy* 12, no. 1:20–39.

———. 2003. *Toward a phenomenology of sexual difference: Husserl, Merleau-Ponty, Beauvoir.* Lanham, Md.: Rowman and Littlefield.

Kruks, Sonia. 1990. *Situation and human existence: Freedom, subjectivity and society.* New York: Routledge.

———. 2001. *Retrieving experience: Subjectivity and recognition in feminist politics.* Ithaca, N.Y.: Cornell University Press.

Linsenbard, Gail. 1999. Beauvoir, ontology, and women's human rights. *Hypatia: A Journal of Feminist Philosophy* 14, no. 4:145–62.

Merleau-Ponty, Maurice. 1962. *Phenomenology of perception.* Translated by Colin Smith. London: Routledge and Kegan Paul. (First French edition: 1945.)

Moi, Toril. 1999. *"What is a woman?" and other essays.* Oxford: Oxford University Press.

Sartre, Jean-Paul. 1956. *Being and nothingness.* Translated by Hazel E. Barnes. New York: Philosophical Library. (First French edition: 1943.)

CHAPTER 4

Testimony, *Historicité*, and the Intellectual in Simone de Beauvoir's *The Mandarins*

Ursula Tidd

A fundamental and complex problematic in Simone de Beauvoir's *The Mandarins* ([1954] 1957) is the political and ethical implications of truth-telling, the intellectual's role in truth-production and his or her responsibility to history and to the Other. These were not entirely new questions for Beauvoir in *The Mandarins*; in *Le sang des autres* (*The Blood of Others*) (1945) and *Tous les hommes sont mortels* (*All Men Are Mortal*) (1946) the interweaving of personal and collective "histoires" propels the protagonists into assuming their responsibilities to act upon and engage with history. But the ethical dilemmas of *Le sang des autres* and *Tous les hommes sont mortels* are centered mainly around the necessity of action, represented as *distinct* from speech both within the personal and political domains, whereas in *The Mandarins* speech and, by implication, literature become politicized as modes of action. For, as Sartre notes in *What Is Literature?*:

> [T]he serious error of pure stylists is to think that the word is a gentle breeze which plays lightly over the surface of things, grazing them without altering them, and that the speaker is a pure witness who sums up with a word his harmless contemplation. To speak is to act; anything which one names is already no longer quite the same; it has lost its innocence. ([1950] 1983, 12)

Indeed, the very possibilities of committed speech and literature as action in the immediate postwar period are interrogated by Beauvoir in *The Mandarins.*

A further difference between Beauvoir's "ethical" fiction of the 1940s, namely *Le sang des autres* and *Tous les hommes sont mortels,* and her 1954 text—which are all nevertheless marked by Beauvoir's recognition of *historicité* (or involvement as a concrete being in an actual world so as to have a "history")[1]—is that the ethico-political dilemmas of *The Mandarins* are explored in a self-consciously intellectual milieu, similar to Beauvoir's own in the mid-to-late 1940s. In short, despite her claims that *The Mandarins* was not a roman à clef (a novel that thinly disguises its roots in real situations and people), there is nevertheless an autobiographical metacommentary in *The Mandarins* in which Beauvoir reflects on the function of the intellectual and, by implication, her own role as a committed intellectual (Beauvoir 1968, 279–80).[2] This apparently reflexive relationship with regard to her intellectual activity is not unusual, for there have been many discussions—by intellectuals—of the intellectual role, as will be briefly outlined below. This effectively means that intellectuals have reflected upon and delimited their own activity at the same time as they have performed as intellectuals. In short, it appears that the intellectual has had a reflexive relationship to himself or herself, at the same time as he or she may have assumed a representative relationship to and for others within the public domain. This reflexivity of the intellectual's role is important and is apparent throughout *The Mandarins.* It is indeed this self-critical intellectual metacommentary on Beauvoir's part and her semifictionalized portrait of the dilemmas of the French left-wing that contributes to the novel's importance as a portrait of the French intelligentsia in crisis in the immediate postwar period.

It will be the purpose of this discussion to analyze the function of the intellectual in *The Mandarins* and the notions of testimonial speech and truth production at work in the text. In this context, it will be argued that the polarization of the intellectual sphere, as the cold war gains momentum, constrains the possibilities of speech as action—possibilities that are already circumscribed by the French experience and aftermath of the Holocaust, as illustrated for example by Anne Dubreuilh's work with concentration camp survivors.

Initially, it will be useful to examine the notion of the intellectual mobilized by the text. It is specifically a French notion of modern intellectual activity, inaugurated in France at the end of the nineteenth century at the time of the Dreyfus affair.[3] Pascal Ory and Jean-François Sirinelli argue in *Les intellectuels en France: De l'Affaire Dreyfus à nos jours* that the noun "intellectuel" was not in common French usage until used by Georges Clemenceau, Maurice Barrès, and Lucien Herr, among others, in the French press of the 1890s, at the time of "l'Affaire Dreyfus" (1986, 6–8). Christophe Charle similarly dates the birth of the public intellectual in France (functioning as a contestatory and autonomous figure) from 1898, when "le manifeste des intellectuals" was published in support of Dreyfus (1990, 7).

When Simone de Beauvoir was born in 1908, it was only approximately ten years since this new function of the intellectual had come into being. In *Mémoires d'une jeune fille rangée* (*Memoirs of a Dutiful Daughter*), her first volume of memoirs, published only four years after *The Mandarins*, Beauvoir relates, at ironic expense to her father, how he used the new term "intellectuel" pejoratively, viewing teachers as members of "the dangerous sect that had stood in defence of Dreyfus: the intellectuals" ([1958] 1963, 178). For Georges de Beauvoir, (left-wing) intellectuals were dangerous, because

> Blinded by their book-learning, taking a stubborn pride in abstract knowledge and in their futile aspirations to universalism, they were sacrificing the concrete realities of race, country, class, family and nationality to those crack-pot notions that would be the death of France and of civilization: the Rights of Man, pacifism, internationalism, and socialism. ([1958] 1963, 178)

Cast in the *Mémoires* as a threat to a perceived integrity of French national identity by Beauvoir's extremist right-wing father, left-wing intellectuals are represented in *The Mandarins* as ethically compromised architects of France's postwar identity seeking to navigate their way through a cold war landscape precisely toward human rights, pacifism, internationalism, and socialism.

But who specifically is Beauvoir's intellectual in *The Mandarins*? First and foremost, a committed, usually male figure, broadly Marxist but not a member of the French Communist Party, as exemplified by Henri Perron and Robert Dubreuilh. The intellectuals in the text have little in common with Julien Benda's right-wing formulation of the intellectual's role in his influential *La trahison des clercs* (1927), in which Benda argued that the intellectual (conceptualized as a male figure) forms part of a politically disinterested elite and that he should concern himself with transcendental values rather than practical, collective issues. Although she did not expound at length on the function of the intellectual in her nonfictional writings, Beauvoir's notion of the intellectual in *The Mandarins* is, as we will see, consonant with left-wing notions of the intellectual articulated by the Italian Marxist Antonio Gramsci, by Jean-Paul Sartre, and, more recently, by Edward Said.

In his *Prison Notebooks*, written between 1929 and 1935, Gramsci focuses on the intellectual's function in society and states that "all men are intellectuals . . . but not all men have in society the function of intellectuals" (1971, 9). He views the intellectual as a product of specific social relations, and as being centrally involved in the class struggle. Gramsci's notion of the intellectual as product of and protagonist in the class struggle is echoed later by Jean-Paul Sartre ([1972] 1974, 228–85) in "A Plea for Intellectuals," which is discussed below. Gramsci differentiates between traditional and organic intellectuals. The traditional intellectual is a member of a historically continuous group, which comprises priests, teachers, scholars, scientists, and administrators, among others. They perceive themselves as autonomous and independent of the dominant social group. The organic intellectual, however, is created whenever a new social group comes into existence and organizes, directs, and reflects upon its function and development within economic, political, and social fields. The organic intellectual can therefore be viewed as legitimating and furthering the group's interests.

In "A Plea for Intellectuals," Jean-Paul Sartre argues that the intellectual is the product of a society divided by the class struggle, and a figure able to bear witness for that divided society.[4] He says:

> The intellectual is thus someone who becomes aware of the opposition, both within himself and within society, between a search for practical truth . . . and a ruling ideology. . . . This new awareness . . . is nothing other than an unmasking of the fundamental contradictions of the society: that is to say, the struggle between classes and within the dominant class itself, the organic conflict between the truth the latter needs for its own purposes and the myths, values and traditions with which it seeks to infect other classes in order to ensure its own hegemony. The intellectual, the product of a class-divided society, testifies to these conflicts because he has interiorized them. He is thus a product of history. In this sense no society can complain of its intellectuals without accusing itself, for it has the intellectuals it makes. ([1972] 1974, 246)

More recently, in *Representations of the Intellectual: The 1993 Reith Lectures*, Edward Said argued that

> The intellectual is an individual endowed with a faculty for representing, embodying, articulating a message, a view, an attitude, a philosophy or opinion to, as well as for, a public, in public. And this role has an edge to it, and cannot be played without a sense of being someone whose place it is to raise embarrassing questions, to confront orthodoxy and dogma (rather than to produce them), to be someone who cannot be easily co-opted by governments or corporations, and whose raison d'être is to represent all those people and issues who are routinely forgotten or swept under the rug. (1994, 9)

Certain points emerge from these accounts of the intellectual's role that are relevant to this discussion of the role of the intellectual in *The Mandarins*. The descriptions given by Gramsci, Sartre, and Said are inspired or influenced by Marx (see Wright 1979, 191–211).[5] Following Marx, they view the intellectual as both the product of, and engaged in, the class struggle. Sartre argues that a divided society produces the intellectual who then bears witness to the social ruptures he or she has internalized. But he warns against false universalism on the part of the bourgeois intellectual. Sartre maintains that the intellectual needs to have an awareness of the society within which he or she works and a self-awareness of how he or she has personally absorbed bourgeois ideology (and is therefore likely to reproduce it) ([1972] 1974, 248–50). Consequently, for Sartre the intellectual has a contestatory role both in relation to the society in which he or she lives and in relation to himself or herself.[6] This notion of intellectual activity as reflexive and socially transformative is derived from the Marxist concept of "revolutionary praxis," according to which social change is mirrored on an individual basis by self-transformation. Thus, to transform society is tantamount to transforming oneself (see McLellan 1980, 226).

In the late 1970s, in a rather different conceptualization of the intellectual role, Michel Foucault distinguished between the "universal" and the "specific" intellectual; he characterized the universal intellectual as a now obsolete figure who once acted as society's consciousness and conscience (Foucault [1977] 1991b, 67–74). Such a figure acted as the individual representative for the proletariat, which is the collective, unconscious bearer of the universal truth of its oppression. Foucault cites writers such as Voltaire (and more recently, by implication, Sartre), as the prototype for this kind of intellectual. The specific intellectual, however, has derived from the savant or expert, and is no longer characterized as a writer, but more probably as a nuclear scientist or computer specialist. This figure has emerged since the Second World War, as a result of the development of technico-scientific structures. More generally, Foucault proposes that the future, fundamentally changed role of the intellectual might be to explore ways of developing a new politics of truth from the particular position that he or she occupies. This figure will no longer be a writer who acts as a bearer of meanings and values in which all can recognize themselves, but someone who acts at a local level in specific everyday struggles. This shift in the function of the intellectual has happened because intellectuals have become much more closely involved in specific struggles and have forged a closer connection to the proletariat and the masses. In Foucault's view, left-wing intellectuals were then (in the late 1970s) confronted with the same adversaries as the proletariat—for example, multinational corporations, the judiciary, and the police ([1977] 1991b, 68).

With these points in mind, we can now focus in more detail on Beauvoir's notion of the intellectual in *The Mandarins*, and observe that she appears to share with Sartre the notion of the intellectual acting as a contestatory figure in relation to society and in relation to himself or herself. She views the intellectual as a figure implicated in the class struggle, as we see in Henri and Dubreuilh's respective notions of action as needing to occur in collaboration with the proletariat. More particularly, Beauvoir conceptualizes the intellectual as a figure who should not serve the interests of the bourgeoisie. Henri fails to fulfill his intellectual mission in this respect, however, when he temporarily eschews probity and perjures himself to save the bourgeois Josette. Moreover, Beauvoir perceives the intellectual as having a privileged, testimonial function, according to which he or she bears witness and speaks for those who are in some way marginalized and unable to represent themselves. To some extent, then, a universalist notion of the intellectual is at work in *The Mandarins*, although (noting Foucault's analysis of the postwar shift in the function of the intellectual), this universalist intellectual function played out in the post-Holocaust era and during the onset of the cold war is represented as being in crisis in the text. For the intellectuals of *The Mandarins* become keenly aware of their diminishing power of influence, stranded as they are between respective Soviet and US expansionist aspirations. In this way, in *The Mandarins*, Beauvoir charts a pivotal moment of transition in the function of the French intellectual.

If we turn to the text in more detail now, the title itself, *The Mandarins*, foregrounds this crisis of intellectual function. Beauvoir did not choose the title until after completing the manuscript (Fallaize 1988, 92). Initially, she had considered *Les suspects* (*The Suspects*) and *Les survivants* (*The Survivors*) as possible titles. The first of these has an accusatory tone that resonates strongly with the climate of *épuration* in the text in which Second World War collaborators are pursued and brought to justice, although it also incriminates intellectuals, casting moral doubt on their probity and implying that they might have acted differently. The second title, *Les survivants*, is hardly less accusatory, as it provokes speculation as to the means and price of surviving the war. It refers much more directly to the Holocaust dimension of the novel—for example, to the survivors treated by Anne in her psychoanalytic practice. *Les survivants* is in fact used in the novel as the title for Henri's play. The final title, *Les mandarins*, shifts the focus away somewhat from issues of guilt, responsibility, and survival, and is, as Beauvoir explained in an interview with *L'Humanité-Dimanche* in 1954, rather ironic but also sympathetic toward the intellectuals represented in the novel (Beauvoir 1979, 360). In its original meaning, the term "mandarin" refers to a Chinese imperial official from the seventh century onward, although more recently it has come to mean—sometimes pejoratively—an influential figure in the possession and deployment of knowledge. In the 1954 interview, Beauvoir points out that many Chinese mandarins were in fact figures of resistance who participated in the democratic revolution and that, in the current situation, intellectuals have to confront the difficulties of their position amid the cold war and act.

Early in *The Mandarins*, the precarious position of French intellectuals in Libération France is highlighted by an outsider, Scriassine, a Russian émigré who has been living in the USA and is very critical of the Soviet Union. Summarizing the plight of the French population as not knowing whether they won the war or lost it, he observes:

> French intellectuals are facing an impasse. It's their turn now. Their art, their philosophies can continue to have meaning only within the framework of a certain kind of civilisation. And if they want to save that civilisation, they'll have no time or energy left over to give to art or philosophy. (Beauvoir 1957, 39; 1954, 34)

In this new postwar context, assuming a responsibility toward history is unavoidable and—according to Scriassine's analysis—literature, philosophy, and art are humanistic indulgences. He asks Anne: "[W]hat weight will the message of French writers have when the earth is ruled either by Russia or the United States? No one will understand them anymore; very few will even speak their language" (1957, 41; 1954, 35). Anne interprets this statement to Dubreuilh as sounding the death knell for French intellectuals, and this assertion is tested in much of the remainder of the novel (1957, 46; 1954, 39).

Early on, in Henri's chapters, an interrogation of various types of intellectual activity is foregrounded, which prefigures Foucault's later analysis of the "universal intellectual" in crisis. Henri is, of course, a writer and editor of *L'Espoir*, a left-wing, nonaligned newspaper. He is positioned as a descendant of Jean Blomart of *Le sang des autres* or Hugo Barine in Sartre's *Les mains sales* (*Dirty Hands*) (1946)—namely, as a young bourgeois who has aligned himself with leftist causes through hatred for his own class and a desire to fight injustice in solidarity with the proletarian masses. Henri's admiration for Dubreuilh will cause him to realize early in chapter 1 that he has "to prove himself. The trouble was that the struggle had shifted form. The Resistance was one thing, politics another" (Beauvoir 1957, 15; 1954, 15). It is not enough to have acted heroically in wartime; the Resistance bequeaths a legacy that must not be betrayed and entails further (and less-well-defined) responsibilities to speak and to act. However, Luc's assertion with regard to the independent editorial policy at *L'Espoir* that "we don't want any political programme; we want to preserve the unity of the Resistance" is rapidly shown to be out of touch with the emerging dynamics of the cold war precisely because it does not recognize the contemporary exigencies of speech and action (1957, 25; 1954, 22).

Drawing on Foucault's genealogical method of understanding history's operation as a complex interrelationship of discontinuous and contingent discourses that produce different "truths" and knowledge at certain moments, it can be argued that Henri and the other characters of *The Mandarins* slowly come to realize that they have to operate within a shifting set of powerful discourses beyond their individual control ([1977] 1991a, 76–100). Foucault's critique of traditional notions of history as falsely celebrating great events such as "war," "Resistance," and "Liberation" that eventually lead to a more liberal society is repeatedly illustrated in *The Mandarins.* For example, as Anne observes early in the novel, "the dead are dead; for them there are no more problems. But after this night of festivity, we, the living, will awaken again. And then how shall we live?" (Beauvoir 1957, 34; 1954, 30). Although the event of the Libération is recognized in *The Mandarins* as crucial, it cannot in itself guarantee what Foucault calls "the practices of freedom" necessary to establish new forms of existence and of society (1988, 114). The atrocities committed during wartime and the Libération pose a moral challenge to those who have survived. Rapidly the characters come to understand that such events have an ambiguous if not negative legacy. Aware of the often arbitrary nature of their survival, most of the main characters are traumatized in one way or another by their experience of war and are still paying its heavy psycho-affective cost: for example, Vincent, who drinks heavily and spends his time tracking down and killing collaborators; Nadine, who deadens her grief over the death of her Jewish lover, Diégo, in the camps by sleeping around indiscriminately; and Sézenac, who takes drugs to deaden his feelings about his activities as a double agent who denounced Jews to the Gestapo. Set against the appalling and continually emerging cost of war, the necessity to speak and to act effectively assumes increasing importance.

In Henri's case, his trip to Portugal in chapter 3 sharply reminds him of his responsibilities as an intellectual and of the ethico-political importance of speaking out. This episode approximately echoes Beauvoir's own trip to Spain and Portugal in early 1945 to lecture at the Institut français in Lisbon and act as official correspondent for *Combat*, the left-wing Resistance newspaper edited by Albert Camus. That Henri should visit Portugal is, of course, not accidental, as both Spain and Portugal, under the fascistic dictatorships of Franco and Salazar, respectively, had not been liberated from their particular oppressive regimes. Henri's visit to Portugal, accompanied by the absolutist Nadine, forces him to confront the suffering of the seven million Portuguese people—of which only seventy thousand have enough to eat. This early example of the respective ethical weights of the plights of the majority versus the minority is later inversely echoed when Henri has to decide if the suffering of fifteen million workers in the Soviet labor camps is outweighed by the Soviet promise of a rosy socialist future for thousands of millions of workers. In this episode, as both Britain and America have economic and political interests in Portugal that prevent them from opposing Salazar's dictatorship, France (here in the shape of Henri) seems their only hope. Henri is told: "Tell the people of France the truth. They do not know; if they knew they would come to our rescue" (Beauvoir 1957, 106; 1954, 88). Nadine, however, is contemptuous of the Portuguese resistance intellectuals, because, in her view, they talk too much and to no effect, a view that offers an early example in the novel of intellectual speech functioning as ineffective action. She consequently tries, unsuccessfully, to persuade Henri to assassinate Salazar. Henri does, however, agree to speak out and to act by publicizing the situation in Portugal and by contacting a former friend in the French Resistance, who is now in government, to mediate a deal between the French government and the Portuguese resistance to Salazar. Henri's actions here are replicated in Beauvoir's autobiographical account of her own return from Portugal in 1945, as represented in *Force of Circumstance*; she similarly delivered a letter from Portuguese resistance intellectuals to the French government (1968, 36).

The aftermath of the visit to Portugal is presented in *The Mandarins* as the first important example of how the exigencies of cold war politics constrain French intellectual activity. As Dubreuilh observes to Scriassine, "The Stalinist menace is purely an American invention . . . when you attack America, they accuse you of playing into the hands of the fifth column" (Beauvoir 1957, 134; 1954, 110). Although Henri clings onto his belief that *L'Espoir* can still act as a subversive, independent force in the French political arena, Dubreuilh condemns his stance: "If your paper pleases everybody, it's because it disturbs nobody. It attacks nothing, defends nothing, evades every problem" (Beauvoir 1957, 137; 1954, 113). However, *L'Espoir*'s subsequent reporting of the situation in Portugal and criticism of US policy in the Mediterranean lead to its paper supplies being withdrawn. Henri's abortive interview with Tournelle to try and broker a deal with the French government on behalf of the Portuguese resistance intellectuals leads him to recognize that France lacks influence and is unable to help itself, let alone other countries.

France's vulnerability in the face of emerging cold war politics is heightened in chapter 5 when Henri reads that one hundred thousand people have been killed in Hiroshima. Dubreuilh observes that America would not have dared to drop an atomic bomb on a German city, populated by white people, and that such an attack is intended to demonstrate the supremacy of American power to the world, especially to the Soviet Union. In this way, "no one will dare to speak up," as Dubreuilh observes, to condemn US policies. From here on, characters will not only be working in the shadow of the Holocaust, as Anne is only too well aware, but also in the "ruins of Hiroshima" with ever-decreasing possibilities of speaking out effectively (Beauvoir 1957, 273; 1954, 222).

Yet the urgent need to speak out is dramatized in chapters 5 and 7 in what is the most pivotal political event of the novel—namely, whether to expose in *L'Espoir* the existence of Soviet labor camps. The staging of this event in *The Mandarins* and the crisis of truth that it brings is interesting, because immediately prior to this episode there are three seemingly minor events in chapter 5 that foreground the question of silence, memory, guilt, and suffering. First, Henri tells Paule that he no longer wants to sleep with her or live in the same apartment. He accuses her of betraying the memory of their earlier relationship when she will not recognize that it is over. This evidently has a wider political echo, in that many of the characters in the novel are slow to recognize that the Resistance is finished and its memory must not be betrayed. As Henri leaves, he is perturbed by the silence of the apartment, signifying Paule's oppressed, hopeless state: "[T]here was only silence. Going down the stairs, Henri thought of the dogs whose vocal cords are severed before they're subjected to the tortures of vivisection. Not a sign in the world of their suffering; it would be far less intolerable to hear them howling" (Beauvoir 1957, 350; 1954, 285). Interestingly, Beauvoir uses exactly the same symbol here as Richard Wright in the second volume of his autobiography, *American Hunger* (1977), when he describes his work assisting a Jewish doctor using vivisection in a medical research institute in Chicago in 1933. Wright recalls the severing of the dogs' vocal cords as being "a symbol of silent suffering" (1983, 48). Although *American Hunger* was not published until 1977 in book form, it was originally conceived as the second part of Wright's autobiography, *Black Boy* (1945), and was published in essay form in journals in the mid-1940s. Beauvoir knew Wright and his work well and would have undoubtedly read the second part of his autobiography, especially since she was planning to work on her own autobiography from at least the mid-1940s. In this image used by both Beauvoir and Wright, there is a recent historical echo of the medical research on concentration camp inmates carried out by Joseph Mengele and others from 1939 to 1945 for the Nazi regime and its attendant silent suffering. The medical abuse of camp inmates constituted part of the criminal charges against high-profile Nazis tried at the Nuremberg Trials from 1945 to 1946, of which Beauvoir would have been aware at the time of writing *The Mandarins*.[7] Importantly, Henri's silencing of Paule here and his later role in silencing the Dachau witnesses, discussed below, suggest that his evolving position is ethically complex. The silencing and anaesthetizing effects of Paule's later psychoanalytic "cure" are also anticipated here. In this context, Henri's ethical speech functioning as testimony to the existence of the Soviet camps will act as a reparative force against the silent suffering of victims at both a political and personal level.

The second significant staging event in chapter 5 is when Vincent tells Henri that Josette and her mother frequented German officers during the war, again highlighting the issue of silence, guilt, and the burden of memory. The third is when, just before the question of the existence of the Soviet camps is raised, Henri hears that Lambert's father has been assassinated, despite having been acquitted of war crimes. These three juxtaposed incidents all foreground the interrelation of silence, guilt, memory, and suffering in the post-Holocaust climate, thereby preparing the ground for the crisis of truth and testimony over the Soviet camps. They all similarly highlight the complexities of "speaking out," of attributing responsibility and obtaining appropriate justice.

Initially, when a former high-ranking Soviet civil servant, George Peltov, claims that there are at least fifteen million people interned in Soviet labor camps, Dubreuilh and Henri are skeptical, questioning Peltov's reasons for divulging this information and requesting further proof. The possible existence and extent of the Soviet labor camps constitute a crisis of truth that, as Henri recognizes, exposes the complexities of the Liberation:

> Telling the truth—up to now it had never posed any serious problems. . . . Obviously, George hadn't invented everything. Maybe, even, it was all true! There were camps in which fifteen million workers were being reduced to a sub-human state, but thanks to those camps Nazism had been defeated and a great country was being built, a country which held out the only hope for a thousand million sub-humans slowly dying of hunger in China and India, the only hope for millions of workers enslaved to inhuman conditions, our only hope. (Beauvoir 1957, 369; 1954, 300)

In this context, Henri realizes that "whatever he did, he'd be wrong: wrong if he printed a garbled truth; wrong if he hid the truth, even though it was garbled. . . . If evil is everywhere, there's no way out, neither for humanity nor for oneself" (1957, 370; 1954, 301).

The fate of fifteen million prisoners in Soviet camps is weighed here against the future of thousands of millions of enslaved workers. Already, however, implicit comparisons are being made between the Nazi use of concentration camps and the Soviet use of gulags, when Lambert comments: "When I was in Germany last year, rumor had it that there had never been as many prisoners in Buchenwald as since the Russian liberation," Buchenwald having been sequentially used both as a Soviet and a Nazi concentration camp (Beauvoir 1957, 363; 1954, 295).

Truth-telling is consequently problematized and represented as ideologically bound when Peltov's motives are questioned by both Henri and Dubreuilh. Both are (made to be) conscious of their responsibility as intellectuals, as Anne reminds Dubreuilh: "As an intellectual, you've taken on certain commitments—to tell the truth, among others" (Beauvoir 1957, 408; 1954, 334). But this reminder is revealed to be out of step with Dubreuilh's perception of the current moral complexities of intellectual speech as action when he responds: "My duties as an intellectual, my respect for the truth—that's all just so much idle chatter! The only question is to know whether, in denouncing the camps, you're working for mankind or against it" (1957, 409; 1954, 335).

By the start of chapter 7, Lambert has accumulated the evidence that convinces Henri that "the camps existed on a large scale and in an institutionalized manner," causing him to reflect that "It has to be brought out in the open, if not, I'll be an accessory to the crime, an accessory and guilty of abusing my readers' confidence" (Beauvoir 1957, 436; 1954, 357). At this stage in *The Mandarins*, Henri is implicated in what Foucault has described as "the parrhesiastic game"—that is to say, he has the moral qualities to know the truth and to convey that truth to others (Foucault 2001, 15; see also 11–24). "Parrhesia," as analyzed by Foucault in lectures given at the Collège de France and the University of California at Berkeley in 1983–84, was a type of "free" or "fearless" speech found in Greek literature from the fifth century B.C. to the fifth century A.D. Foucault was interested in a type of parrhesia that involves speaking the truth, where truth-telling coincides exactly with knowledge and belief. Parrhesia requires certain conditions: that there is a risk to the speaker in speaking the truth, that the truth might damage the interlocutor or the speaker, that the speaker is in a position of inferiority to the interlocutor, and that speaking out is undertaken freely and out of moral duty. In Henri's case, speaking out and exposing the existence and extent of the Soviet labor camps and, toward the end of the novel, condemning as without proper judicial sanction the brutal and illegal repression of anticolonial forces in Madagascar constitute examples of parrhesia, because he speaks out at certain risk to himself and in accordance with what he perceives is his moral duty to the readers of *L'Espoir* and *Vigilance.* Conversely, however, Henri will fail to produce parrhesia when, in a bid to help Josette, he provides false testimony to clear Mercier, a blackmailer and Gestapo informer, of denouncing two Jewish women. In so doing, he contradicts the testimony of two Dachau survivors, who then withdraw their accusation. Ironically, Henri's (false) testimonial speech carries more authority in court than the speech of these survivors. As a Resistance hero, it is assumed that he is telling the truth and that the survivors are mistaken. Henri also acts in direct opposition here to Anne in her work as a facilitator of survivor testimony, for he effectively silences the two Dachau survivors in his double abuse of testimony and parrhesia—both of his own capacity for testimonial, parrhesiastic speech and of the testimonial, parrhesiastic speech of the Other.

Dubreuilh, however, consistently has a more nuanced, strategic view of truth-telling. In the case of the Soviet camps, he advises Henri to let the right-wing press expose their existence to avoid *L'Espoir* and the SRL being perceived as anti-Communist and critical of the Soviet regime. In this way, we might see Dubreuilh as more attuned to a Foucauldian notion of truth-telling as a regime that structures, produces, and recognizes particular types of statements as true and false according to the power relationships in play (Foucault [1977] 1991b, 74). As Foucault observes, the problem for intellectuals is to "ascertain the possibility of constituting a new politics of truth" (74). The constitution of a new post-Liberation politics of truth is labored and complex in *The Mandarins*, as the weight of recent history constrains and restructures the possibilities of truth-telling. This is indicated by Dubreuilh's anguish over his failure to speak out over the camps: "[W]hen I refused to speak out against the labor camps, it was because the truth seemed noxious to me . . . either you speak the truth or you don't. If you can't make up your mind to speak it always, the best thing is to remain silent and not interfere" (Beauvoir 1957, 499; 1954, 409). However, his view changes, as indicated by his reaction to Henri's false testimony when he tells him: "You can't lead a proper life in a society which isn't proper. Whichever way you turn, you're always caught" (Beauvoir 1957, 597; 1954, 489–90).

In counterpoint to Henri's and Dubreuilh's wrestling with the politics of truth-telling, in Anne's chapters there is a similar meditation on speaking the truth or remaining silent both in the political and personal spheres. In her professional practice, as already noted, she hears the testimonies of concentration camp survivors; however, this specific form of truth-telling, as Derrida observes, commits the witness to a repetition of the same and, as such, annuls its own indivisible possibility in the moment of its enactment (Derrida 2000, 33). For the witness testifies to an indivisible moment of experience that cannot be divided without losing its value of veracity and reliability. Yet that indivisible moment is also temporally situated and must promise its own repetition, thereby destroying itself in the process. In this way, the witness is placed in the position of effecting the destruction of his or her own testimony, as it falls away as "dead" speech. Anne acts here as the receiver of these fractured Holocaust testimonies, which are often articulated, significantly, through image rather than through word, as if the words and the speakers do not exist to articulate them. But this testimony functions as dead speech in that there is no real catharsis brought by its articulation. As she sees it (and she understands this much earlier in the novel than either Henri or Dubreuilh), it involves a mutilation and an adaptation to the sick society that itself created the survivors' traumatic experience of the concentration camp. In her work with survivors, Anne is horrified at having "to drive that stranger, who had died two years earlier at Dachau, from his son's heart" (Beauvoir 1957, 69; 1954, 57). Here and in the later description of Paule's gradual descent into madness and subsequent psychoanalytic "cure," speech is not represented as therapeutic, as a means to palliate trauma; speech acts as a reactionary and adaptive force that mutilates individuals both morally and affectively, as it effects their adaptation to a morally sick society. Through this process, speech is abused and appropriated by clinical regulatory mechanisms to normalize and nullify traumatic experience. For this reason, it can be argued that it is all the more important to Anne that the traumas of recent French history are not turned into an American "wax legend," as illustrated in chapter 10 when she visits a waxworks display at a fair in America and is disturbed to see scenes from "Buchenwald and Dachau withdrawing into history" (Beauvoir 1957, 635; 1954, 522). Such scenes contrast sharply with the fractured images produced by survivors in her consulting room, and as staged scenes, they are in effect prey to manipulation. So it is not only a question of remembering history in *The Mandarins* but also a question of *who* remembers and *how* to remember history. Indeed, partly because of Anne's profession as a psychoanalyst and her role in facilitating the narrative staging of memory, the reader is regularly reminded of the problematic issue of how to remember wartime suffering ethically. For example, in chapter 11, during the discussion relating to how Sézenac should be punished for acting as a double agent and denouncing Jews to the Gestapo, Anne tells Nadine:

> What good will it do to make him pay for it? You can't bring the dead back to life. . . . We have forgotten them. Maybe it isn't our fault, but it means that we no longer have any rights on the past. . . . You have forgotten. And if you're so set on having Sézenac punished, it's because you want to prove the opposite to yourself. And that is being dishonest. (Beauvoir 1954, 681–82; 1954, 561)

In *The Mandarins*, Beauvoir frames the crisis in intellectual function in the post-Holocaust and early cold war period specifically around the possibilities of speech, action, and remembering, which are revealed to be necessary but vulnerable and complex forms of ethical engagement that often fail. As Henri reflects, "You don't prevent a war with words. But speaking was not necessarily a way of changing history; it was also a certain way of living it" (Beauvoir 1957, 695; 1954, 571). Similarly, as Dubreuilh explains to Henri, action is a matter of preference: "[I]f you wait until you meet absolute perfection before getting involved, you'll never love anyone and never do anything" (1957, 673; 1954, 554). The confrontation with history is represented as potentially traumatic and ethically complex but nevertheless unavoidable. By the end of the novel, history is revealed as something that must be faced and not to be used as an alibi of guilt to avoid speech and action in the present or future. If the intellectuals of *The Mandarins* are sometimes lacking in ethical substance and fail to produce parrhesia, it is because, in the moral chaos of the post-Libération, France's intellectuals are a product of that time and are seeking to testify somehow to the conflicts that they have internalized. They may be in parrhesiastic crisis, but they still attempt in a modest if not consistent way, as Said terms it, "to raise embarrassing questions, to confront orthodoxy and dogma (rather than to produce them) and . . . to represent all those people and issues who are routinely forgotten or swept under the rug" (Said 1994, 9). For Beauvoir, also implicit in the ethical crises facing the intellectuals of *The Mandarins* is an interrogation of the role of literature. Henri's decision to stay in France so that he can remain politically involved and write implies a recognition that politics and literature are mutually dependent. In this way, Theodor Adorno's return to his famous dictum that "After Auschwitz, it is no longer possible to write poems" finds an echo in Beauvoir's novel (Adorno [1949] 1973, 362). Adorno explained subsequently that he had "no wish to soften the saying that to write lyric poetry after Auschwitz is barbaric but . . . literature must resist this verdict. . . . It is now virtually in art alone that suffering can find its own voice, consolation, without immediately being betrayed by it" (Adorno 1982, 312). *The Mandarins* demonstrates that literature must resist its own deathly silencing but only through its ethico-political commitment.

Notes

1. This definition of "historicity" is taken from the glossary provided by Hazel Barnes in her translation of Sartre (Sartre 1989, 632).

2. See Beauvoir's dismissal of *The Mandarins* as "un roman à clé" in *Force of Circumstance.*

3. The Dreyfus affair involved Captain Alfred Dreyfus, a Jewish officer serving with French Military Intelligence. He was accused (erroneously, as it was later proven) in 1894 of spying for the Germans and was sentenced to life imprisonment. Dreyfus was not exonerated until 1906. The affair became a major political cause in 1897—following revelations of corruption and intrigue at the highest levels of the French army—that divided France and saw the emergence of the figure of the twentieth-century French intellectual.

4. In his definition of the intellectual's role, Sartre refers directly to the Gramscian concept of hegemony, according to which the ruling class (the bourgeoisie) imposes its ideology on the rest of the population who assimilate it as "common sense" (the term is used by Gramsci to mean "the uncritical and largely unconscious way of perceiving and understanding the world that has become "common" in any given epoch" (1971, 322)); this, Sartre explains, is why revolutionary praxis requires self-transformation as well as social transformation.

5. Eric Olin Wright argues that there are at least five interpretations of the class position of intellectuals in Marxist theory: firstly, that all intellectuals who work to earn their living are part of the working class; secondly, that intellectuals can be viewed as belonging to three categories—the working class, the bourgeoisie, and the precapitalist classes; thirdly, that intellectuals represent one sector of the "new" petty bourgeoisie; fourthly, that intellectuals largely belong to the "professional and managerial class," which represents a class distinct from the working class and petty bourgeoisie; and lastly, that intellectuals should be considered as individuals occupying contradictory positions within class relations at economic and ideological levels. Olin Wright asserts that the latter interpretation is "the most comprehensive basis for a rigorous understanding of intellectuals" (1979, 193).

6. It should be noted that Sartre's views on the role of the intellectual were changing both during the 1960s and as a result of the events of May 1968; by the late 1960s, he envisaged that the "nouvel intellectuel" should play a more populist, less individualistic role; see Beauvoir's summary of his views ([1981] 1984, 4).

7. In *Force of Circumstance*, Beauvoir refers to her friend Jacques Bost as having been among the first war correspondents to enter Dachau shortly after its liberation; she also refers to her viewing and reading of US films and reports immediately after the war on the Nazi concentration camp atrocities (see 1968, 40).

Works Cited

Adorno, Theodor. [1949] 1973. *Negative dialectics*. Translated by E. B. Ashton. New York: Continuum.

———. 1982. Commitment. In *The essential Frankfurt School reader*, edited by Andrew Arato and Eike Gebhardt. New York: Continuum.

Beauvoir, Simone de. 1954. *The mandarins*. Paris: Gallimard.

———. 1957. *The mandarins*. London: Collins.

———. [1958] 1963. *Memoirs of a dutiful daughter*. Harmondsworth, England: Penguin.

———. 1968. *Force of circumstance*. Harmondsworth, England: Penguin.

———. 1979. Interview de Simone de Beauvoir par J.-F. Rolland. In *Les écrits de Simone de Beauvoir*, edited by Claude Francis and Fernande Gontier, 358–62. Paris: Gallimard.

———. [1981] 1984. *Adieux, a farewell to Sartre*. Translated by P. O'Brian. Harmondsworth, England: Penguin.

Benda, Julien. 1927. *La trahison des clercs*. Paris: Grasset.

Charle, Christophe. 1990. *Naissance des "intellectuals."* Paris: Minuit.

Derrida, Jacques and Maurice Blanchot. 2000. *Instant of My Death/Demeure: fiction and testimony*. Translated by Elizabeth Rottenberg. Stanford: Stanford University Press.

Fallaize, Elizabeth. 1988. *The novels of Simone de Beauvoir*. London: Routledge.

Foucault, Michel. [1977] 1991a. Nietzsche, genealogy, history. In *The Foucault reader*, edited by Paul Rabinow, 76–100. Harmondsworth, England: Penguin.

———. [1977] 1991b. Truth and power. In *The Foucault reader*, edited by Paul Rabinow. Harmondsworth, England: Penguin.

———. 1988. The ethic of care for the self as a practice of freedom. In *The final Foucault*, edited by J. Bernauer and D. Rasmussen, 113–31. Cambridge, Mass.: MIT Press.

———. 2001. *Fearless speech*. Los Angeles: Semiotext(e).

Gramsci, Antonio. 1971. *Selections from the prison notebooks of Antonio Gramsci*. Edited and translated by Quintin Hoare and Geoffrey Nowell Smith. London: Lawrence and Wishart.

McLellan, David. 1980. *The thought of Karl Marx*. 2nd ed. London and Basingstoke: Macmillan.

Ory, Pascal, and Jean-François Sirinelli. 1986. *Les intellectuels en France: De l'affaire Dreyfus à nos jours*. Paris: Armand Colin.

Said, Edward. 1994. *Representations of the intellectual, The 1993 Reith lectures*. London: Vintage.

Sartre, Jean-Paul. [1948] 1950. *What is literature?* London: Methuen; Qu'est-ce que la littérature? In *Situations II* (Paris: Gallimard, 1948). New York: Harper Collins.

———. [1972] 1974. A plea for intellectuals. In *Between existentialism and marxism*. London: NLB.

———. [1950] 1983. *What is literature?* New York: Harper Collins.

———. 1989. *Being and nothingness*. Translated by Hazel Barnes. London: Routledge.

Wright, Eric Olin. 1979. Intellectuals and the class structure of capitalist society. In *Between labour and capital*, edited by Pat Walker. Hassocks, England: Harvester Press.

Wright, Richard. 1983. *American hunger*. New York: Harper and Row.

CHAPTER 5

The Return of Commitment

Simone de Beauvoir's The Mandarins *Revisited*

Karen Vintges

A resumption of hope when hope which is too easy has gone, a difficult optimism which is simultaneously a contested optimism; that is what I wanted.

—Simone de Beauvoir, *Une interview par Madeleine Chapsal*

This article focuses on the theme of political commitment in Simone de Beauvoir's *The Mandarins.* It will be argued that Beauvoir's approach is a topical one, since it offers a way out of the current dilemma about how to take a stance in politics and ethics without falling back on political doctrines or truths. I will first discuss Beauvoir's concept of the ethical-political *way of life.* I will then argue that *The Mandarins* approaches the theme of political commitment from this perspective. I conclude that in this way Beauvoir proclaimed and anticipated a return to a new form of commitment that is fitting and timely for today. This new type of commitment can be characterized as a political commitment without Truth.

The Ethical-Political Way of Life

"But was she happy?" Time and again I have to come back to this question whenever discussing in some context or another the ideas of Simone de

Beauvoir. This time the question was asked of me in a radio program to which I was invited in order to comment on the news through the eyes of Simone de Beauvoir. I said that she would have considered the so-called preemptive war on Iraq as motivated by neocolonialism. Beauvoir was among the first French intellectuals to oppose the French wars in Vietnam and Algeria. We can be fairly certain that she would have had great difficulties with the image of Western culture—that is, the combination of capitalism and liberalism—as the superior model of society to be exported on a global level. She would have been far more suspicious of the fuss many French and other Western Europeans make about Muslim women wearing head scarves in public places, than her self-proclaimed heirs, such as Elisabeth Badinter, contend she would have been. She would have sided with the European intellectuals Habermas, Derrida, Eco, Vattimo, and others in their recent defense of a European identity and their plea for a common European foreign policy in reaction to the US's current unilateralism.[1] "But," the interviewer interrupted, "was she happy?"

Toril Moi has pointedly remarked that people tend to have interest only in the personal side of intellectual women and not in their work: "[W]hatever a woman says, or writes, or thinks, is less important and less interesting than what she *is*" (Moi 1990, 27, emphasis in the original). After many years of periodic Beauvoir activities I can confirm and capture this in the following way: a woman can have written masterpieces, be a great politician, have made an interesting career, but the only thing that seems to matter is: WAS SHE HAPPY?

In the introduction to *The Second Sex* Beauvoir herself commented on the theme of women and happiness.

> Are not women of the harem more happy than women voters? Is not the housekeeper happier than the working-woman? It is not too clear what the word *happy* really means and still less what true values it may mask. There is no possibility of measuring the happiness of others, and it is always easy to describe as happy the situation in which one wishes to place them. In particular those who are condemned to stagnation are often pronounced happy on the pretext that happiness consists in being at rest. This notion we reject.

She concludes, "I am interested in the fortunes of the individual as defined not in terms of happiness but in terms of liberty," and she notes: "for our perspective is that of existentialist ethics" ([1949] 1974, 28, 29).

I have argued elsewhere that Beauvoir's own ethical theory as worked out especially in her essay *The Ethics of Ambiguity* forms the principal theoretical framework of the rest of her oeuvre, including *The Second Sex* and her literary works.[2] Here I want to show in detail how this is the case for the novel *The*

Mandarins. Both the plot of this novel and its characters draw heavily on *The Ethics of Ambiguity*.

Ethics in this essay comes forward as an attitude—namely, one of "willing oneself free"—an attitude that has to be practiced constantly and that extends to one's whole mode of being. Beauvoir points out that existential philosophy holds that every human being is free and has to invent his or her own ethical behavior. There are no universally applicable maxims or moral rules: we ourselves are responsible and have to judge each particular case ourselves—in the terms of Hannah Arendt, "without a banister." The only code or rule we have is that by willing ourselves free we commit ourselves to freedom as such and therefore to the freedom of everyone. Beauvoir holds that people have to be socially free to be able to realize their freedom, and our commitment to freedom thus implies that we actively have to strive for the social freedom of everyone. "To will oneself free is also to will others free. This will is not an abstract formula. It points out to each person concrete action to be achieved" (Beauvoir 1948, 73). Since Beauvoir believes that we have to intervene in power relations that violate people's social freedom, politics comes into the picture right away.

The ethical-political attitude of willing ourselves and others free, and of taking responsibility, is not an easy one and demands constant exercise, because we are tempted to avoid the anguish of this permanent choice "in laziness, heedlessness, capriciousness, cowardice [and] impatience" (Beauvoir 1948, 25). Beauvoir specifies several attitudes in which one tries to flee or refuse freedom. She describes the attitude of "seriousness" in which one holds to absolute values—thus denying the fact that we ourselves are responsible—and the opposite attitude, nihilism, a denial of every value whatsoever. She then goes into the attitude of "the adventurer" who asserts himself as pure freedom and "shares the nihilist's contempt for men" (61). Next she discusses the maniacal-passionate attitude of the person "who sets up the object as an absolute, not like the serious man as a thing detached from himself, but as a thing disclosed by his subjectivity." One claims the object of his passion and closes off the communion of freedom (64). Then there is the attitude of the intellectual who "sets up a superior, universal and timeless value, objective truth," thus denying his particular situation in the world (68). Finally, she talks about the aesthetic attitude, as exemplified by the tourist who looks at the world in detached contemplation (75).

The last forty pages of the essay are the least interesting sections and the reason why Beauvoir later distanced herself from the work, describing it as her "moralist period." In two subsections entitled "The Present and the Future" and "Ambiguity" she tries to develop a *method* for making moral judgments and acting ethically. By formulating methodological rules like "the means have to correspond to the ends" she comes close to proposing a type of Kantian maxim that she herself had criticized in the first 115 pages of her text, as she acknowledged herself later on (1962, 547). However, in the body of her text she does succeed in amending Sartre's original ontology and in transforming it into an ethics.

She accepts Sartre's ontological definition of man as being no thing but a consciousness, empty and therefore free. But she claims that in addition to this we have to assert and realize our freedom by acting in the world as *incarnated* consciousnesses. For the existentialist Sartre freedom basically meant experiencing the emptiness of consciousness. Beauvoir, on the contrary, emphasized our bodily existence in the world.[3] She argued that since we are both empty consciousness and incarnated beings, the human condition is ambiguous. The ethical attitude implies that we—through a "moral conversion"—accept our bodily and emotional dimension and transform our pure freedom into a concrete commitment to the freedom of our fellow men.[4] We have to rise up, so to speak, from the empty consciousness to the level of the senses, emotion, and connectedness to others. Beauvoir's plea for the moral attitude of "willing oneself free" thus implies a plea for a sensitive self that engages itself in the world with body and mind, heart and soul. Ethics for Beauvoir comes down to an ethical-political *way of life.*

In this respect her approach belongs to the tradition of "philosophy as a way of life." The classicist Pierre Hadot has written much about this tradition in a book that bears this same title. According to Hadot, the ancient Greeks thought of philosophy as "spiritual exercises" or *askesis.* Exercises, such as writing, meditation, dialogue with oneself, examination of conscience, exercises of the imagination and of the styling of daily behavior, were not only about transforming one's mind but also one's entire *mode of being.* This is one of the main reasons why Hadot speaks in terms of "spiritual" exercise: "None of the other adjectives we could use—'psychic,' 'moral,' 'ethical,' 'intellectual,' 'of thought,' 'of the soul'—covers all the aspects of the reality we want to describe. . . . [T]he word 'thought' does not indicate clearly enough that imagination and sensibility play a very important role in these exercises" (Hadot 1995, 81–82). In other words, here we are dealing with exercises that "engage the totality of the spirit" (127).

According to Hadot, who himself was influenced by French existentialism, the existential aspects of ancient philosophy have never completely disappeared. They can be found in the works of Descartes, Spinoza, Nietzsche, Schopenhauer, Marx, and even Husserl, and last but not least in "the movement of thought inaugurated by Heidegger and carried on by existentialism (that) seeks—in theory and in principle—to engage man's freedom and action in the philosophical process." But he then concludes that existentialist philosophy "in the last analysis" is "primarily a philosophical discourse" (Hadot 1995, 272). This may be the case for Sartre; but Beauvoir's approach can be characterized throughout as "philosophy as a way of life" that engages the "totality of the spirit."

She once described Sartre's philosophy precisely from this perspective in an article that was originally headed "Sartre" but was published under the misleading title "Jean-Paul Sartre: Strictly Personal" (1946).[5] Here she took Sartre's life and work together, and dealt with his existentialist thought as a "mode of being" [mode d'existence]. Sartre believed that man as free consciousness has to constantly tear himself loose from the "sticky" mass of the given. In her article Beauvoir shows how Sartre lived his philosophy of freedom, opposing objects, neglecting his body, and trying to escape his own past.

Beauvoir herself interestingly concentrated on ethics as a mode of being.[6] It was not so much philosophy as a way of life but ethics as a way of life that interested her, more precisely the ethical-political way of life that strives for freedom for itself and for all people. In line with this Beauvoir wrote diaries and letters, as well as five volumes of autobiography, as spiritual exercises in order to create herself as an ethical-political self that works to enhance the freedom of her fellow human beings (see Vintges 1996 and 1999).

The Mandarins Revisited

If we take a closer look now at *The Mandarins*, we find that this novel is likewise centered around the theme of the ethical-political way of life that aims for freedom for all and that demands constant "ethical-spiritual" exercise. In *The Mandarins* Beauvoir describes the lives of a group of intellectuals and friends in Paris in the years after the Second World War. The main plot revolves around the dilemmas the writers Henri Perron and Robert Dubreuilh are facing in regard to their political activities. Henri is the editor-in-chief of the paper *L'Espoir*. He is persuaded by his friend Robert Dubreuilh—a former professor and a Marxist—to affiliate the paper with a political party, the SRL, which was founded by Dubreuilh. The SRL's aim was to offer a so-called third alternative to capitalism and communism, that is, an alternative to the United States and the Soviet Union. But then Henri and Dubreuilh receive irrefutable evidence of the existence of mass concentration camps in the Soviet Union. Should they publish? Dubreuilh is against doing so. In the prevalent political climate, he says, it would mean a definitive shift of *L'Espoir* and the SRL to the right. Henri, however, decides in favor of publication, which means he loses Dubreuilh as a friend.[7]

The paper is embraced by the Right. The other editors want to shift allegiance to the Right. Henri is against this move and is forced to resign. He plans to devote himself to writing in the Italian countryside, but finally reinforces his chosen identity and life's work as a politically committed writer. Dubreuilh's doubts also increase as the story progresses. The SRL falls apart, but Dubreuilh and Henri start a new political weekly.

Certainties have vanished, the hope that the Soviet Union may present a good way of life to humanity has been dashed, and the notion of becoming a writer in the service of world peace has proved unfeasible. But this does not mean political action has disappeared from their agenda. The loss of the socialist ideal, and the disappearance of political certainties, does not mean political action has become superfluous. Henri concludes that it is not enough to say that history is sad in every way. "But then again, if you attach importance to misery, to death, to individual men, it isn't enough to say to yourself, 'Anyhow it's a sad business,' to feel authorized to wash your hands of it. It is essential that it be more or less sad" (Beauvoir 1956, 734).

In a comment on *The Mandarins* Beauvoir said,

> One of the principal themes that emerges from my story is that of *repetition* in the sense in which Kierkegaard uses that word: truly to possess something, one must have lost it and found it again. . . . Instead of being content with facile optimism, they [the main characters] take upon themselves all the difficulties, the failures, the scandal implied in any undertaking. (1968, 282)

Elsewhere she stated that this book was "a resumption of hope when hope which is too easy has gone, a difficult optimism which is simultaneously a contested optimism; that is what I wanted" (1960, 395). Henri and Dubreuilh have lost the certainties that guided their political decision-making. But in the end they again take political initiatives, with modest expectations, not pretending to save humanity. Henri concludes, "You don't prevent a war with words. But speaking was not necessarily a way of changing history; it was also a certain way of living it" (1956, 752). And Dubreuilh says:

> We weren't modest enough . . . you've got to work in the actual present. . . . It's modest because we aren't organising in terms of a lot of preconceived ideas we'd like to impose upon the world. . . . The SRL had a constructive programme and it was necessarily utopian. What I am doing now is much more like what I was doing in '36. We're trying to defend ourselves against a given danger by employing whatever means are at hand. That's far more realistic. (728)

Later he adds:

> Reality isn't frozen. . . . It has possibilities, a future. But to act on it—and even to think about it—you've got to get inside it and stop playing around with little dreams. . . . We don't always realize it,

> but it takes a hell of a lot of arrogance to place your dreams above everything else. When you're modest, you begin to understand that on the one hand, there's reality, and on the other, nothing. (730)

Henri and Dubreuilh have become aware that political commitment cannot consist of applying blueprints but involves engaging politics on a case-by-case basis and with more modest goals; and they are aware that it requires that we approach issues not from some point outside reality but from the inside.

Earlier in the novel one of the young people in Henri's circle asks him for advice: "They beat us over the head with politics, but why side with one party rather than another? First of all we need an ethics, an art of living."[8] Henri answers: "An ethics necessarily includes a political attitude. . . . And on the other hand, politics is itself a living thing" (Beauvoir 1956, 180). *The Mandarins* puts forward the idea that politics is not a matter of "imposing preconceived ideas upon the world." Instead, political commitment in the novel comes forward as the ethical-political way of life that demands "ethical-spiritual" exercise such as inner dialogue and discussing one's behavior with a friend. This theme also comes up in the life of the other main character, the psychiatrist Anne, who has a daughter with Dubreuilh named Nadine. Anne faces a dilemma as well. Having lost her lover in America, she feels desperate and does not want to live any longer. But she nevertheless opts for life and returns to her work as a psychiatrist, trying to make other people's lives more bearable and to alleviate their suffering. She, in the end, assumes the ethical-political way of life, willing herself and others free.

The Mandarins thus follows up on the main theme of *The Ethics of Ambiguity*. There are also a number of attitudes that Beauvoir distinguished in this essay that are present in the novel as lived positions. In the character of the communist Lachaume, we see the serious man who believes in absolute values. Anne and Dubreuilh's daughter, Nadine, tries to be the nihilist. Then there is Vincent the adventurer, who, like Nadine, shows contempt for the lives of others. Henri's mistress, Paule, is the maniacal-passionate person who is not prepared to let go of Henri because she is the only one who really recognizes his superior quality. The psychiatrist Anne and the writer Henri, the two narrators who tell the story in alternating sections, are the ones who explicitly struggle to assume the ethical-political way of life: Anne struggles with the passionate attitude, Henri with the aesthetic one, a fact that is immediately obvious from the first pages in which he makes plans to travel abroad as a tourist. Dubreuilh is the intellectual who claims to have access to objective truth, thus forgetting that "what he defines as objective truth is the object of his own choice. . . . He does not merely describe. He takes sides" (1948, 68–69).

All in all, we can conclude that *The Mandarins* is a literary-philosophical work pleading the ethical-political way of life and a political commitment without Truth.

A Return of Commitment

It is common nowadays to hear that political commitment is dead. But it is only a specific kind of commitment that is dead—namely, the old dogmatic type that wanted to impose doctrines and truths. Today all kinds of "isms" indeed are fading away, but in the meantime a new type of commitment seems to have crystallized, and it is time that it is recognized in these terms.

What does this new type of commitment look like? Today many people are trying in their own lives to really contribute something to the quality of life of others. Many, for instance, support various groups of people in the third world by sending them money and basic goods or actively participate in development projects to improve people's immediate life-conditions. Others are active in aiding refugees—for instance, in the Netherlands people hide in their homes asylum seekers who are under threat of being expelled from the country. Many people are active in projects that strengthen the social cohesion in neighborhoods or try to provide deprived people with jobs or education; others are organizing all kinds of intercultural contacts and exchanges.[9] And social and political movements (for example feminism) are reentering the public sphere in the form of a shared ethics instead of a dogma; people organize on the basis of a shared ethical-political inspiration and are thus *creating* politics on the individual and collective level instead of simply applying political blueprints. This new type of political commitment has done away with the belief that society can be molded into preconceived models; it does not try to apply any objective truth or doctrine. Rather it comes down to the attitude that was characterized earlier as the ethical-political way of life. Commitment in its new form is not based on isms and total truths but on ethical-political (self)creation on the individual and collective level.

And it wants everyone to have the possibility to engage in ethical-political self-creation. It wants access for all to this way of life throughout cultures, and it takes the form of a cross-cultural coalition and cooperation. Furthermore, instead of looking to social blueprints, the new type of commitment "works on the limits." It wants the free ethical-political life for everyone, but it works bottom up, and from within the existing institutions and practices in a process of "trial and error" and "piecemeal engineering."[10] The new commitment without Truth does not conceive of itself as unilateral charity but is based on respect for other possible ways of leading the free ethical-political life.[11] This new type of commitment does not want to export Western institutions or practices, because it is aware that Western liberal democracies impose the model of consumer and client and obstruct the ethical-political way of life.

Beauvoir was always critical of the Enlightenment "dream dreamed by reason" (1948, 121). French existentialism stands "in the most ferocious opposition to the Enlightenment faith in a self-grounding, self-evident Reason, in progress through the extension of rationality and in the natural and unquestionable universality of rational rules and norms" (Levin 1990, 81). Beauvoir would have opposed Western liberalism's triumphalism, which claims to bring progress through reason on a global level, and which we are experiencing today. She would have sided with all those that try in intercultural coalitions to fight any type of fundamentalism, including the Western one. But she detested any political dogmatism that has an answer to all problems and demands blind faith in the creed.

> I regret that the non-Communist left should have grown as monolithic as the Party itself. A left-winger must necessarily admire China without the least reservation, take Nigeria's side against Biafra and the Palestinians' against Israel. I will not bow to these conditions. (1988, 437)

In *The Mandarins* she expressed that politics should be an open creative process and should not be derived from doctrines. Political commitment in this novel is not the prerogative of intellectuals, as is shown by the case of Anne. But if we focus on the role of the intellectuals, we can conclude that Beauvoir offered a way out of the current dilemma of how to take a stance in ethics and politics without falling back on political dogmas or truths that we nowadays know to be historical constructions themselves. Today's postmodern thinkers have emphasized the historical contingency of all truth-tales and absolutes, unmasking the transparency and neutrality of language. Language is no longer seen as a descriptive medium, but as a field in which terms only refer to each other. Thus, Truth has been knocked off its pedestal. We can no longer claim that a series of terms describe or reflect reality.[12] Apart from postmodern thinking, the developments in the theory of science since Thomas Kuhn's major work on the importance of "paradigms" in legitimizing empirical "facts" have contributed to the historicization of truths. But when there is no longer any strict relation between theory and reality, what criteria or which values could guide intellectuals in politics? During the last two decades many intellectuals have responded to this quandary with a loss of faith in their position and with self-doubt.

The philosopher Michel Foucault introduced the concept of the "specific intellectual" in order to replace the old concept of political commitment of the intellectual.[13] Foucault presented his concept in opposition to the so-called universal intellectual who "purported to make himself heard, as the spokesman of the universal," in other words as "the master of truth and justice." The specific intellectual, on the contrary, is an expert in a local field. Foucault explains that he is talking of the intellectual not in the sociological sense but in the political one, that is, of "the person who utilizes his knowledge, his competence, and his relation to truth in the field of political struggles" (Foucault 1984, 70).

"It is, rather, he who, along with a handful of others, has at his disposal, whether in the service of the state or against it, powers which can either benefit or irrevocably destroy life" (Foucault 1984, 71). The specific intellectual should not again climb the stage as a "bearer of universal values," but should try to rework the truth-power relations within his own field" (73). Foucault never reconsidered his aversion to the universal intellectual in his later work (see note 6). In my view, Beauvoir's thinking is preferable on this matter because she envisioned a role for the universal intellectuals outside the notion of the masters of truth and justice or "mandarins."

In *The Mandarins* she put the role of intellectuals into perspective, as is also clear from the title of her book.[14] She was well aware of the negative connotation of the word "mandarin" as a pompous and pretentious person. For example, she protested when the press reported Sartre had been received in China as a mandarin (see Beauvoir 1957, 350). She explained her choice of title as follows: "[T]here is a little irony in the word, but also a lot of sympathy. It is true intellectuals have their own problems and preoccupations. But they should not deny their destiny; that destiny is difficult, they have to assume it" (Beauvoir 1954b, 360). For Beauvoir, the intellectual is certainly no philosopher-king. On her own life as writer, she commented that "It's as good a life as any other" (Beauvoir 1968, 664), displaying again her deeply held belief that being an intellectual is a way of life.

In *The Mandarins* she tried to show how the universal intellectual can be politically committed on behalf of his ethical-political way of life. *The Mandarins* shows that universal values can be put forward within such a framework, whereas Foucault never explicitly reconsidered his concept of the specific intellectual who was supposed to limit himself only to specific topics and issues. Foucault's concept of the specific intellectual is insufficient, because we need intellectuals who speak publicly about their times and oppose various forms of dominance, oppression, and neocolonialism, the way Foucault himself did, and just as some European and American writers and philosophers recently did regarding the war on terrorism and the war in Iraq. In their common letter, entitled "After the War: The Rebirth of Europe" (see note 1), Habermas and Derrida propose a role in the world for "a pacific, cooperative Europe that is open to other cultures and dialogue."[15] However, they add,

> Today we know that many of the political traditions that command obedience by virtue of their natural character were in fact "invented." In light of this, a European identity, sprouted under the sunshine of a public forum, will always remain somewhat contrived. Ultimately, only what has been based on the arbitrary is free of artificial ambition. The political-ethical ambition, that is hermeneuti-

> cally expressed through processes in which the relation one has with himself is collectively made explicit, is not arbitrary. The difference between the heritage that we have assumed and that which we hope to reject demands as much circumspection as the decision on the way in which we interpret this heritage in order to appropriate it. (2003)

Habermas and Derrida claim that their proposal is based on an ethical-political appropriation of history, through a will that reflects on itself. We thus find that they are emphasizing the contingency of their own normative stances, but nevertheless putting them forward. Beauvoir's novel *The Mandarins* in a brilliant way announces the return of the universal intellectual's commitment in this new form.

When Nadine asks Henri whether he would be happy living in Italy, he reconsiders his plans to leave for the Italian countryside, "Happy. The fact was that the word no longer had any meaning. You can never possess the world and protecting yourself against it is out of the question, too. You're in it, that's all" (Beauvoir 1956, 755). In her essay *The Ethics of Ambiguity* Beauvoir stated that man must not aim at an impossible state of equilibrium and rest. "Whatever the problems raised for him, the setbacks that he will have to assume, and the difficulties with which he will have to struggle, he must reject oppression at any cost" (1948, 96). Happiness according to Beauvoir is not to be found in withdrawal or apathy but in getting involved. At the end of *The Mandarins*, Anne concludes: "Either one founders in apathy, or the earth becomes repeopled. I didn't founder. Since my heart continues to beat, it will have to beat for something, for someone. Since I'm not deaf, I'll once more hear people calling to me. Who knows? Perhaps one day I will be happy again. Who knows?" (1956, 763).

Notes

1. On May 31, 2003, these European intellectuals published a wave of articles in Europe's top daily newspapers in reaction to the support of eight European countries for the US's "preemptive" war in Iraq. I will discuss the common letter of Habermas and Derrida in the last section (see Habermas and Derrida 2003).

2. See Vintges (1996).

3. As has been pointed out by several Beauvoir scholars by now. See, among others, Bauer (2001), Bergoffen (1997), Lundgren-Gothlin (1996), and Simons (1998).

4. This attitude has to be practiced constantly, since in Beauvoir's philosophical framework one finds both phenomenological sensitivity to our always being situated and incarnated beings as well as the insistence that pure, empty, consciousness (Sartre's

"nothingness") is also an element of our human condition—indeed, the element that separates us from ourselves and from other people. For Beauvoir, incarnation and pure consciousness are the two sides of our ambiguous condition, and their reconciliation comes by way of a moral conversion through which we accept this incarnated dimension and commit ourselves to things and people. For this reason she calls her ethics an "ethics of ambiguity." Yet the pure, empty consciousness always remains, which is why the moral conversion has to be practised constantly, and why there will never be complete harmony between people, as Beauvoir emphasizes in all of her work, including *The Second Sex*. See Vintges 1996.

5. Only recently Sylvie le Bon de Beauvoir found the original French version of this essay, which is fifty-five lines longer. The title and organization of the article turn out to be composed by the editors. The fifty-five cut lines are about Sartre's philosophy and his philosophical way of life ("mode d'existence"). The last of these lines, concluding the article, read: "If Sartre's attitude may seem paradoxical, it is because the human condition is ambiguous, and Jean-Paul Sartre is a man who has fully assumed his condition as man." Beauvoir here refers to her own ethics of ambiguity. An English translation of the original French version appears in Simons 2004. See also my introduction to this text in the same volume.

6. Here we see a striking parallel between Beauvoir's approach to ethics and that of the later Michel Foucault who—informed by Hadot's approach to ancient philosophy—also focused on the ethical-political way of life, introducing the concepts of "ethos" and "aesthetics of existence." See especially Foucault 1997a and 1997b; see also Vintges 2004a.

7. The way Henri arrives at his decision is dealt with more extensively in Vintges 1996.

8. Beauvoir uses this phrase to indicate the creative moment of ethics. I do however prefer to speak in terms of the ethical-political way of life to avoid any possible mistake about Beauvoir's political intentions. In my quotation I do not follow the English translation because it imprecisely translates "une morale" and "art de vivre" as "a set of principles" and "an approach to life," respectively. [Beauvoir 1956, 180] [Beauvoir 1954, 134, 136].

9. The antiglobalization movement is an exemplary case, but the old dogmatic type of commitment runs through it as well.

10. I make use here of two terms of the philosopher Karl Popper.

11. Ways that turn out to be present in principle in all cultures as soon as religious contexts are taken into account. I deal with this extensively in Vintges (2004a).

12. For a summary of the main discussion on this topic in today's political and social philosophy, see Kelly 1994.

13. He did so in 1972, in a conversation with Gilles Deleuze, and in the 1977 interview "Truth and Power" (Foucault 1984). I refer here only to the interview.

14. Beauvoir soon saw the French intelligentsia's pretension of making world history as rather naïve. Her travels to the United States in 1947 and the years of contact with American intellectuals that followed would play a decisive role in this realization.

15. See http://watch.windsofchange.net/themes_63.htm (obtained August 24, 2004). One may find it a little unexpected that Habermas and Derrida are writing a common letter. Although Habermas composed the letter, in an introduction Derrida

declares himself to be totally in accordance. Kelly (1994) convincingly argues that Habermas is close to postmodern thinking in the sense that he is aware of the contingent historical character of Western reason. Habermas himself goes at length into the concept of modernity as awareness of contingency (Habermas 1987).

Works Cited

Bauer, Nancy. 2001. *Simone de Beauvoir: Philosophy and feminism*. New York: Columbia University Press.

Beauvoir, Simone de. 1946. Jean-Paul Sartre: Strictly Personal. Translated by Malcolm Cowley. *Harper's Bazaar*, January, 113, 158, 160.

———. 1948. *The ethics of ambiguity*. New York: Philosophical Library.

———. [1949] 1974. *The second sex*. Harmondsworth, England: Penguin.

———. 1954a. *Les mandarins* Paris: Gallimard.

———. 1954b. Interview de Simone de Beauvoir par J.-F. Rolland. In *Les écrits de Simone de Beauvoir*, edited by C. Francis and F. Gontier, 358–62. Paris: Gallimard, 1979.

———. 1956. *The mandarins*. Translated by Leonard M. Friedman. Washington, D.C.: Regnery Gateway.

———. 1957. *La longue marche*. Paris: Gallimard.

———. 1960. Une interview par Madeleine Chapsal. In *Les écrits de Simone de Beauvoir*, edited by C. Francis and F. Gontier, 381–96. Paris: Gallimard, 1979.

———. 1962. *The prime of life*. Translated by Peter Green. Cleveland: World.

———. 1968. *Force of circumstance*. Translated by Richard Howard. Harmondsworth, England: Penguin.

———. 1988. *All said and done*. Translated by Patrick O'Brian. London: Fontana.

Bergoffen, Debra. 1997. *The philosophy of Simone de Beauvoir*. New York: State University of New York Press.

Foucault, Michel. 1984. Truth and power. In *The Foucault reader*, edited by P. Rabinow. New York: Pantheon.

———. 1997a. The ethics of the concern for self as a practice of freedom. In *Ethics: Subjectivity and truth. Vol. 1 of Essential works of Foucault 1954*–1984, edited by P. Rabinow, 281–301. New York: New Press.

———. 1997b. On the genealogy of ethics. In *Ethics: Subjectivity and truth. Vol. 1 of Essential works of Foucault, 1954–1984*, edited by P. Rabinow, 253–80. New York: New Press.

Habermas, Jürgen. 1987. *The philosophical discourse on modernity*. Cambridge: Polity, in association with Basil Blackwell.

Habermas, Jürgen, and Jacques Derrida. 2003. Nach dem Krieg: Die Wiedergeburt Europas. *Frankfurter Allgemeine Zeitung*, May 31, 2003. English translation: http://watch.windsofchange.net/themes_63.htm.

Hadot, Pierre. 1995. *Philosophy as a way of life: Spiritual exercises from Socrates to Foucault*, edited and with an introduction by A. Davidson. Oxford: Blackwell.

Kelly, Michael. 1994. *Critique and power*. Cambridge, Mass.: MIT Press.

Levin, D. M. 1990. Existentialism at the end of modernity: Questioning the I's eyes. *Philosophy Today*, Spring 1990, 80–85.

Lundgren-Gothlin, Eva. 1996. *Sex and existence*. London: Athlone.

Moi, Toril. 1990. *Feminist theory and Simone de Beauvoir*. Cambridge, Mass.: Blackwell.

Simons, Margaret. 1998. *Beauvoir and the second sex*. Lanham, Md.: Rowman and Littlefield.

———. 2004. *The Beauvoir series vol. 1: Philosophical Writings*. Champaign: University of Illinois Press.

Vintges, Karen. 1996. *Philosophy as passion: The thinking of Simone de Beauvoir*. Bloomington: Indiana University Press. (Dutch original: 1992.)

———. 1999. Beauvoir's autobiography: "Autofiction" or "selftechnique"? In *Simone de Beauvoir: 50 Jahre nach dem "Anderen Geschlecht,"* edited by Y. B. Raynova and S. Moser. Vienna: Institut für Axiologische Forschungen.

———. 2004a. Endorsing practices of freedom: Feminism in a global perspective. In *Feminism and the final Foucault*, edited by D. Taylor and K. Vintges. Champaign: University of Illinois Press.

———. 2004b. Introduction to "Jean-Paul Sartre (1945)." *The Beauvoir Series*, volume I: *Philosophical writings*, edited by M. Simons, 223–28. Champaign: University of Illinois Press.

Chapter 6

"Politics Is a Living Thing"

The Intellectual's Dilemma in Beauvoir's The Mandarins

Gail Weiss

"A set of principles necessarily includes a political attitude," Henri said. "And on the other hand, politics is itself a living thing."

"I don't think so," Lambert replied. "In politics, all you're concerned with are abstract things that don't exist—the future, masses of people. But what is really concrete is the actual present moment, and people as separate and single individuals."

"But each individual is affected by collective history," Henri said.

"The trouble is that in politics you never come down from the high plateau of history to the problem of the lowly individual," Lambert said. "You get lost in generalities and no one gives a damn about particular cases."

—Simone de Beauvoir, *The Mandarins*

[W]e must, I think, ask ourselves why a professor of philosophy, driven to ask the sort of philosophical question that no science can answer, should be considered especially qualified to penetrate and solve daily problems better than others. I always wonder why the philosopher (in the particular academic sense of the term) should be expected to have unique insight and expected even to bear a special responsibility. Shouldn't the clergyman, the doctor, the schoolteacher, the judge, even the journalist *exercise a far greater influence on events, and therefore bear a far greater responsibility for the present and future?* [emphasis added]

—Hans-Georg Gadamer, "The Political Incompetence of Philosophy"

Can politics positively transform the everyday life of specific individuals through appealing to their collective history, as Henri suggests above? Is Lambert's pessimistic view that politics never addresses the concrete individual justified? Should some people be held more responsible for their politics than others, as Gadamer asserts, asking his readers to discount Martin Heidegger's Nazi past so that his philosophy can be judged "neutrally," that is, apolitically? Professors of philosophy, Gadamer implies, are dealing with matters too abstract to be held accountable for the social and political situation in which they (happen to) find themselves. Indeed, he claims, they do not bear the same responsibility for the present and future as those whose professions demand that they concern themselves continuously with the welfare of other human beings—namely, clergymen, doctors, schoolteachers, and judges. How does the journalist fit into this list? Should we agree with Gadamer that the philosopher's speculative reflections render him less responsible than others for the daily events that unfold around him?

These questions invoke some of the specific ethical and political dilemmas faced by leading intellectuals during and after World War II, dilemmas that Beauvoir and Gadamer respond to quite differently. While Beauvoir, in *The Mandarins*, embraces these difficult questions and works out concrete solutions to them through her various characters, Gadamer attempts to dissolve the tensions they generate. For if, as Gadamer implies, we can make hard-and-fast distinctions between politics and philosophy, then it seems we can distinguish between those who bear ethical and political responsibility for the mundane world in which we live (and philosophize!) and those who have a "higher calling," namely, philosophers such as Heidegger, who are motivated purely by ontological questions that seemingly have no bearing on the everyday world whatsoever.

While Beauvoir does not provide us with a clear road map for how to resolve the issues raised above about individual as well as collective responsibility, her novel emphatically communicates the importance of these questions themselves, and, contra Gadamer, she seems to place a special responsibility on the intellectual for raising and addressing these questions. Gadamer's attempt to exempt the intellectual from responsibility for the present and future and Beauvoir's affirmation that each individual must bear this responsibility for himself as well as others together capture some of the most important features of what I am calling "the intellectual's dilemma." The intellectual's dilemma, as I am defining it here and as it appears in the dialogue between Henri and Lambert above, arises in response to the question of whether and how to become engaged politically *as an intellectual*, that is, as one whose mode of assessment of the situation takes the form of a theoretical analysis of that situation. In the essay that follows, I will argue that in her novel *The Mandarins* Beauvoir offers us a much more satisfactory (albeit more complicated) picture of the dilemma itself, how it unfolds differently for different people, and the various responses that it provokes than does Gadamer in his philosophical defense of Heidegger's affiliation with the Nazi Party throughout World War II.

In the dialogue between Beauvoir's main character, Henri, and his junior journalist colleague Lambert, the pragmatic efficacy of politics is itself called into question. Prematurely jaded by the expedient political collaborations with the Germans that characterized the Vichy government's policies and actions during the Occupation, Lambert's cynicism about the relevance of politics in the daily life of concrete individuals is understandable. Indeed, he suggests that individuals are better off without politics, since the latter has no bearing on "the actual present moment, and people as separate and single individuals" (Beauvoir 1991, 147). Henri, on the other hand, is not willing to accept Lambert's binary distinction between an abstract realm of politics based on "the future, masses of people" and the concrete domain of everyday existence where each individual is unique and irreducible in her particularity to any other.[1] For Henri, this simplistic distinction fails to acknowledge the historicity of the individual, specifically her participation in a "collective history" that binds her socially and politically to past, present, and future others. Henri affirms that far from consisting in formal abstract principles, politics is "a living thing," an animate, evolving entity that depends upon concrete individuals in their collective history to keep it alive, that is, to give it its purpose, meaning, and direction (*sens*).

In Gadamer's apologia for Martin Heidegger's politics, he argues that philosophers should not have a special (political) responsibility for the present and the future. This stands in marked contrast to Henri's and even Lambert's perspectives. Clearly troubled by the ways in which what has come to be known as "The Heidegger Scandal" has tainted Heidegger's philosophical legacy, Gadamer takes up his philosophical cudgels on his old professor's behalf, urging us to acknowledge "the political incompetence of philosophy" and to assign political responsibility to others who play a more active role in public life. His attempt to exempt philosophers from having to occupy themselves with political matters sets both Gadamer and his work apart from the lives as well as the literary, philosophical, and political concerns of his existentialist colleagues, most notably Beauvoir and Jean-Paul Sartre. Indeed, as Beauvoir was writing her political novel *The Mandarins* in Paris in the aftermath of the German Occupation, Sartre was writing a series of essays on literature and proclaiming that both speakers and prose writers must be politically committed at all times to fighting injustice and improving human existence. In Sartre's words:

> Thus, by speaking, I reveal the situation by my very intention of changing it; I reveal it to myself and to others *in order* to change it. I strike at its very heart, I transfix it, and I display it in full view; at

> present I dispose of it; with every word I utter, I involve myself a little more in the world, and by the same token I emerge from it a little more, since I go beyond it towards the future.

And, he adds,

> The "committed" writer knows that words are action. He knows that to reveal is to change and that one can reveal only by planning to change. He has given up the impossible dream of giving an impartial picture of Society and the human condition. (Sartre [1948] 1988, 37)

Far from maintaining with Gadamer that the philosopher should be considered politically incompetent and therefore must be judged solely on her/his purely philosophical contributions, Sartre affirms that all prose writers bear a special political responsibility to transform positively the world in which they live *through* their writing. If they have not assumed this responsibility, he implies, then the writing and the thinking that motivates it are themselves politically suspect.

The intellectual's dilemma, for both Beauvoir and Sartre, then, is not *whether* to engage in political struggle, but *how* to do so in a manner that does justice to one's own personal principles and political ideals. While Sartre offers writers an eloquent intellectual exhortation to be politically committed in their writing, Beauvoir's *The Mandarins* provides us with a whole host of idiosyncratic individuals whose complex interactions reveal the difficulties of making and honoring such commitments but, at the same time, the absolute necessity of doing so. In what follows I will discuss the significance of Beauvoir's philosophical and literary depictions of the intellectual's political dilemma in *The Mandarins.* My focus will be not only on the intellectual writer and journalist Henri, who embodies this dilemma through and through, but also on other central characters in the story, who experience different versions of this dilemma. Beautifully illustrating the alterities that separate and even alienate the various characters and their life histories from one another, Beauvoir shows us that one can only take political responsibility for the future by taking responsibility for one's present and one's past. Since each individual's past, present, and future differ from those of other individuals, so, too, do their means of political engagement. Rather than prescribe a single mode of "authentic" political commitment, Beauvoir's existentialist perspective demands that we individualize our collective responsibility to ensure a future based upon human freedom.[2]

Henri's and Lambert's disagreement about the relevance and efficacy of politics in daily life offers a perfect example of how difficult it is even for two intellectuals who share basically the same liberatory goals to find a common ground or point of departure. Consumed with the particularities of his own past—

namely, his privileged bourgeois heritage and his collaborationist father—Lambert continually feels the need to prove that he is independent of them both, an attempt that miserably fails in the face of his girlfriend Nadine's relentless attacks and his own uncertainty about how to address the demons of the past he wants to repudiate in order to reinvent himself in the present and the future. At the other extreme, Henri is continually conscious of the complex ties that bind him to a collective past as well as his personal past, a past that includes his relationship with his intellectual mentor and longtime friend, Robert Dubreuilh, and with his wartime lover Paula. Henri sees these ties as non-negotiable obligations, that is, as moral constraints that continually remind him that it is impossible ever to assert oneself as a pure individual: "'It's funny,' he said to himself, 'but whenever you do the decent thing, instead of it giving you certain rights it only creates more obligations'" (Beauvoir 1991, 156).

In the course of the novel, Henri discovers that the fluidity of human relationships and the contingencies of one's situation allow these obligations to be realized in more than one way, thereby revealing that the past must be accepted but that its meaning can also be transformed through one's actions in the present and one's commitments to the future. The key to integrating past, present, and future in a decisive political commitment, as he suggests to Lambert in a later conversation, is to recognize that "In order to know who you are and what you want to do, you have to decide where you stand in the world" (1991, 274). That is, rather than figuring out one's place in the world by appealing to one's individuality and what one aims to accomplish, one must *begin* (rather than end) with one's participation in a collective history; the individual must define her own place in the world *through,* and not in spite of, her relationships with others. Rejecting Louis's seductive vision of a "pure literature" that is not burdened by the past, present, or future, a vision that mirrors Gadamer's own position and that Lambert finds incredibly appealing, Henri affirms that it is only by acknowledging the facticity of my situation, "where I stand in the world," that I can discover who I am and the meaning of my actions. The enormous (and often paralyzing) responsibility that attends this realization is conveyed by Henri as he contemplates writing an autobiographical novel: "[T]he truth of one's life is outside oneself, in events, in other people, in things; to talk about oneself, one must talk about everything else" (275).

The question that remains, of course, is how best to do justice to one's situation in order to define oneself and exercise political agency. This is precisely the question that dogs Henri, his friends, and his colleagues throughout *The Mandarins,* just as it dogged Beauvoir, Sartre, and their compatriots in the economic, social, political, and personal upheavals that followed World War II. For, as not only Beauvoir but many others have shown, war changes everything; the situation one inhabits before, or even during, a war is transformed permanently once the war is over.[3] If an individual (and a society as a whole, for that matter) fails to acknowledge and adjust to these transformations in the situation (as Paula's refusal to face the present and the future in order to cling to an illusory past amply illustrates), the results can be tragic for everyone involved in and/or affected by that situation.[4]

Thus, it is impossible to discuss the intellectual's dilemma in *The Mandarins* without acknowledging the specific post–World War II context that situates the novel, Beauvoir's own writing of the novel, and the actions of all the characters within it. As Henri struggles to write his own autobiographical text that will span the pre- and postwar years, his task is complicated by his realization that

> he had nothing in common with the person he had been in 1935. His political indifference, his curiosity, his ambition, all that foolish insistence on individualism—how quickly it passed, how foolish it was! It presupposed a future without obstacles, with guaranteed progress, the immediate brotherhood of man, and peace everlasting. Above all it presupposed selfishness and thoughtlessness. (1991, 150)

Like Henri, Anne is also aware of the idealistic illusions one must give up in order to acknowledge the reality of one's present situation. This reality includes not only broader political concerns but all the volatile intricacies of concrete, lived experience. To appraise her situation honestly in light of the latter, Anne must come to terms with her daughter Nadine's hostility (a hostility directed at Anne but which she realizes stems from Nadine's heartbreak and bitterness over the sudden death of her young wartime lover), with her own fears of aging and losing her sexuality, and with her increasing realization that her husband, Robert, does not depend on her presence to validate his own existence. As Anne's own therapeutic work with Holocaust survivors reveals, the price of such honesty for some individuals can be too high. Indeed, as we shall see, there are times when Anne actually envies Paula and her patients for being able to dwell in a fantasy world in order to escape from the terrible painfulness of their actual situations.

When Anne decides to go to the United States for three months on a lecture tour, leaving behind Robert and Nadine to manage without her, she does so based on the painful recognition that her own physical presence is not essential to the daily well-being of her husband and daughter. This recognition, in turn, leads Anne to question the very meaning of her own existence as a wife, mother, and therapist dedicated to healing the pain of others. As she attempts to seek self-fulfillment outside these roles by plunging herself into an entirely new situation and an entirely new set of relationships, Anne must confront afresh her own capacity for survival. Recognizing what is lost and what is gained in the very act of survival, Anne observes: "To survive is, after all, perpetually to begin to live again. I hoped I would still know how" (1991, 234).

As a psychoanalyst who treats Holocaust survivors, Anne is well-aware of the fragility of the survivor; for this reason she is the most sympathetic of all the characters to Paula's stubborn refusal to accept the demise of her former life as Henri's lover. Realizing the untenability of Paula's refusal to acknowledge the end of her relationship with Henri, a refusal that itself guarantees that which it seeks to prevent, Anne anticipates Paula's breakdown, helping to gather up the pieces of her psyche as she gathers up the pieces of the broken mirrors that are strewn across Henri's and Paula's apartment in the wake of Paula's final rampage. In the course of the novel, Beauvoir's characters each develop their own strategies for survival, and the means they utilize to survive form the basis for their judgments of each other as well as the reader's judgment of them.

Confronting her own psychic fragility at the end of the novel, Anne realizes that the divide that separates herself as a professional therapist from Paula and her patients is not nearly as secure as it had once seemed. Paula's choice after her breakdown to survive through resignation alarms Anne as much, if not more, than her previous refusal to accept a life without Henri. This new Paula, Anne observes, has adapted by insuring

> herself once and for all against tragedy; she was reconciled to everything and anything. But I couldn't resign myself to her resignation. In fact, it saddened me to such an extent that I became more and more disgusted with my profession; often I felt like saying to my patients, "Don't try to be cured; you'll heal as much as you need to by yourself." I had many patients, and that winter, as a matter of fact, I met with success in several difficult cases. But my heart wasn't in it. I really no longer understood why it is proper for people to sleep at night, make love with ease, be capable of acting, choosing, forgetting, living. Setting free all those neurotics imprisoned in their narrow misfortunes—when the world, after all, was so vast—used to seem terribly important to me. Now, however, when I tried to rid them of their obsessions, I was merely obeying a set of old slogans. Now I myself was becoming like them! The world was still as vast as ever, and I was no longer able to take an interest in it. (1991, 537)

The obsessive neurotic, Anne implies, at least has her motivating passion, a passion that gives significance (albeit pathological significance) to the rest of her life. The high price one may pay for giving up this passion is illustrated through Paula herself. Paula's attempt to keep her relationship with Henri at the center of her existence ultimately fails for the simple reason that Henri no longer loves her and that a relationship cannot be sustained by one person alone. In the absence of his present love, his past love, precisely because it is grounded solely in memories and not in the present or future, can no longer serve as a secure anchor for her psyche. Paula's passionate refusal of Henri's refusal to rekindle their love in the present leads to neurosis and eventually a psychotic breakdown; nonetheless, the emotional and intellectual energy required to sustain her illusion that Henri still loves her continues to provide Paula's life with a meaning and purpose. To be healed, for Paula, is to become resigned to a life without this passion, and yet, lacking passion it is unclear how she will be able to commit herself to the formidable task of reconstituting the very meaning of her life.

Unlike Paula, Anne is committed (like Beauvoir herself) to a clear-eyed recognition of her situation, and this means that she is much quicker than Paula to realize that her own life-affirming love for Lewis Brogan cannot be sustained without Lewis's reciprocal love for her. Convinced that this transatlantic love can be preserved and can continue to flourish if she and Lewis are totally honest with one another, Anne is forced to realize that for Lewis, honesty and passion from a distance cannot overcome the reality of their daily physical separation. Despite their love for one another, Lewis resigns his passion for Anne rather than resigning himself to sharing only a small part of her life.

Anne's unwillingness to choose Paula's path of self-delusion leads her to forgo her passion for Lewis, even though she recognizes at the same time her husband Robert's and her daughter Nadine's self-sufficiency, the fact that they do not need her love to give their own lives meaning and purpose. To accept the end of the relationship with Lewis, Anne fears that she must, like Paula, accept the path of resignation. For Anne, giving up their love means resigning herself to becoming an old woman (at age 39!); she is convinced that the long-dormant sexuality that Lewis has reawakened in her will never surface again, consigning her for the remainder of her life to an absence of sexual desire and sexual satisfaction. After all, with the birth of Nadine's and Henri's baby, Anne has herself become a grandmother.

In the final chapter of the book, Anne, the professional "healer" of others' pain, prepares to express her own resignation to the "vastness" of a passionless world (and to the meaninglessness of her own life within it) through suicide. For, she dully concludes, "whether you're killed or whether you die doesn't make very much difference. And everyone dies, at about the same age, at about forty" (1991, 606).[5] However, as she contemplates the effect her death will have on those she loves—on Robert, on Nadine, and yes, even Lewis—Anne decides not to overdose on the vial of drugs she took from Paula's purse in order to prevent Paula from doing the same thing:

> How could I not have thought of it? I can't impose my corpse and everything that would come after that on their hearts: Robert

> bending over this bed, Lewis in his house in Parker with words dancing before his eyes, Nadine sobbing furiously. I can't. . . . It's strange. I would die alone; yet it's the others who would live my death. (1991, 609)

Facing what Camus has famously called the "one truly serious philosophical problem"—namely, suicide—Anne decides that the love of others indeed makes life worth living. Like those whom she has successfully healed, she affirms the promise as well as the pitfalls of intersubjective existence as the very meaning of survival:[6]

> For a long time, I sat before the mirror, looking at my face, the face of a survivor. The lips would have become blue, the nostrils pinched. But not for me: for them. My death does not belong to me. The vial is still here, within reach of my hand; death is still present. But the living are even more so. (1991, 609–10)

Returning to her family in the garden outside, listening to Robert enthusiastically share his and Henri's latest plans for a new political weekly that will rise like a phoenix in the ashes of *L'Espoir*, Anne wonders, "How could I ever have been such a fool?" And, she silently observes, "For a moment I had really passed over to the other side, there where nothing counts any more, where everything is equal to nothing" (1991, 610). What has pulled her from the "other side," from her solipsistic, fatalistic reverie, is the love of others and their own passion for life:

> "Are you listening to me?" Robert asked. He smiled at me. "Where are you?"
>
> "Here," I replied.
>
> I am here. They are living, they speak to me, I am alive. Once more, I've jumped feet first into life. Words are entering my ears; little by little, they take on meaning. Here are the estimates for the weekly and the layouts Henri suggests. Do I have an idea for a name? None of the ones they've thought of so far are suitable. I try to think of a name. I say to myself that, since they were strong enough to wrest me from death, perhaps they will know how to help me to live again. They will surely know. Either one founders in apathy, or the earth becomes re-peopled. I didn't founder. Since my heart continues to beat, it will have to beat for something, for someone. Since I'm not deaf, I'll once more hear people calling to me. Who knows? Perhaps one day I'll be happy again. Who knows? (1991, 610)

It is no accident that Anne's "rebirth" coincides with the rebirth of Henri's and Robert's friendship, intellectual solidarity, and political commitment to doing whatever is in their power to denounce oppression and realize their shared idealistic vision of a liberatory future. Through all of these characters' different experiences, Beauvoir reveals that a passion for intellectual activity receives both its greatest challenges and its highest validation through political engagement. Moreover, the converse is also true: political engagement must, to be efficacious, involve serious, ongoing intellectual inquiry even when the result of the latter is to produce more questions than answers as to how to proceed.

What Anne's experience in particular reveals is the importance of passion in committing oneself to life with all the complex relations to others that this latter entails. Just as Beauvoir's existentialist predecessor, Søren Kierkegaard, proclaimed over a century earlier, it is passion that motivates one to seek the truth of one's existence, and it is passion that provides one with the motivation to transform one's present situation. In his words: "[P]encil-pushing modern speculative thought takes a dim view of passion, and yet, for the existing person, passion is existence at its very highest—and we are, after all, existing persons. In passion, the existing subject is infinitized in the eternity of imagination and yet is also most definitely himself" (Kierkegaard [1846] 1992, 197). A little later he continues, "In forgetting that one is an existing subject, one loses passion, and in return, truth does not become a paradox . . ." (199). Kierkegaard's claim that "passion is the highest pitch of subjectivity" resonates with Anne's recognition that "Either one founders in apathy, or the earth becomes re-peopled." However, while Kierkegaard emphasizes the ways in which passion animates an individual's own existence, deepening her subjective inwardness and enhancing the paradox of truth, Beauvoir emphasizes the intersubjective dimensions of passion revealing how the passion of others can reanimate one's own passion for existence (as Anne seeks to recover her passion for life through the love of her family). In short, truth, for Beauvoir, is not subjectivity as it is for Kierkegaard, but intersubjectivity. More precisely, it is the active presence of intersubjectivity at the heart of subjectivity that, for Beauvoir, produces the paradoxical nature of truth.

For Kierkegaard, by contrast, the paradox of truth embraced in subjective passion is the logically impossible yet nonetheless lived union of the finite (mortal existence) and infinite (spiritual existence) within a singular human existence. Kierkegaard's primary concern, throughout his various discussions of truth, is the passion and subjectivity of the single individual culminating in the religious journey of the knight of faith. For Beauvoir, on the other hand, a focus upon any particular individual always leads to those other individuals whose existence is intimately bound up with her own. Thus, it is not surprising that Anne's solitary meditation on suicide in the bedroom upstairs leads her back out to her family in the garden, where the very flowers that "people it" are themselves a symbol of integrated, communal life: the loveliness of each flower is displayed and accentuated by all of those that surround it, together creating the beauty of the garden as a whole.

The passion Beauvoir embraces at the end of the novel, through the characters Anne, Henri, Nadine, and Robert, is not merely a passion for others, or for intersubjective existence more generally, but rather is a passion to help transform the present and past by working with others to build a new future. Although Henri feels compelled to relinquish *L'Espoir*, and continually questions his own idealistic hopes concerning the power of ideas and the written word to enact genuine social change, at the end of the novel he and Robert are planning to start a new weekly that will thrust them once again into the very center of political life, working together to help France achieve a new image in the wake of its own wartime transformation under the German Occupation. That they will frequently disagree on how to accomplish this goal is inevitable, given their past history; however, by attempting once again to work together and to confront their differences, they are indeed affirming that "the truth of one's life is outside oneself . . ." and that this truth can and must be realized in passionate collaboration with others (1991, 275).

In the context of *The Mandarins*, as well as in the context of Beauvoir's own life, Gadamer's claim that philosophy (and the philosopher) is politically incompetent is far from compelling. As I mentioned at the outset, the intellectual's dilemma, for Beauvoir, is not whether to make a political commitment but how best to do this in a manner that does justice to one's moral and intellectual beliefs. Nonetheless, Beauvoir recognizes the profound feelings of impotence that can plague the intellectual as she is forced to acknowledge her own limited role in bringing about lasting change in the world. As Robert Dubreuilh observes, joining with others to form the Resistance is one thing, since all those involved are committed to a joint project—namely, opposing the enemy (i.e., the Nazis and the French citizens who collaborated with them) by any and all means at one's disposal. Committing oneself to rebuilding France after the liberation is an entirely different project that is grounded in instability, uncertainty, and dissenting views. While Henri is convinced that even a minority can do effective work to achieve this goal, Dubreuilh points out that this was only true for the Resistance, not for the larger task of creating a new political future:

> For the Resistance, fine! A handful of men was enough; all we wanted, after all, was to stir up trouble. Stirring up trouble, sabotage, resisting—that's the job of a minority. But when you set out to build, that's an entirely different story. We thought all we had to do was take advantage of the running start we had gotten, while actually there was a radical difference between the Occupation period and the one that followed the liberation. (1991, 515)

In response to Dubreuilh's pessimism regarding the power of the minority to make a significant political contribution in the urgent task of rebuilding France after the liberation, Henri wonders, "Perhaps Dubreuilh was right; but if that was the case, then it was all one big joke" (1991, 516). Why should a minority make the effort at all, if it is doomed to failure from the outset? Despite the seductiveness of being able to relinquish one's political responsibility for creating a new future because one believes that nothing one does will have any lasting impact, Henri refuses to accept Dubreuilh's exhortation "to resign yourself to impotence" (516). Indeed, later on in the novel Dubreuilh himself rejects this view, hurling himself back into political life with the full force of his formidable intellect and a passionate belief in the ability of the few to affect the many.

In the end, Beauvoir implies, the intellectual can and must preserve her idealistic vision of a future grounded in freedom, and she must continually commit herself to realizing this future in concert with others, even while recognizing that other people's methods for obtaining this goal may be strongly at odds with her own. Thus the question of *how* to engage oneself politically must be confronted over and over again—the intellectual's dilemma, as stated earlier, can never be surpassed or overcome. Moreover, Beauvoir suggests that each individual has her own unique contribution to make to realize a collective vision for the future; she affirms in both her literary and her philosophical works that every person is irreplaceable, that freedom cannot be secured for some without, at the same time, attempting to realize the freedom of all. As Beauvoir famously declares in *The Ethics of Ambiguity*:

> To will oneself free is also to will others free. This will is not an abstract formula. It points out to each person concrete action to be achieved. But the others are separate, even opposed, and the man of good will sees concrete and difficult problems arising in his relations with them. ([1948] 1997, 73)

Returning to *The Mandarins*, to recognize the differences that divide one person from another, even in the face of a shared political vision that is intended to apply to them all, requires that one recognize, in Anne's words, that: "One man plus one man doesn't make two men; it will forever make one plus one" (1991, 359). This raises the political stakes considerably for Beauvoir, for "[t]he ambiguity of freedom, which very often is occupied only in fleeing from itself, introduces a difficult equivocation into relationships with each individual taken one by one" ([1948] 1997, 136). Negotiating this equivocation is a crucial part of what I have called the intellectual's dilemma. It is a dilemma that Beauvoir believes must be lived with passion, committed to with love. As she observes,

> [I]n order for the idea of liberation to have a concrete meaning, the joy of existence must be asserted in each one, at every instant; the movement toward freedom assumes its real, flesh and blood figure in the world by thickening into pleasure, into happiness. ([1948] 1997, 135)

The fact that there is real suffering in the world, that the goal of realizing the "joy of existence" for each and every individual seems impossible to achieve, should not, for Beauvoir, lead the intellectual to turn away from the demands of everyday existence in order to embrace the types of theoretical abstractions that encourage political impotence. Henri's and Robert's decision to start a new weekly and Anne's decision to rejoin the world of the living at the end of *The Mandarins* are marked by the awareness that there are no guarantees that their efforts will be rewarded with success and happiness. Nonetheless, they start out afresh, with confidence in their fellow human beings, hoping to make lasting change in the world. Anne, we are led to believe, will continue to help Holocaust survivors work through their traumas so that they can once again embrace life. She must accept the impossibility of achieving happiness with Lewis and nonetheless reaffirm her own passion for life by throwing herself into Robert's and Henri's new project, acceding to their demand that she be intellectually and emotionally involved rather than a vicarious bystander.[7] In so doing, she charts her own course as a survivor.

What distinguishes Beauvoir's depiction of the political demands of everyday life from those provided by many of her own existentialist interlocutors at the time, especially Sartre, is her continued insistence upon the intersubjective ground for all individual inquiry and action. As Beauvoir rightly insists, it is in and through the inevitable conflicts that arise out of our life with others that political commitments must be negotiated and renegotiated. This means that there will always be new intellectual dilemmas to replace the old ones; interpersonal conflicts (even with one's allies) are unavoidable and must be confronted in their potential for hindering as well as facilitating political action. For Beauvoir, if politics is to survive as a "living thing," the intellectual's response to these dilemmas requires that she passionately embrace the ongoing demands of communal life, as opposed to seeking the end of all demands through resignation to impotence/death.

In contrast to Sartre, Beauvoir emphasizes that the intellectual's message can never be a purely individual expression of how best to transform a common situation, since it emanates from and is always directed toward a life with others. Moreover, pace Kierkegaard, the passion that animates an individual's existence is not grounded in love for a transcendent God, but in her concrete relationships with her fellow human beings. And, pace Gadamer, an apolitical philosophy is not a viable option. Philosophers, and intellectuals more generally, Beauvoir is suggesting, must refuse the false seduction of a world of pure ideas; it is a false seduction precisely because it is not a world at all; it lacks passion, flesh, and blood. Through *The Mandarins*, Beauvoir teaches us that the intellectual must abandon her calm meditations in the armchair by the fire to become capable, not only of transforming the world, but also of being transformed by it—lacking the stability and permanence of the Cartesian cogito, the intellectual must be more dynamic and fluid, like Descartes's ball of wax as it encounters the flames.

Notes

1. Lambert's advocacy of the concrete, allegedly apolitical realm over the abstract, historical realm seems to mirror the arguments of those who champion the relevance and importance of an individual's private existence over the anonymity of public life. Henri's response, by contrast, deconstructs this distinction in ways that anticipate 1960s' feminists' battle cry that "the personal is the political!"

2. Sartre also emphasizes that each person must choose their own form of political engagement; however, *The Mandarins* provides a much richer account of how the facticity of each individual existence creates a different context for action than Sartre is able to offer in the "What is Literature?" essays. Sartre's own post–World War II play *Dirty Hands* poignantly and painfully reveals the high personal and political stakes of the intellectual's dilemma, yet the focus there is primarily upon how this dilemma is lived by a single character, while Beauvoir, in *The Mandarins*, allows us to inhabit the idiosyncratic perspectives of several characters, including Henri, Anne, Robert, Paula, Nadine, Lambert, Lewis (who always remains somewhat inscrutable), and Vincent.

3. The irrevocable changes brought about by war are masterfully depicted in so many literary texts; the ways of coping and failing to cope with these changes run the gamut from Septimus Warren Smith, the World War I veteran in Virginia Woolf's *Mrs. Dalloway* who commits suicide because he cannot vanquish the demons of his wartime past to Vladek Spiegelman, the Holocaust survivor (and the author's own father) who begins a new life in the USA in Art Spiegelman's *Maus* volumes.

4. In Paula's case I say an illusory past, because it becomes evident from the text that Paula has liberally reinterpreted key events in her past relationship with Henri so that they will confirm her desperate belief that he always loved her and loves her still. Given the interconnectedness of past, present, and future, it is not surprising that Paula resorts to the creation of an elaborate, phantasmic past in order to support and justify her refusal to face the reality of a loveless present and the prospect of a future life without Henri. Ultimately, Paula's refusal to confront the demands of her new situation is precisely what precipitates her mental breakdown.

5. Although it is beyond the scope of this paper to enter into a discussion of Beauvoir's rather startling views about the onset of old age, it is not incidental that she

herself was in her early forties while she was writing *The Mandarins* and that her transatlantic relationship with her American lover, Nelson Algren (to whom the book is dedicated), had also recently ended because Algren was unwilling to accept the limited role in her life that she was willing to give him. To get a better sense of Beauvoir's views on love and aging, see her monograph *The Coming of Age*.

6. It is worth citing the opening lines of Camus's 1942 essay "An Absurd Reasoning" in their entirety: "There is but one truly serious philosophical problem, and that is suicide. Judging whether life is or is not worth living amounts to answering the fundamental question of philosophy. All the rest—whether or not the world has three dimensions, whether the mind has nine or twelve categories—comes afterwards" (Camus [1955] 1983, 3).

7. The ever-petulant Nadine, too, is happy at the end of the novel, though her own political engagement seems to take the form of supporting Henri and her father, Robert, rather than making unique contributions of her own. Nadine is a thorny character in this novel, and to do justice to the complexities of her character would require a separate essay. Through her character as well as through the other angry young people in the novel (such as Vincent, who savagely murders a Nazi collaborator and brings the dead body to the Dubreuilh's summer cottage), Beauvoir shows that the violence of the war extends through all the generations and has the potential to compromise a society's entire future. Nadine, Lambert, and even Vincent must come to terms with their own difficult memories in order to move beyond their private vendettas and embrace a common liberatory vision. They will each, presumably, do this (or fail to do this) in their own way: Nadine, through her new life with Henri and their daughter; Lambert, by coming to terms with the fact that Louis, his new intellectual mentor, was a collaborator; and Vincent, by refusing any longer to destroy himself as well as others in order to overcome his anger with everything and everyone. Of these three characters, Vincent, a drug addict and murderer, seems the least likely to survive, much less attain happiness. For Vincent, there is no intellectual dilemma at all—political engagement can only be violent, ending life rather than affirming it.

Works Cited

Beauvoir, Simone de. [1948] 1997. *The ethics of ambiguity*. Translated by Bernard Frechtman. Secaucus, N.J.: Citadel Press.

———. 1972. *The coming of age*. Translated by Patrick O'Brian. New York: Putnam.

———. 1991. *The mandarins*. Translated by Leonard M. Friedman. New York: W. W. Norton.

Camus, Albert. [1955] 1983. *The myth of Sisyphus and other essays*. Translated by Justin O'Brien. New York: Vintage Books.

Descartes, René. 1979. *Meditations on first philosophy*. Translated by Donald A. Cress. Indianapolis: Hackett.

Gadamer, Hans-Georg. 1992. The political incompetence of philosophy. In *The Heidegger case: On philosophy and politics*, edited by Thomas Rockmore and Joseph Margolis. Philadelphia: Temple University Press.

Kierkegaard, Søren. [1846] 1992. *Concluding unscientific postscript to Philosophical fragments*. Translated by Howard V. Hong and Edna H. Hong. Vol. 1. Princeton, N.J.: Princeton University Press.

Sartre, Jean-Paul. [1948] 1988. *"What is literature?" and other essays*. Cambridge, Mass.: Harvard University Press.

———. 1976. Dirty hands. In *No exit and three other plays*. New York: Vintage Books.

Spiegelman, Art. 1986. *Maus: A survivior's tale*. New York: Pantheon Books.

Woolf, Virginia. 1981. *Mrs. Dalloway*. San Diego: Harcourt Brace Jovanovich.

Chapter 7

Personal Choice and the Seduction of the Absolute in *The Mandarins*

Shannon M. Mussett

Simone de Beauvoir's novel *The Mandarins* offers insight not only into the personal and political lives of post–World War II French intellectuals, but also into the difficulties of concretely struggling with certain vital (but oftentimes abstract) philosophical concepts. One such concept that surfaces repeatedly, albeit in different manifestations of Beauvoir's philosophy, is the idea of the absolute. In many cases throughout her theoretical works, Beauvoir critiques the positing and allegiance to external absolutes. In these instances, existents either adopt a prefabricated absolute such as the State or a particular religion, or they create their own absolutes such as Wealth or Power, to which they abdicate their freedom. In either case, there is a disingenuous move on the part of the agent to constrict choice and responsibility by swearing submission to an abstraction. However, Beauvoir also acknowledges that there is an absolute that, if it serves as both the foundation and goal of our actions, is to be embraced. This absolute is freedom. As Beauvoir makes explicit in her ethical works, freedom is the only absolute that does not stand over against the subject as a dominating and authoritarian force, but rather forms the very basis of the existent's praxis.[1]

The tension created by the individual's struggle with the absolute is concretized in the character of Anne Dubreuilh in *The Mandarins*.[2] Although many of the characters, such as Henri Perron, Robert Dubreuilh, and Gerard Lambert, face crises of social and *political* absolutes (such as the struggle between communism and capitalism, the role of the writer in society, and the morality of seeking revenge after the time of political urgency has passed), no character more reveals the existential turmoil and allure of absolutism for the *individual* than Anne. Certainly, Anne's personal struggles serve as a mirror to the political struggles of her various companions, but more importantly, her story shows the deeply personal underpinnings of all public action. Through Anne, we are given a window into the profoundly lonely nature of choice, which struggles to be in community with others despite its recondite singularity.

Anne is alienated and alone. Her story is the long and arduous narrative of the existent who must come to learn the interconnectedness of all human actions, and thus all human beings. This journey of association is portrayed through her efforts to rid herself of dependence upon foreign absolutes; it is a journey that only concludes when she finally makes a deliberate choice that acknowledges not only her own freedom, but embraces her connection to others.

To fully grasp the magnitude of Anne's final decision not to end her own life, it is necessary to trace the philosophical backdrop to Beauvoir's fictional setting. It is thus fitting to begin with Beauvoir's critique of absolutism in *Pyrrhus et Cinéas* and *The Ethics of Ambiguity* in order to highlight how seductive foreign absolutes are, as well as to show how freedom alone should be set up as absolute. Much of this discussion takes up the motif of death as the absolute and how Beauvoir ultimately rejects the early Heideggerian emphasis on being-toward-death in favor of a being from and toward freedom. Anne's struggle with death and freedom comes through most strikingly in her relationships with the two most significant men in her life: her husband, Robert, and her American lover, Lewis Brogan. In both cases, albeit in different ways and with different results, Anne sets up each man as an absolute that has replaced her childhood relationship to God as the supreme adjudicator of existence.

Beauvoir's development of Anne's story requires a mirror narrative that parallels and apes it: the story of Paule Mareuil. Paule's addiction to love (in the form of Henri) leads to a dark descent into madness and eventually a total break from others. Anne, unable to bring herself to show Paule the destructiveness of her addiction, instead sees Paule as a mirror through which she reflects upon her own dependency on foreign absolutes. Whereas Paule's forced break from Henri leads to madness and isolation, Anne's break from her dependency on Robert and Lewis leads to reconnection, hope, and the opening of future action.

The Absolute: Seriousness, Death, and Freedom

The problem of the individual's relationship to the absolute appears directly in all of Beauvoir's theoretical writings and at least indirectly in her works of fiction. This is due to the fact that one simply cannot grasp the idea of concrete, embodied freedom without understanding it in relationship to and in contrast with the absolute. In some cases, such as in *The Second Sex*, Beauvoir indicates the danger and damage due to the characterization and misappropriation of absolutes ([1949] 1976a, 15).[3] In others, such as *La vieillesse*, she illustrates the mechanism of oppressive concepts (in this instance "old age") and how such concepts serve as greater and more feared absolutes than death itself ([1972] 1996, 539). Her most direct, and for my purposes important, references to the absolute come from her ethical treatises: *The Ethics of Ambiguity* and *Pyrrhus et Cinéas*. In these two works, Beauvoir makes clear her philosophical orientation toward the posture of absolutism, being-toward-death, and freedom—all of which become central themes in *The Mandarins* in general and Anne's story in particular.

In *Pyrrhus et Cinéas*, Beauvoir had already formulated the hazards of setting up absolute values. This tendency is most clear in the description of the serious person who "claims to separate the end from the project which defines it and to recognize in it value in itself. He believes that values are in the world, before man, without him" (1944, 29).[4] The serious person believes that there are certain values that are more permanent, stable, and intrinsically valuable than the human beings that create them. This problematic idea that the end of action can be separated from (and therefore be more true than) the actor who wills it forms the backbone of her more elaborate study of seriousness in *The Ethics of Ambiguity*.

In her discussions of the nihilist, the subman, the child, and so on, we find brief but powerful sketches of those who do not yet have or acknowledge their freedom. All of these illustrations are related in some way to the attitude of seriousness. Whether it is the child who plays at being serious or the adventurer who almost escapes its pull, moral action is necessarily put into a relationship with the attitude of seriousness. This is due to the fact that action cannot exist without positing some form of absolute. And in many ways, the *easiest* way to achieve a goal is to adopt an external ideal that stands as a measure and judge of action.

Beauvoir expands upon the idea of the serious person as one who draws a sharp (and wrongheaded) distinction between the agent and goal of action. For her, the two are inseparable, but for the serious person, the goal stands outside of the agent. As such, the goal becomes the "object" of action or authority, and the agent becomes the "subject" seeking to achieve it. The objectification of the goal is the direct result of its being excised from the existent and consequently seeming to take on a life of its own.[5] For Beauvoir's existentialism, life is much more ambiguous and fluid than the strict subject/object dichotomy allows, but for the serious person life is clearly and unambiguously divided between these two poles. In one sense, this makes life much easier, because it does away with (at least temporarily) all of the uncertainty and anxiety that necessarily accompany ambiguous existence where actor and goal are mutually implicated. However, a much more pernicious result of the attitude of seriousness is that the individual flees his or her freedom by trying to lose subjectivity into the object, thus avoiding the ethical onus to choose and take responsibility for action. In harmony with Sartre's descriptions of bad faith in *Being and Nothingness*, Beauvoir describes the serious person as seeking to get

> rid of his freedom by claiming to subordinate it to values which would be unconditioned. He imagines that the accession to these values likewise permanently confers value upon himself. Shielded with "rights," he fulfills himself as a *being* who is escaping from the stress of existence. . . . There is the serious from the moment that freedom denies itself to the advantage of ends which one claims are absolute. ([1948] 1997, 46)

The attitude of seriousness thus seeks to flee the stresses of existence by claiming devotion to an unconditioned—and thus distinctly inhuman—absolute. In so doing, this attitude tries to deny freedom even as it employs it in its flight.

Rather than recognizing the absolute as a human construction—either on the individual or cultural level—the serious person sees the absolute as a timeless, monolithic thing that serves both as the model of behavior and the goal of all action. The danger of this kind of attitude lies in its personal and social impact. On the social level, the attitude of seriousness inevitably leads to tyranny and violence, because the Cause, in whatever form it is manifest, takes priority over the individuals that it serves, orders, or supports. On the personal level, it often leads to frustration, humiliation, and sometimes even despair. Because each action unfolds in the thoroughly temporal world of shifting norms, values, and situations, one cannot but be disappointed in the world (nihilism) or in oneself (masochism) for failing to ever achieve or embody the absolute.

Beauvoir's corpus shows that there are a number of different ways in which existents seek to deny their freedom by positing ends as absolutes. Some specific attitudes of seriousness that illuminate the personal anguish of setting up a foreign absolute are the passionate person from *The Ethics of Ambiguity* and the *amoureuse* (the woman in love) from *The Second Sex*. Both of these types posit the beloved as an idealized object worthy of idolatry. The passionate person (which is the precursor to the *amoureuse*) elevates the beloved into an almost mythical status. In *The Ethics of Ambiguity*, Beauvoir explains that the passionate person desires to attain existence by immortalizing and adulating another person—a person who, by definition, is also an ambiguous, temporal, and free being who cannot possibly embody any kind of perfection. Thus, the passionate individual is a tragic character:

> Having involved his whole life with an external object which can continually escape him, he tragically feels his dependence. Even if it does not definitely disappear, the object never gives itself. The pas-

> sionate man makes himself a lack of being not that there might *be* being, but in order to be. And he remains at a distance; he is never fulfilled. ([1948] 1997, 65)

By setting up the beloved as the absolute, the passionate person both inspires admiration and horror, according to Beauvoir. Passionate individuals are commendable because they set up the free other as the object worthy of esteem. But the horror of loneliness that such a project engenders is unavoidable, and we find that the one who loves another with such fierceness is one who is most alone.

Beauvoir develops the sketch of the passionate person further in *The Second Sex*, but in that book there is very little that inspires admiration, and much that inspires aversion. As such, the *amoureuse* in *The Second Sex* darkens the similar attitude of the passionate person found in *The Ethics of Ambiguity*. The woman in love is a desperate and maniacal figure who has emptied her own hopes and aspirations into a mania for another. By devoting herself completely to her only project—to love and dote on a man—she becomes an empty shell of a person, eventually becoming deranged, delusional, and annoying. As Beauvoir points out,

> Even if the chosen is deserving of the profoundest affection, his truth is terrestrial: it is no longer him that the woman loves as she kneels before a supreme being; she is duped by the spirit of seriousness which refuses to place values "between parentheses," that is, to recognize that they have their source in human existence; her bad faith raises barriers between her and the man whom she adores. ([1949] 1976b, 562)

Drawing the clear association between the *amoureuse* (a form of the passionate person) and the spirit of seriousness, Beauvoir drives home the way in which even our most intimate connections with others are open to the seduction of absolutizing them. Indeed, our very love can turn into a stone with which we bludgeon ourselves as well as the beloved. Such behavior is at the heart of the spirit of seriousness. That which we set up as an external absolute inevitably turns on us and transforms us into dependent, diminished, and self-denying individuals. This attitude, however, is neither inevitable nor impossible to overcome. At any point, we can make an authentic choice and take responsibility for what we do.[6]

Why is the attitude of seriousness so ubiquitous in human experience? An easy answer is given by Beauvoir, who draws the conclusion from the simple but astute observation that all human beings begin as children and thus have many years as unwitting apprentices of seriousness ([1948] 1997, 46). But an even more fundamental insight into the seduction of seriousness is found in the Heideggerian study of our anxiety and the self-dissolving fear of our own finitude. Many scholars have noted the varying degrees of influence that Heideggerian philosophy has had on Beauvoir's metaphysics and ethics.[7] However, few commentators develop the role of one of the cornerstones of Heidegger's philosophy on Beauvoir's analysis: being-toward-death.[8] In order to understand Beauvoir's critique of the absolute fully, it is necessary to see how being-toward-death figures into her ethical theory.

As Heidegger explains in *Being and Time*, we care because we are finite, but our finitude is essentially marked by the fact that we die. The experience of our own possibility of not existing causes us tremendous anxiety: "Thrownness into death reveals itself to it [*Dasein*] more primordially and penetratingly in the attunement of *Angst*" (Heidegger 1996, 232). For Heidegger, our being-toward-death causes us deep angst because it reveals the impossibility of our own permanence or being. Because we feel anxiety at our own impermanence, we often attempt to evade our being-toward-death in what Beauvoir will later call attitudes of seriousness. Heidegger explains: "Temptation, tranquillization, and estrangement . . . characterize the kind of being of *falling prey*. Entangled, everyday being-toward-death is a constant *flight from death*" (235). Attitudes of seriousness that deny the ambiguity of existence by seeking verification in absolute values are all enactments of the flight from death Heidegger describes.

The Ethics of Ambiguity struggles to define an existentialist ethics against the pervasive spirit of seriousness that desires universal and deathless truth against the ever-changing world. Beauvoir even opens this work with a quote from Montaigne on the work of life as that of building death, adding "Man knows and thinks this tragic ambivalence which the animal and the plant merely undergo" ([1948] 1997, 7). According to Beauvoir, the ambiguity of existence is firmly rooted in the idea that while we live, we know we are going to die. And much of the spirit of seriousness is born of our incessant denial of this very finitude.[9] What Beauvoir offers in place of the spirit of seriousness that seeks to avoid death in a multitude of ways is an ethics of the here and now. As she concludes *The Ethics of Ambiguity*: "If it came to be that each man did what he must, existence would be saved in each one without there being any need of dreaming of a paradise where all would be reconciled in death" (159). This goal, however, requires that each person take responsibility for his or her existence and refuse to be seduced by the foreign absolute.

The Ethics of Ambiguity argues against the human tendency to deny death by positing forms of eternity—be they heaven, country, God, or love. However, Beauvoir does not adhere entirely to Heidegger's ideas of our being-toward and flight-from death. In fact, in *Pyrrhus et Cinéas*, she had challenged Heidegger on the grounds that death cannot be the quintessential absolute toward which we are projected. In this early text she writes: "[O]ne must not say with Heidegger that man's authentic project is being for death, that death is our essential end, that there is no other choice for man than between the flight from or the assumption of this ultimate possibility" (1944, 61–62). It might seem surprising that Beauvoir, who consistently maintains a criticism of foreign ideals, would not accept Heidegger's being-toward-death as the most original and intimate absolute, especially since Beauvoir agrees that our finitude is defined, to a large extent, by our death and the possibility of our own nonexistence. However, she argues that "The nothingness that anguish reveals to me is not the nothingness of my death" (63). What, then, does our anguish reveal to us, according to Beauvoir? Quite simply, our own essential nothingness, our own lack of being: "the negativity that allows me to continually transcend all transcendence" (63). In short, anguish reveals to us not our being-toward-death but our very freedom. Beauvoir concludes her critique of Heidegger by writing, "The human being exists in the form of projects which are not projects toward death, but projects toward singular ends" (64).

Choice, although often tarrying with the problem of death in the setting up of projects, is only authentic with freedom as its genesis and goal. Thus, what Beauvoir begins in *Pyrrhus et Cinéas* she brings to fruition in *The Ethics of Ambiguity*—namely, the idea that the only absolute that we should set up as a goal is freedom. Freedom alone is the "universal, absolute end" ([1948] 1997, 58). Only freedom avoids the pitfalls of becoming solidified into an abstract, and therefore necessarily dangerous, absolute. It accomplishes this by the simple fact that human freedom is *nothing*, and therefore can never become an objectified ideal that stands over and against human beings engaged in concrete activity. If we actively will freedom through a fundamental assumption of our own freedom, we engage in ethical activity that is true to the ambiguity and dynamism of existence. However, as Beauvoir illustrates in her examples of attitudes of seriousness, as well as later in the lives of her characters in *The Mandarins*, to will freedom from the assumption of freedom is not easy, straightforward, or guaranteed. In fact, Anne's journey spans many pages and many years before she is able to engage in a truly free choice.

Anne's Struggle with and against the Absolute

Just as *The Ethics of Ambiguity* opens and closes with an emphasis on the experience of death, so too is *The Mandarins* framed by profound confrontations with death. Given the dynamics of the text as a whole—consisting of constant discussions and allusions to the Holocaust, the war, and personal loss—Anne's own struggle with and against death seems to point to the Heideggerian insight that our being-toward-death is the axiomatic absolute and it is only by confronting this that we achieve authentic existence. Only in the very last lines of the book do we come to see that the confrontation with death is merely a step in achieving genuine freedom.

When we first meet Anne, she is in the middle of a crisis. She cannot sleep, her dreams are tormented, and she feels acutely isolated and alone. She tells herself: "No, I shall not meet my death today; neither today nor any day. I will be dead for others without ever being dead for myself" (1954, 26; [1956] 1999, 30 TA).[10] Anne's dilemma is not meant to be an ordinary anxiety attack but an existential crisis that takes the entirety of the novel to work through. Anne immediately clues us in to what fills her with the thoughts of death that are haunting her very being: she has yet again lost the security that the adoption of a foreign absolute provides for the individual.

Anne explains that she had not always been prey to the fear or even knowledge of death. When she was a child, the figure of God had given her the stability necessary to deny the limitations and inevitability of her own finitude. As a little girl, she would imagine that she was dead, but the thought of God would reassure her with promises of eternity (1954, 26; [1956] 1999, 31). Yet, mirroring Beauvoir's own adolescent crisis, the child Anne realized that God as the absolute guarantor against finitude was a mendacious abstraction.[11] At fifteen years of age, Anne renounced God but then quickly realized that in giving up God as the absolute, she had condemned herself to death (1954, 26; [1956] 1999, 31). For four years, she experienced the anguish of one who truly confronts being-toward-death. In a very pronounced sense, then, Anne's loss of God as the absolute forced her to confront her finitude. But then something happened to rescue Anne from this existential quandary: she met Robert Dubreuilh.

Anne recalls: "From the moment I loved Robert, I never again felt fear, of anything. I had only to speak his name and I was secure" (1954, 27; [1956] 1999, 31 TA). In marrying Robert, Anne replaces God with another object of adoration who offers her the same kind of inoculation from change, time, and death. She recalls, "[A]t nineteen, it seems as natural to be loved by the man with whom you're in love as by doting parents or all-powerful God" (1954, 46; [1956] 1999, 52). Robert is described as one of the greatest minds of his age—devoted to his cause to such a degree that, in many ways, he is indistinguishable from it. Active in the Resistance and faithful to the future revolution, he is at one with his project such that the personal man *is* the political activity into which he throws his energy. The kind of assurance that Robert offers Anne replaces her childhood need for God. Teaching her about politics, eroticism, and professionalism, Robert gives Anne the reassurance against age and death that she had lost in her youth. Explaining the world to her in an orderly manner—where there is purpose and clarity—he provides Anne with a surrogate to replace the authority of her lost God.

Seeking permanence and weight in his books, Robert is a figure like an Aristotelian prime mover. He needs nothing outside of his own self-contained passion, and because of his completeness and self-sufficiency he draws others to him through their desire to be near, like, or useful to him. Anne remembers that when she first fell in love, all she wanted was "to be like him. . . . From chaos, Robert had drawn a full, orderly world, cleansed by the future he was helping to produce. And that world was mine" (1954, 46; [1956] 1999, 52–53). Anne later observes that "Robert always felt fine. . . . He was never cold; it is probable that he produced his own warmth, like the yogis" (1954, 65; [1956] 1999, 72 TA). Ageless, timeless, permanent—Robert is the embodied absolute for many, but especially for Anne. He has so come to replace God for her, that she even ceases to engage in acts of physical love and affection with him and instead sees him as a remote, yet perfect pillar of her existence.

But then something happens. Just as Anne's crisis of adolescence shattered her security and forced her to confront her finitude, so a new crisis emerges when Robert's seeming perfection and counterpoise falter. After signaling a loss of enthusiasm about his literary and autobiographical writing, Robert's placement as the untouchable is scrutinized by Anne. He who had been so unfaltering and whose destiny had been written in the stars now appears to be just another man with doubts, questions, and uncertainties. Anne experiences a shift in her entire worldview as Robert questions his projects:

> Suddenly I saw everything with perfect clarity. The war was ending and a new history was beginning in which nothing was guaranteed. And Robert's future wasn't guaranteed; it was possible for him to stop writing and even for his completed *oeuvre* to be swallowed up into emptiness. (1954, 42; [1956] 1999, 48 TA)

Rather than seeing in this shift a radical opening of the future, Anne experiences tremendous anxiety at the loss of her mainstay. It is particularly important that the dispossession of Robert as a figure of the absolute leads immediately to another confrontation with death for Anne.

In a rare heated exchange with Robert, Anne argues that the living continue to live in spite of their inevitable betrayal of those who have died. Robert confronts her, saying, "We'll also die, you know; that brings us very close them" (1954, 43; [1956] 1999, 49). Just as her adolescent loss of faith forced Anne to confront the reality of her own mortality, her loss of faith in Robert as the buttress of her world forces her to confront the very same thing. And with this disruption of her assurance, Anne suffers the same crisis as in her youth: "I was weeping, and for the first time in twenty years I was alone, alone with my remorse, my fear. I fell asleep and dreamed I was dead" (1954, 43; [1956] 1999, 49). Profoundly alone, isolated from the man to whom she is most intimately tied, Anne again confronts one of the most radically solitary experiences an individual faces: her own death and all the uncertainty, fear, and anxiety that such a thought engenders. With Robert no longer protecting her from her death, Anne falls again into despair.

The monument that was Robert in Anne's eyes proceeds to crumble—a degeneration that is accelerated by an invitation to attend a conference in New York. In trying to decide whether or not to go, she thinks to herself that leaving would be unfavorable to him, whereas she would have never thought so before. But ever since he descended to the ranks of the merely human, Anne looks at him (and as a direct result, herself) differently: "Robert wasn't invulnerable. And suddenly he seemed even fragile" (1954, 173; [1956] 1999, 189).

Anne is decidedly unsuccessful in her somewhat unreflective attempts to find in Robert the absolute that she had lost in her youth. On one level, she recognizes the falseness of using a foreign absolute to give meaning to her life, yet she admits, "[N]o doubt, I haven't completely eliminated my old dreams of the absolute" (1954, 47; [1956] 1999, 53 TA). It is because she has not entirely kept from using the crutch of external absolutes that she must engage in a form of repetition. Beauvoir admits, "One of the principal themes that emerges from my story is that of *repetition* in the sense in which Kierkegaard uses that word: truly to possess something, one must have lost it and found it again" (1992a, 270).[12] In one way, Anne's affair with the American writer Lewis Brogan functions as a repetition of her love of Robert as she finds a new reason to live in her deep love of this new man. However, like the repetition found in Kierkegaardian philosophy, Anne's repetition is not an exact mirroring, but contains within it critical differences from her relationship with Robert. These differences allow Anne to come to terms once and for all with her dependence on foreign absolutes.

There is no question that Lewis is not the same kind of man as Robert. Rather than presenting the persona of stability, timelessness, and dependability, Lewis is constantly in flux—unpredictable, emotional, and erratic. Whereas Robert calmed the nineteen-year-old Anne, twenty years later Lewis excites and awakens the thirty-nine-year-old woman into an emotional delirium. Just as Robert had put the confusion of life into order for Anne, Lewis breaks down the steadiness and routine that she had constructed for herself. Her sexual life over with Robert, Lewis transfigures her into a living being yet again (1954, 319; [1956] 1999, 341). Drawn out of herself, she is transformed by Lewis into a "perfect marvel" (1954, 319; [1956] 1999, 342 TA). In the erotic embrace, Anne is able to overcome (albeit temporarily) the gnawing anxiety of death and age. At its greatest intensity, Anne's love for Lewis places her squarely in the eternity of the present, rather than rushing her forward into her future death. She discovers that in their early lovemaking, "The past, the future, everything that was separating us died at the foot of our bed. Nothing separated us any longer. What a victory! Lewis, complete, was in my arms, and I in his. We wanted nothing else; we had everything, forever" (1954, 328; [1956] 1999, 350). The victory she experiences is the victory over time and finitude. Their love is, for Anne, the absolute truth of existence. But this absolute still remains outside of her as she proceeds to raise Lewis into a position of adulation. And, as do all foreign absolutes, Lewis fails to give Anne the protection against time and death that she desires. Even before Anne expresses the preceding assertion of perfect unity, there is the specter of time, change, and death haunting their relationship.

Echoing the opening confrontation, the book's midpoint is punctuated by the unwelcome but inevitable return of death. Despite the passion and loss of self that Anne experiences in the first throes of her affair with Lewis, insecurity and uncertainty eventually creep in between the lovers. In their second American rendezvous, Anne reunites with Lewis and immediately feels apprehensive about the reliability of their relationship and their feelings for each other. Almost in a state of panic as to the inconsistency of Lewis' mannerisms, Anne is confronted by a striking comment from Lewis in the cab. In a most unexpected manner, Lewis explodes: "Don't you ever want to kill everybody, and yourself, too?" to which Anne replies, "No. . . . And especially not when I'm with you" (1954, 322–23; [1956] 1999, 345). Given Anne's opening and closing encounters with mortality, this is a most significant proclamation from the new absolute in her life. Not allowing Anne to continue with the charade of timelessness and protection against death, Lewis reminds her sharply that nothing—not even the most intense of love affairs—can provide her with the endurance she craves.

Once this turning point has been initiated, the love affair takes a decidedly darker path and the phantom of death is never far away. Even though she overcomes her insecurity to reclaim her intense love for Lewis in their second liaison, he is unable to remain her pillar against decay.[13] As she prepares to leave him for Paris, she notes that her unpacked suitcases carry with them "a smell of love, of death, of disaster. In truth, it was a funeral home, and all those objects were the relics of a dead woman, the sacraments she would carry with her to the hereafter" (1954, 330; [1956] 1999, 352). The reintroduction of death into her life carries over even more starkly back in Paris. Her doubts about Robert intensify, and she finds herself once again meditating on death, which "nibbles at everything" (1954, 336; [1956] 1999, 359).

In fact, in direct denial of the eternity of her rapture with Lewis in America, Anne announces to Robert definitively that "Things are never as important as they seem; they change, they end and above all, when all is said and done, everyone dies" (1954, 337; [1956] 1999, 359). In response, and in a crucial moment of foreshadowing, Robert responds: "One proves that one chooses to believe in life by living; if one sincerely believes that death alone is real, then one should kill oneself" (1954, 337; [1956] 1999, 360 TA). Thus, Robert, echoing and answering Lewis's question to Anne in the New York taxi, forces her to confront her being-toward-death and to decide if, in fact, this is the *only* absolute against which no God, no cause, and certainly no love can shield her. It remains for Anne to determine whether or not the Heideggerian absolute is the only absolute that is truly and authentically one's own.

Mirroring Anne: Paule and the Absolute of Love

Anne's struggle is clearly the struggle of any existent to find value in a world in which truth is neither given nor guaranteed. Thus, her struggle with absolute values through her relationships to God, Robert, and Lewis are illustrative of the human condition in general, which seeks meaning that is given more often than meaning that is created. But Anne's struggle traverses the entirety of the book and requires a shadow story that parallels it to throw it into perspective. This shadow story is manifest in the relationship between Paule Mareuil and her chosen absolute, Henri Perron.[14] Paule's love affair with Henri mirrors and, in many ways, apes Anne's love affair with Lewis, and it is only through Paule that Anne is finally able to overcome her dependence upon the foreign absolute. In short, Anne mediates herself through Paule in order to confront her own inauthenticity and to shatter the final illusion that there can be any other absolute than freedom.

Paule's devotion to Henri serves as the foil to Anne's devotion to Lewis. It has been well noted that Paule is a fictionalized representation of the attitude of the *amoureuse* from Beauvoir's *The Second Sex*.[15] As explained in the first section of this essay, the *amoureuse* is a prime example of an existent who wishes to bury her freedom in an external object that is consequently raised to superhuman status. The greater the object of love, the emptier the lover; that is, the more she loves, the more unhappy and frustrated the *amoureuse* becomes. Beauvoir explains that authentic love assumes the lacks and limitations of the beloved, but "Idolatrous love confers an absolute value to the loved one" ([1949] 1976b, 562). In other words, the beloved becomes the absolute that bestows purpose to the lover's existence. However, the *amoureuse* does not experience an elevation along with her beloved, but rather a diminishing sense of self. Relegating herself to inessential alongside the essential, the woman in love loses any sense of integrity. Beauvoir writes, "There is for her no other way out than to lose herself, body and soul, in him who is designated as the absolute, as the essential" (547). As Beauvoir shows us (through the unfortunate depiction of Paule), the *amoureuse* not only loses herself in the beloved, but can very easily slip into irrationality and insanity.

Even though Henri's story is told through third-person narrative in order to accentuate the public dimension of the novel, the book opens with the private relationship between him and Paule. This positions the reader to see Anne's story (told through first-person narrative in order to highlight the private dimension) as both similar to and distinct from Paule. Immediately, we find that Paule is immersed in Henri. Paule constantly frets over Henri's safety, career, and happiness to the complete detriment of her own. Once a promising singer, she gave up pursuing such a career in order to devote herself more fully to her love of Henri. Dabbling in writing throughout the story, she never devotes herself with any passion and admits that she only engages in such projects for Henri. Paule often makes references to the total unity between her and Henri and the eternal nature of their love. She explains to Anne, "[F]undamentally, we're one single being. I used to feel it often; in fact, I clearly remember my first awareness of it. I was almost terrified; it's strange, you know, to lose yourself absolutely in another. But how rewarding it is when you find the other in yourself" (1954, 178; [1956] 1999, 195). Despite the distance that grows between Henri and Paule throughout the book (leading to their eventual break and Paule's plunge into derangement) Paule continues to insist that nothing is amiss and whatever tensions they have are cosmetic, rather than foundational. Even after their split and Henri's choice of Josette as a partner, Paule insists on continuing to sacrifice herself to her absolute. She tells him in an embarrassing exchange at the office of *L'Espoir*, "There is only you; me, I am nothing" and further down, "The way of self-denial isn't easy. But now I swear to you: I'll ask nothing more for myself. You alone exist, and you can demand anything of me" (1954, 379; [1956] 1999, 404 TA). Paule's self-abjuration leads her to avoid *doing* anything at all. Rather, she locks herself away in her private abode and dreams of her past relationship with Henri and of inflated images of his future success. One might here recall Beauvoir's words in *The Ethics of Ambiguity*, as they are particularly poignant regarding Paule: "There are people who are filled with such horror at the idea of a defeat that they keep themselves from ever doing anything. But no one would dream of considering this gloomy passivity as the triumph of freedom" ([1948] 1997, 29). Such inactivity is not simply a fear of failure, but as Paule's character shows us, it is often rooted in a fear of the ultimate failure of existence: death.

In many ways, Paule's behavior allegorizes the psychic crises that result from the threat and manifestations of death that all people, but especially those who are victims of war and violence, must confront. Paule's character is supposed to inspire revulsion because of her weakness and inability to extract herself from her obsession, but we are also supposed to feel pity and even empathy for her. She too had to face the Occupation and the constant fear that her beloved, who was an active and very public figure of the Resistance, would be killed. As with all of the characters, Paule has been forced to confront death as an immediate threat, rather than as an abstract future event. She portrays the tendency of many, if not most, human beings to avoid rather than endure the anxiety of mortality. Instead of accepting her being-toward-death, Paule engages in constant self-delusions to hide from it.

To return to a crucial point: one of the main motivations to flee into the spirit of seriousness is to find permanence and stability in the face of acute finitude. Not only did Paule face the threat of the German Occupation, but she was once beautiful and talented, and now faces the threat of her own aging with horror. As such, she clings even more tenaciously to Henri, in whose eyes she wants to remain forever young and beautiful. In part, her superficial concerns show her vanity and weakness, but much more significantly they show a very human reaction to the absolute of death. To Paule, it is much better to immerse her freedom in an idealized love object than to confront herself—her limitations, her age, and the inevitability of death.

But Paule is not only a tragic figure, but quite clearly a comic one as well. Her spectacular breakdown shows the supreme irrationality of the serious mentality that places faith in unchanging and eternal absolutes. Even in her greatest swings of passion, Paule's histrionics are transparent to those around her and even to herself. When Robert and Anne finally convince a deranged Paule to check herself into a hospital, she has a moment of clarity about her situation. Catching a look shared between her friends, Paule responds, "'Yes, it's an act (*comédie*),' she said wearily. 'Now I'm beginning to ape myself.' She took off her coat, threw it on a chair. 'That's an act, too. I saw myself, throwing off my coat. . . . I'm always seeing myself!" (1954, 419; [1956] 1999, 446).[16] In the end, Paule's delusion is little more than an intricate act of bad faith, and even in her delirium she recognizes it as nothing more than a very convincing but ultimately self-defeating exhibition. It is this performance that shows Anne the ultimate failure of the project of absolutizing the beloved as a way of immunizing oneself against time.[17]

Beauvoir explains in *Force of Circumstance* that Anne's story struggles with the question: "Is there any possible reconciliation between fidelity and freedom? And if so, at what price?" (1992a, 124). In answering this question, Beauvoir masterfully uses the motif of the mirror in order to show how Anne mediates through Paule so as to come to full awareness and acceptance of her ultimate freedom and responsibility. Whereas Paule unquestioningly transfers her freedom to her love, Anne struggles with this dilemma almost from the very beginning of her affair with Lewis. When trying to decide whether or not she will attend the conference in New York, Anne immediately calls Paule. She thinks to herself, "I am really quite fond of Paule, but at the same time she frightens me a bit. Often, in the morning, I feel a suffocating shadow spread over me, the shadow of all the misfortunes that are awakening, and my first thought is of her" (1954, 174; [1956] 1999, 190). What frightens Anne about Paule is that she implicitly recognizes the possibility of herself becoming Paule—even if this does not become explicit to Anne until well into the throes of her affair with Lewis. In short, Anne requires Paule as the mirror and foil who sets up the picture of the maniacal woman in love that Anne secretly fears and eventually rejects.

Paule—a once beautiful woman—must break from her need to see herself reflected back to her from the outside. She recalls her first dance with Henri ten years earlier at the appropriately named Palais des Mirages, where "everywhere around them they had seen themselves endlessly multiplied in a forest of mirrored columns" (1954, 12; [1956] 1999, 14). Obsessed with how others (especially Henri) see her, Paule is so immersed in the external gaze that she avoids any independent introspection on her career and love choices. Paule's mirage is only broken with the shattering of all of the mirrors in her apartment on the fateful eve of her final breakdown (1954, 418; [1956] 1999, 445). Unlike Paule, who must split from the superficial addiction to her own reflection (and consequently her addiction to her absolute, Henri), Anne believes that she has "always been able to avoid being caught by the snare of mirrors" (1954, 37; [1956] 1999, 43).[18] Beauvoir shows us that where Paule's problems lie in her addiction to how she appears to those outside of her, Anne's problem lies, to a large extent, in her inability to thoroughly reflect upon her own addiction to the absolute. Because she is unwilling to reflect back onto herself, Anne watches Paule's deterioration with an almost detached interest. This invariably leads to the fundamental question that is raised by the relationship between Paule and Anne: given that Anne is both a therapist as well as Paule's best female friend, why doesn't she do more to show Paule what she is doing to herself? Why, in other words, doesn't Anne try to get Paule to snap out of it?

The answer lies in the fact that Anne is not ready to face her own self-delusion about her reliance upon love as a foreign absolute that gives her life meaning. To tell Paule that she is acting, at best, in the spirit of seriousness, and at worst irrationally or insanely, would be to admit that Anne is also somewhat guilty of the same self-deceptions. When discussing Henri's relationship with the beautiful Josette (herself a mirror to Paule, as she is a vain, young, aspiring actress), Paule continues to deny the status of her relationship with Henri. Instead of setting her straight, though, Anne stops herself: "I felt like saying to her, 'Stop lying to yourself!' But what right did I have? And in a way, I even admired her obstinacy" (1954, 342; [1956] 1999, 365). What right, indeed, since Anne was simply waiting until she could return to America to reclaim her new beloved. Anne is unable to challenge Paule, because she is unable to challenge herself. She cannot, in short, look in the mirror. Even in a moment of sincerity, when Paule asks Anne why she, as her closest friend, didn't warn Paule that she was on a foolish and degrading track, Anne waffles. Confronting Anne, Paule retorts, "'I know I'm a little idiotic, but when I understand, I understand" (1954, 345; [1956] 1999, 368).

Anne, however, has yet to understand. Even as Paule sinks deeper into madness, Anne outwardly comforts her: "'You'll get well, you've got to get well. Love isn't everything . . . ,'" and inwardly thinks: "And I knew very well that in her place I would never want to get well and bury my love with my own hands" (1954, 413; [1956] 1999, 439). Anne does not yet realize that she is watching the development of a choice that she herself could make. Preoccupied with the American to whom she will return, transitioning from the absolute that Robert was for her to the absolute that Lewis promises to be, Anne does not want to admit the danger of devotion to external absolutes. And as such, the very lines before her return trip to Chicago are devoted to her thoughts of Paule's fate as she is carried off to the hospital for the analysis that Anne refused to give her. Cynical about Paule's treatment, Anne hints that the treatment will more likely rob Paule of her reason to live, rather than make her "better" in any way. She muses that after rehabilitation, Paule would be like Anne herself, "like millions of others: a woman waiting to die, no longer knowing why she's living" (1954, 420; [1956] 1999, 447).[19] In other words, once Paule's absolute love is taken from her, Anne knows she will be forced to take comfort in the only other absolute, death. This is a most unhappy substitution and one that Anne herself refuses to make until she returns from America and her broken relationship with Lewis to confront love, death, and ultimately, freedom.

Conclusion

Anne's contest with her own dependence upon the absolute provides us with a glimpse into what Beauvoir considers to be an essential component of the human condition. Whether it is because we have all shared the position of childhood or because we often find ourselves in situations defined by rules, laws, and norms that are not of our choosing, we must all confront the artificiality of foreign absolutes by freely choosing to accept or reject them—thereby asserting rather than fleeing our freedom. Only then can we be said to be responsible and mature and therefore, only then can we be said to be free.

Anne's lifelong journey from absolute to absolute is not a solipsistic struggle of a woman against the world. Rather, she mediates through others in her discovery that independence requires *inter*dependence. In this light, we can see that Anne needs the shadow story of Paule as the *amoureuse* in order to see the pitfalls of inauthenticity mirrored back to her. And whereas Paule cannot be said to have taken up her freedom in any kind of meaningful way at the conclusion of the story, we find that Anne's resolution of her dependency must be viewed in a different light than Paule's. Consequently, we cannot properly consider Anne as an illustration of the *amoureuse* as put forth in *The Second Sex*. Instead, Anne is much more accurately characterized as an example of the passionate person from *The Ethics of Ambiguity*. And if we see Anne as exemplary of the passionate attitude, we can see Beauvoir's own suggestion for one way to overcome the spirit of seriousness through an existential conversion. As previously discussed, there is a striking similarity between the passionate person and the *amoureuse* in that both are tragically dependent upon an idealized and absolutized love object. But whereas Beauvoir concludes that the *amoureuse* is at heart a justification for bad faith, the passionate attitude contains the possibility for an ethical conversion.

Beauvoir writes that "a conversion can start within passion itself. The cause of the passionate man's torment is his distance from the object; but he must accept it instead of trying to eliminate it" ([1948] 1997, 66). Clearly, Beauvoir's depiction of the affair between Anne and Lewis provides all the criteria to consider Anne a passionate person. She begins by setting up Lewis as a kind of absolute to replace Robert, who has become frail and human in her eyes. But throughout their love affair, she in fact refuses to give herself completely to him (by refusing to stay in America and leave Robert and her life in Paris completely). In addition, there is a *concrete* distance separating them, as Anne resides in another country than her beloved. In the end, despite her protestations to the contrary,[20] it is through renouncing her love for Lewis as a surrogate absolute that she comes to make an authentic choice. That is, because she accepts the distance between her and Lewis (literally and emotionally), she can encounter death and freedom directly.

At the conclusion of the book, Anne returns to the almost identical discovery conveyed by her opening words: that her death is not her own, and that it is left for others to experience it. Meditating on Paule's vial of prussic acid, she imagines ending her life. Coming full circle, she notes that "once more, as on that day when I was fifteen, when I cried out in fear, death is stalking me" (1954, 575; [1956] 1999, 606). Invoking her initial loss of God, Anne has traversed two substitute absolutes, as different from each other as they could be, yet both temporarily fulfilling her desire to have an extrinsic absolute that puts her universe in place and gives her life meaning.

Yet, Anne is not the same person that she was years earlier at the beginning of the story. She has learned multiple lessons that have lead up to her pivotal moment of choice. For one, she is able to remove the specter of death as the only true absolute against which all else is meaningless. Holding the vial of prussic acid in her hand, she thinks, "Death has won; death is now the only truth. A single move and that truth will become eternal" (1954, 577–78; [1956] 1999, 609). But she does not kill herself, thus negating the assertion that the only truth, the only absolute, is the lonely desert of the Heideggerian being-toward-death.

Another step that Anne makes is that she has learned that no matter how isolated she feels in her confrontation with loss, she is interconnected with those around her. Imagining her husband, daughter, and lover experiencing her suicide, she concludes with finality that although she would die alone, the experience of her death would fall on others who would undergo it with horror and feelings of profound betrayal. Thus, Anne accepts that "My death does not belong to me" (1954, 578; [1956] 1999, 610). Reminiscent of *The Ethics of Ambiguity* where Beauvoir emphasizes that freedom is not isolated but is dependent upon the interweaving of other free projects, Anne is forced to recognize that her actions ripple out into and are defined by the world of others.

But the discovery of her interconnection is contingent upon the much deeper discovery. Anne discovers the only true absolute that can lead to an authentically lived existence—not God, nor love, nor even death, but freedom. In her darkest confrontation with suicide, Anne finally breaks with the foreign absolute: "Dead the little girl who believed in paradise, dead the young girl who thought immortal the books, the ideas and the man she loved, dead the young woman who walked overwhelmed in a world promised to happiness, dead the woman in love (*amoureuse*) who woke up laughing in Lewis's arms" (1954, 577; [1956] 1999, 608 TA). In short, dead are the absolutes that had been the signposts and crutches of her life.

Unlike Paule who sits among the shattered glass of her identity, Anne courageously faces her reflection in her moment of deepest despair. With the final dismissal of all foreign absolutes (even the most personal absolute of death itself) Anne is able to look at herself in the mirror and discover her freedom: "For a long time, I sat before the mirror, looking at my face, the face of a survivor" (1954, 578; [1956] 1999, 609). As Beauvoir argues in *Pyrrhus et Cinéas*, death is not the only true absolute, because death is never really here. It belongs to others (such as Anne's family and friends) to experience it. What *is* here is life, and what is human life if not freedom? Echoing Robert's prophetic words that to live is to *choose* life, Anne chooses not to kill herself. And this choice is Anne's epiphany at the conclusion of the book: that she must choose life over suicide and, as such, accept her absolute freedom and responsibility.

Does this mean that the book has a happy ending? Most assuredly no. But Beauvoir has never made the equation of freedom with happiness. As she explains in *The Second Sex*, "[W]hat interests us about the fortunes of the individual we do not define in terms of happiness, but in terms of liberty" ([1949] 1976a, 32). The authentic assumption of freedom does not necessarily make one happy, but Beauvoir hints that it is the precondition for any real sense of happiness. Thus, when Anne concludes the novel with the words: "Who knows? Perhaps one day I'll be happy again. Who knows?" (1954, 579; [1956] 1999, 610) we are not to read it as a depressing resignation, but as a hopeful opening to future possibilities. When Anne elects not to kill herself despite her brokenhearted loneliness and the extreme difficulty of taking responsibility for her life, she chooses freedom over all other absolutes.

Notes

1. This is not to ignore the complexities of Beauvoir's treatment of freedom, which differs, for example, from Sartre's autonomous agent in his early metaphysics. There is much that can be said about Beauvoir's treatment of *situated* freedom—what Sonia Kruks defines as "an embodied consciousness, a socially situated and conditioned freedom" (Kruks 1995, 82). However, in this paper I begin from the assumption that all freedom is situated and that choice is always conditioned by certain factical considerations.

2. In finding an intricate philosophical critique of absolutism in *The Mandarins*, I argue against those who do not find any philosophy in this novel. For example, Maryse Choisy writes, "I know well that Mme de Beauvoir is a philosopher. Nevertheless, I have read and reread with a sustained attention, and I have not found a shadow of philosophy in *The Mandarins*" (Choisy 1954, 522; translation my own).

3. Specifically, she points out how woman is "the sex" absolutely, whereas man is the absolute subject. Both positions are harmful, both are untrue, and both require a faith in the primacy of the absolute over the living existent. All citations from *The Second Sex* are my own translations from the original French.

4. All translations from *Pyrrhus et Cinéas* are my own.

5. The division between the subject and the goal of action recalls the Marxist discussion of fetishization in which the object of labor, through its alienation from the laborer, seems to take on an exaggerated and more real existence than the one who produced it.

6. This is not to deny that there are, as Kruks calls them, "degrees, or gradations, of freedom" such that not every existent can make a choice at any moment to authentically choose their actions (Kruks 1995, 84). Certainly, the woman in love is a tragic figure precisely because her situation as a woman in the patriarchy is such that she is left little choice but to set up her beloved as an absolute project. However, Beauvoir always maintains that one can find a way out of the hardened facticity of a situation given the right circumstances. This theme is clear in the stories of Anne and Paule, who make dramatically different choices regarding their positions as women in love.

7. Karen Vintges emphasizes Beauvoir's use of Heidegger's existential-phenomenological method to describe the philosophical import of everyday life (Vintges 1996, 142–43). Eva Gothlin argues that *Dasein*, *Erschlossenheit* (disclosedness), and *Mitsein* (being-with-others) are the foundation of Beauvoir's notion of ambiguity (Lundgren-Gothlin 1996, 216; Gothlin 1999, 84). Others, such as Debra Bergoffen and Nancy Bauer, have taken up the controversial usage of *Mitsein* specifically, with Bergoffen arguing that Beauvoir's usage of the term is "brief, complex, and troublesome" (Bergoffen 1997, 168). Bauer, taking note of all the Heideggerian nomenclature employed by Beauvoir, argues the opposite point, claiming that Beauvoir's utilization of *Mitsein* has been misunderstood and is in fact indicative of her own belief that human beings are *not* originally held together by a primordial interconnectedness (Bauer 2001a, 144).

8. Lundgren-Gothlin (1996) and Bauer (2001b) both discuss the role that the fear of death has on Beauvoir's philosophy, but primarily in its relationship to Hegel, not Heidegger.

9. This is why Beauvoir concludes the book by turning, as she does throughout the text, to Hegel's philosophy. Beauvoir writes, "[W]hat it [Hegel's system] had offered me, under a show of the infinite, was the consolations of death; and I again wanted to live in the midst of living men" ([1948] 1997, 158). Thus, the text opens and closes with a call for existents to face, rather than flee, death in order to live a truly free life.

10. I have included both the French and English citations from *The Mandarins*. Where necessary, I have altered the English translation and denoted the change by TA.

11. Beauvoir recounts her own traumatic confrontation with death as a girl in *Memoirs of a Dutiful Daughter*. There she recalls, "I made another discovery. One afternoon, in Paris, I realized that I was condemned to death. I was alone in the house and I did not attempt to control my despair: I screamed and tore at the red carpet" ([1963] 1986, 138).

12. See also Terry Keefe (1983, 196).

13. Regarding the inevitable breakdown of Lewis and Anne's love, Keefe writes, "[A]lthough Anne's American adventure actually ends as it does because Brogan is unable to tolerate the situation, it could not in any case have provided her with any more than temporary relief from her deep preoccupation with aging, decline, suffering and death" (1983, 185).

14. Beauvoir tells us in *The Prime of Life* that she deliberately set up Paule to be Anne's foil (1966, 412). As Keefe observes, "The ways in which Anne and Paule both invest too much of themselves are entirely different but broadly complementary" (Keefe 1983, 191–92).

15. For example, Elizabeth Fallaize writes that "Paule is the complete example of *The Second Sex*'s analysis of the *amoureuse* (the woman who makes a cult of love) who tries to attain her own being vicariously through that of the loved one" (Fallaize [1988] 1990, 109). Sally Scholz concurs, claiming that exactly like the *amoureuse* in *The Second Sex*, "Paule abdicates herself and her independence to be Henri's mistress. When he stops loving her, she turns to self-loathing" (Scholz 2000, 75).

16. In the final stages of her collapse, Paule fittingly tacks a sheet of paper to her door with the phrase "The Society Ape" [Le singe mondain] scribbled on it (Beauvoir 1954, 417; [1956] 1999, 444).

17. This is not to say that Anne does not have moments of recognition about the pitfalls of love without Paule's histrionics, such as when she returns to Lewis the second time and they travel to Mexico: "But suddenly I was afraid: would I be punished some day for having dared to love without giving my whole life?" (1954, 425; [1956] 1999, 452). However, it is crucial to keep in mind that most of Anne's revelations concerning the dangers of self-abdicating love *follow* Paule's final breakdown.

18. A somewhat disingenuous claim, given that Anne immediately goes on to note that she cannot but help to be drawn into the "vertiginous" [vertigineux] looks of others who judge her from the outside (1954, 37; [1956] 1999, 43).

19. Beauvoir opens the very next section with Anne telling herself that back in Chicago, "I would once more rediscover myself in the body of a woman in love (*une femme amoureuse*), a woman loved" (1954, 420; [1956] 1999, 447). The mixture of love, death, and absolutism is unavoidable in this key transition.

20. Speaking of her despair, Anne asserts, "It isn't because of Lewis. It's been two weeks since the huge orchid faded, since I threw it away, a closed affair" (1954, 575; [1956] 1999, 606 TA).

Works Cited

Bauer, Nancy. 2001a. Being-with as being-against: Heidegger meets Hegel in *The second sex*. *Continental Philosophy Review* 34:129–49.

———. 2001b. *Simone de Beauvoir, philosophy and feminism*. New York: Columbia University Press.

Beauvoir, Simone de. 1944. *Pyrrhus et Cinéas*. Paris: Gallimard.

———. [1948] 1997. *The ethics of ambiguity*. Translated by Bernard Frechtman. Reprint, Secaucus, N.J.: Citadel Press. (An English translation of *Pour une morale de l'ambiguité*, published by Gallimard in 1947.)

———. [1949] 1976a. *Le deuxième sexe*. Vol. 1. Reprint, Paris: Gallimard.

———. [1949] 1976b. *Le deuxième sexe*. Vol. 2. Reprint, Paris: Gallimard.

———. 1954. *Les mandarins*. Paris: Gallimard.

———. [1956] 1999. *The mandarins*. Translated by Leonard M. Friedman. Reprint, New York: W.W. Norton & Company.

———. [1963] 1986. *Memoirs of a dutiful daughter*. Translated by James Kirkup. Reprint, Middlesex, England: Penguin Books. (An English translation of *Memoirs d'une jeune fille rangée*, published by Gallimard in 1958.)

———. 1966. *The prime of life*. Translated by Peter Green. New York: Lancer Books. (An English translation of *La force de l'âge*, published by Gallimard in 1960.)

———. [1972] 1996. *The coming of age*. Translated by Patrick O'Brian. Reprint, New York: W. W. Norton & Company. (An English translation of *La vieillesse*, published by Gallimard in 1970.)

———. 1992a. *The force of circumstance*. vol. 1, *After the War, 1944–1952*. Translated by Richard Howard. New York: Paragon House. (An English translation of *La force des choses*, published by Gallimard in 1963.)

———. 1992b. *The force of circumstance*. vol. 2, *Hard Times, 1952–1962*. Translated by Richard Howard. New York: Paragon House. (An English translation of *La force des choses*, published by Gallimard in 1963.)

Bergoffen, Debra. 1997. *The philosophy of Simone de Beauvoir: Gendered phenomenologies, erotic generosities*. New York: State University of New York Press.

Choisy, Maryse. 1954. Psychologie, sociologie et syntaxe des *Mandarins*. *Psyche* (Paris) 9, no. 95 (September): 521–33.

Fallaize, Elizabeth. [1988] 1990. *The novels of Simone de Beauvoir*. London: Routledge.

Gothlin, Eva. 1999. Simone de Beauvoir's notion of appeal, desire, and ambiguity and their relationship to Jean-Paul Sartre's notion of appeal and desire. *Hypatia* 14, no. 4 (Fall): 83–95.

Heidegger, Martin. 1996. *Being and time*. Translated by Joan Stambaugh. Albany: State University of New York Press. (An English translation of *Sein und Zeit*, published by Max Niemeyer Verlag in 1953.)

Keefe, Terry. 1983. *Simone de Beauvoir: A study of her writings*. Totowa, N.J.: Barnes and Noble Books.

Kruks, Sonia. 1995. Simone de Beauvoir: Teaching Sartre about freedom. In *Feminist interpretations of Simone de Beauvoir*, edited by Margaret A. Simons. University Park: Pennsylvania State University Press.

Lundgren-Gothlin, Eva. 1996. *Sex and existence: Simone de Beauvoir's "The second sex."* Translated by Linda Schenck. Hanover, N.H.: Wesleyan University Press.
Scholz, Sally J. 2000. *On de Beauvoir.* Belmont, Calif.: Wadsworth.
Vintges, Karen. 1996. *Philosophy as passion: The thinking of Simone de Beauvoir.* Translated by Anne Lavelle. Bloomington: Indiana University Press.

Chapter 8

Love, Theory, and Politics

Critical Trinities in Simone de Beauvoir's The Mandarins

Jen McWeeny

Simone de Beauvoir's *The Mandarins* (1999b), first published in 1954, is a story of the personal, theoretical, and political trinities that characterize a group of intellectuals in post–World War II France. The central trinity of the novel is that comprised of its two narrators (Anne Dubreuilh and Henri Perron) and the character that each sees herself or himself in relation to—namely, Robert Dubreuilh. This triadic structure is repeated over and over again in the interpersonal relationships of the novel's characters, in the theoretical questions that dominate the characters' thoughts, and in the political poles that loom behind the plot of the story. For example, there are more than seven love triangles mentioned in *The Mandarins*, the most prominent of which is the triangle of Anne, Robert, and Lewis Brogan. In addition, the backdrop of World War II fuels the plot's philosophical problem of trying to reconcile one's abstract intellectual commitments with one's political practice and personal relationships. Furthermore, on a political level, *The Mandarins* tells a tale of the opposition between Soviet communism and American capitalism from the perspective of French socialism.

The trinities in *The Mandarins* are "critical" trinities because Beauvoir's evocations of them serve to form an image of the movement of life, theory, and history that stands in critical juxtaposition to the movement characterized by Hegel's master-slave dialectic and progression of history.[1] In her philosophical works, Beauvoir criticizes Hegel for excluding woman from the dialectic (1989, 435; 1949, 2:235),[2] for reducing woman to a mere negation of man (1989, xxi), for ignoring the ways in which one's situation influences the possibilities for the expression of one's subjectivity (1997, 84), and for his optimistic notion that an individual is a mere moment of a unified history (1962a, 266).[3] These criticisms raise the question of whether Hegel's theory of interpersonal and historical relationships, which also appears to possess a triadic structure, can allow for the separateness and uniqueness of the three terms while situating them within a framework that is exclusive, based on mirrored opposition, inattentive to differing subjectivities, and universalizing. Since the image of relationships that derives from the trinities of *The Mandarins* does not fall prey to these criticisms, one could take this image as a basis for formulating the beginnings of a theory of personal, conceptual, and historical relationships that is an alternative to that of Hegel. The idea that such a theory can emerge out of *The Mandarins* is a sensible one in light of the fact that in her literary writing Beauvoir depicts women, not as she would want them to be, but as she saw them (Beauvoir 1987, 278). As such, the female characters of *The Mandarins* are literary answers to the questions that drive the discourse of *The Second Sex*: "What place has humanity made for this portion of itself [woman] which, while included within it, is defined as the Other? What rights have been conceded to it? How have men defined it?" (1989, 65). Thus, the trinities in *The Mandarins* are "critical" in a second sense of the word in that they are essential for understanding Beauvoir's theories as presented in *The Second Sex*.[4] This understanding in turn uncovers the need for theories, practices, and lives that are capable of creating freedom in the midst of oppression. Such a creation depends upon recognizing the interplay between the personal, the theoretical, and the political that is exemplified in Beauvoir's writing. As she herself intimates, "I see myself reflected no less in *The Second Sex* than in *The Mandarins*, and vice versa" (1987, 332).

The Gifts, Withdrawals, and Solitudes of Love

Nearly all of the characters in *The Mandarins* partake in one or more love triangles throughout the course of the novel. The most prominent love triangles are those that are in part constituted by each of the two focal characters—namely, those of Anne, Robert, and Lewis, and of Henri, Paule, and Nadine. The plot also consists in the love triangles between Nadine, Lambert, and their dead lovers (Nadine, Lambert, and Diego; and Nadine, Lambert, and Rosa), of the love triangle between Nadine, Lambert, and Henri, and of the love triangle between Henri, Paule, and Josette. Personal relationships that take the form of a trio are relationships in which each individual must inevitably view the couples she or he is involved in from the perspective of an outside observer. The adoption of this third-party perspective makes it impossible for one to see an Other as simply a negative or positive reflection of oneself and for one to see oneself as a mere reflection of an Other.[5] As a result, triadic personal relationships are not constituted by oppositional struggles for recognition, but by gifts, withdrawals, and realizations of absolute separateness.

The relationships that comprise the amorous trinities of *The Mandarins* are not oppositional because a relation between three parties cannot be theorized in terms of simple negations. In *The Second Sex*, Beauvoir claims that the master-slave dialectic does not involve true opposition because, within the dialectic, the Other is a mere negative reflection of the Self and thus neither term confronts a distinct freedom (1989, 64–65). Judith Butler rightly summarizes Beauvoir's critique as follows: "The self-asserting 'man' whose self-definition requires a hierarchical contrast with an 'Other' does not provide a model of true autonomy, for she [Beauvoir] points out the bad faith of his designs, i.e. that the 'Other' is, in every case, his own alienated self" (1998, 37). Within a trio, the conflation of the Other and the Self that hinders true autonomy is impossible because each member is never able to look at the Others from the confines of her or his own perspective and thus cannot project her or his own negative Self onto that Other. Lewis comes to this painful realization when Anne refuses to forgo her life in Paris for the sake of giving herself entirely to him. Although Anne tells him "I don't love you any less because other things mean something to me" (Beauvoir 1999b, 462), Lewis's inevitable imaginings of Anne's separateness and of her other life without him eventually cause him to be unable to love her. The ever-present image of France and Robert hinders Lewis's capacity to look at Anne and see his own reflection. By loving Lewis for three months a year, Anne avoids an identity that is constructed solely in relation to one man. In doing so, she follows one of the liberatory proposals Beauvoir makes in *The Second Sex*: "To emancipate woman is to refuse to confine her to the relations she bears to man, not to deny them to her; let her have her own independent existence and she will continue none the less to exist for him also: mutually recognizing each other as subject, each will yet remain for the other an *other*" (1989, 731). However, Lewis's inability to love Anne within the context of the type of reciprocity proposed in *The Second Sex* implies that love is not yet a space where woman is recognized as an autonomous subject with her own unique desires.

Through a disruption of one's capacity to see the Other in the terms of the Self, triadic relations make one aware of one's own unavoidable separateness from other people and of the impossibility of a higher union. According to Beauvoir, this separateness is an ontological fact of the human condition that Hegel's dialectic fails to acknowledge. In *Pyrrhus et Cinéas* Beauvoir writes, "In vain Hegel declares that individuality is only a moment of becoming universal. . . . [Man's] very effort to pull himself up from the earth only digs him his place there" (1962a, 266; my translation). Later in the essay, Beauvoir claims that a "higher reconciliation" of opposed freedoms is not possible, because there can be no free actions unless humanity is "a discontinuous succession of free men who are irremediably isolated by their subjectivity" (285; my translation). Beauvoir summarizes her view when she writes, "Freedoms are neither unified nor opposed, they are separated" (282; my translation).[6] For Beauvoir, the acknowledgment that one is essentially separate from others serves as the impetus for action and responsibility, because it is a recognition that one's life does not derive its meaning from that which stands outside of it. Anne's entrance into a love triangle denies her an identity that can be derived from mirrored opposition. Thus, Anne must recognize herself as standing alone and as such, she realizes her responsibility for constructing her own identity. Similarly, Nadine's birth, by changing the couple of Anne and Robert to a familial trio, forces Anne to acknowledge her separateness from Robert. Anne narrates, "I hadn't wanted her [Nadine]; it was Robert who wanted to have a child right away. I've always held it against Nadine that she upset my life alone with Robert. I loved Robert too much. . . ." (Beauvoir 1999b, 69). Likewise, Henri's love for Josette is what finally makes Paule realize that he no longer loves her and that she is interminably alone. Anne's realizations of separateness that take place in the personal sphere carry over into her political thoughts as well. While trying to calculate the worth of her political action in terms of numbers of lives at stake, Anne concludes, "One man plus one man doesn't make two men; it will forever make one plus one" (359).

If freedoms are neither unified nor opposed, but separated, as Beauvoir suggests, then what is the impetus for human relationships? In short, any connections between individuals must be chosen and continuously sustained. For Beauvoir, not only is it possible for separate consciousnesses to exist in reciprocity where each recognizes the Other as Other, but their very independence from each other is the condition of reciprocal recognition (1989, 731). On this view, to love someone is, at base, a choice, not an inevitable desire for recognition. Thus, the character of a relationship is determined by the attitudes of its individual members; a relationship never has a character all on its own. These attitudes may change as the situation of the individual changes. In the absence of inevitable unifying or opposing forces, human relationships exist and decay as a result of gifts and withdrawals. Anne begins to realize this character of relationships after the end of her affair with Lewis: ". . . I had never understood that love is always undeserved. Lewis had loved me without any valid reason; it hadn't surprised me. Now, he no longer loved me; neither was that surprising, it was even very natural" (1999b, 542). Love triangles, by extracting one from the mirroring perspectives of a couple, are reminders that human relationships exist for no a priori reasons. The notion that relationships and their members are constituted by chosen gifts and withdrawals runs in direct contrast to Lewis's Hegelian notion of manhood. For him, a man is "above all, someone who doesn't resign himself to things, someone who has desires and who fights to satisfy them" (460). For Beauvoir, a lover does not fight people or things to satisfy her or his desires because in those situations where two people "think they confront one another, it is really against the self that each one struggles" (1989, 728). Instead, a lover must assume the ambiguities of her or his situation. In other words, a lover should not fight to define and manipulate the other or to extract love from the other. In a relationship of reciprocal recognition, each "remain[s] for the other an other" (731) by respecting the gifts and withdrawals that the other chooses.

The triadic image of relationships presented in *The Mandarins* is not just characteristic of Beauvoir's fictional romances. When pondered in the context of their own non-monogamous yet committed "arrangement," it is no wonder that Beauvoir discusses how she and Jean-Paul Sartre were both repeatedly drawn to the question of how a third term would affect a binary relation (1962b, 286–313). One of the times in which Beauvoir and Sartre were faced with difficulties because of their arrangement was during Beauvoir's affair with Nelson Algren, which is recounted "very approximately" in *The Mandarins* through the relationship of Anne and Lewis (1987, 133–35). However, the "third party" who came closest to dissolving Beauvoir and Sartre's companionship was one of Beauvoir's students, Olga Kosakievicz. Both Beauvoir and Sartre got along so well with Olga that after they met her, they resolved that "from now on we would be a trio and not a couple" (Beauvoir 1962b, 291).

Beauvoir's first novel, *She Came to Stay* (1999a), which relates many of her experiences as a member of the trio she comprised with Sartre and Olga, is in many ways a premonition of the literary and philosophical themes put forth in *The Mandarins*.[7] In her autobiography, Beauvoir claims that *She Came to Stay* is, in part, her attempt to describe her own threatening realizations, which resulted from her experiences in the trio, that people are unavoidably separate individuals (1962b, 313) and that other people have "rational awareness" that is capable of passing judgment (381). *She Came to Stay* is frequently interpreted as a psychological account of the relationship between Françoise and Xavière that takes the form of a literary depiction of the novel's epigraph from Hegel: "Each conscience seeks the death of the other."[8] However, *She Came to Stay* is not so much the story of two opposed consciousnesses as it is the story of the trio of Françoise, Pierre, and Xavière. Structurally, the novel repeats its triadic theme through its trio of narrators (Françoise, Gerbert, and Elizabeth), its trio of female characters (Françoise, Elizabeth, and Xavière), and its second romantic trio (Françoise, Gerbert, and Xavière). In particular, *She Came to Stay* is a description of the ways in which Xavière (the third party, the "X," the invited stranger) mediates the consuming relationship between Françoise and Pierre so as to enable Françoise to come to her own subjectivity. At the start of *She Came to Stay* Pierre tells Françoise, "You and I are simply one. . . . Neither of us can be defined without the other" (1999a, 25). In contrast, following Xavière's death, the final lines of the novel run, "[N]ow nothing separated her [Françoise] from herself. She had chosen at last. She had chosen herself" (1999a, 404). The interposition of a third party between Françoise and Pierre, a situation that is ultimately rendered eternal through Françoise's crime, allows not only the character of Françoise but also Beauvoir herself to arrive at subjectivity. Beauvoir thus reflects on the ending of *She Came to Stay*: "[A]bove all, by releasing Françoise, through the agency of a crime, from the dependent position in which her love for Pierre kept her, I regained my own personal autonomy" (1962b, 410). Hence, in Beauvoir's own life and in her novels, the third party encourages one to observe one's relationships from a different point of view. This fresh observation disrupts identities based on mirrored opposition or visions of an inevitable synthesis, and as a result serves as the basis for freedom and subjectivity.

The Problem of Reconciling Theoretical, Political, and Personal Commitments

The triadic structure of the personal relationships in *The Mandarins* is repeated in the philosophical problem that each of the characters must solve: How does one reconcile one's abstract intellectual commitments, one's political practice, and one's personal life? This theoretical trinity is rendered concrete in the three character types—namely, lover, intellectual, and activist—that all of the novel's characters move between. The very difficulties that the characters have with separating their intellectual, political, and personal commitments disrupt the notion that these spheres can be separated at all. This inseparability is exemplified most by the fact that Anne's three lovers in the novel (Scriassine, a Russian journalist; Robert, a French intellectual; and Lewis, an American novelist) easily map onto the political and theoretical poles of the novel. The content of what her lovers write, combined with the place that these lovers occupy in Anne's own life, suggests that Scriassine symbolizes the Soviet Union and political practice, Robert symbolizes France and intellectual pursuits, and Lewis symbolizes the United States and the sphere of personal, intimate, bodily relationships. The plot of *The Mandarins* is driven by the ways in which the climate of postwar France makes manifest the mounting incompatibility of these three spheres, and thus, the plot is also driven by a growing need to reconcile them.

Scriassine, who explains to Anne that because he is an outsider he is able to observe the situation of French intellectuals with more clarity than they are able to observe themselves (1999b, 38), is prescient of this need at the start of the novel.[9] From his unique perspective, Scriassine tells Anne, "French intellectuals are facing an impasse. It's their turn now. Their art, their philosophies can continue to have meaning only within the framework of a certain kind of civilization. And if they want to save that civilization, they'll have no time or energy left over to give to art or philosophy" (39). Scriassine's words highlight how the presence of war disturbs and occupies one's identity by placing one's abstract, symbolic pursuits in conflict with one's own existence and the existence of particular others. In response to this occupation, French intellectuals must construct an identity that retains meaning in the midst of this conflict. Scriassine tells Anne that the people of Russia, Austria, and Germany have already experienced the struggle that ensues from the incompatibility of theoretical, political, and interpersonal spheres. He confesses that although he would like to have written literary works, writing anything but factual accounts of political regimes was "out of the question," because "to continue to take an interest in things cultural in the face of Stalin and Hitler, you have to have one hell of a humanistic tradition behind you" (39). However, Scriassine's turn to political practice is not capable of ameliorating the intellectual's impasse, because this impasse is not simply a result of the conflict between the pursuit of art and political participation; it is also a result of the conflict between either of these activities and particular human lives. Lambert points out the similarities between intellectual and political endeavors when he tells Henri, "In politics, all you're concerned with are abstract things that don't exist—the future, masses of people. But what is really concrete is the actual present moment, and people as separate and single individuals" (147). In other words, one must remember, like Anne does, that what is most horrifying about Stalin and Hitler is neither their political regimes nor the theories that found them, but rather that they have murdered concrete people like Rosa and Diego.

The character who struggles most explicitly with the philosophical problem of reconciling intellectual commitments, political practice, and particular lives is Henri, who, as the head of the independent journal *L'Espoir*, is faced with many difficult decisions.[10] Henri, Robert, and Luc constitute the trio of socialist journalists who run *L'Espoir* and who struggle with the question of whether or not to ally their paper with the Communist Party in order to keep it going. They also struggle with the decision of whether or not to print a story about the existence of communist-run concentration camps, because they fear that the capacity of the Communist Party to counter capitalism, which they see as the greater of two evils, will be weakened. Both decisions raise the philosophical problem that Scriassine articulates at the beginning of the novel of whether one should compromise one's abstract intellectual and moral commitments for the sake of influencing the end result of a particular political situation. And, like Scriassine, Henri sees the problem as dialectical in structure; he desires to quell the tension between his theories and the inevitability of political practice. Likewise, Vincent and Sézenac also situate their struggles within a dialectic of theory and practice. But, as foils to Henri and Robert, the two younger men privilege action over theory with their involvement in *épuration* activities.[11] While Vincent is a man of action who kills ex-collaborators and uses their money to fund socialist journals, Henri refuses to accept Vincent's money and insists that one must be true to one's theoretical commitments despite the consequences of that allegiance. However, both Henri and Vincent cannot see beyond the dialectical tension between theory and political practice to the invisible third term that is a particular human life. Because of this blindness, neither extreme of killing, on the one hand, or defending abstract values, on the other, provides a solution to the problem.

Alternatively, the female characters of *The Mandarins* do not see their own psychological struggles as constituted by the opposition between abstract theory and political practice, because their womanly situations do not allow them access to this dialectical construction. Anne, Paule, and Nadine exist almost entirely within the private, personal sphere. Most importantly, none of the female characters write. Paule, who was once a well-known singer, no longer works and puts all of her energy into her relationship with Henri. Nadine, who had no desire to work at the start of the novel, eventually becomes a secretary for her father and spends most of her time moving in and out of romantic relationships. The one time in the novel when Nadine does attempt to be of some public consequence by helping Vincent with an *épuration* mission, she fails miserably because she is unable to walk a significant distance, and Anne ends up having to retrieve her from a roadside ditch in the middle of the night (Beauvoir 1999b, 215–16). Likewise, Anne's attempt to enter into the public realm through work is an ironic one, because her work as a psychoanalyst entails that she develop and sort through personal relationships. Even her intellectual conversations are personal in that she comes to the defense of Robert rather than to the defense of an abstract intellectual theory or political practice (39).

The fact that the female characters in *The Mandarins* inhabit the private sphere of personal relationships echoes Beauvoir's criticism that Hegel's dialectic lacks a place for woman. Eva Lundgren-Gothlin describes this understanding as it is articulated in *The Second Sex* when she writes, "Passages in the *Phenomenology of Spirit* lead the reader to conclude that women are not conceived of as participants in the struggle for recognition. Women belong to the private sphere, and the question of their self-consciousness is of no interest to Hegel" (1996, 72). By relegating woman to the private sphere and emphasizing the importance of man's move to the public sphere, Hegel mistakenly conflates woman's struggle for recognition with that of man (Beauvoir 1989, 64–65) in the same way that Paule mistakenly conflates her own identity with that of Henri. In attending to the lives of particular women, who are positioned outside of the dialectical struggle that seeks to reconcile theory and political practice, Beauvoir sheds light on the fact that human relationships move with more complexity and ambiguity than the movement of Hegelian thesis, antithesis, and synthesis. *The Mandarins* is a novel that describes, with detailed attention, the lives of outsiders. Because it is an attempt to articulate the human particularities and ambiguities that exceed words and current intellectual theories, *The Mandarins* can be likened to the postwar party in its opening scene. As Anne tells Robert: "[W]e went to a very peculiar party tonight, with all the dead who weren't there" (1999b, 49). Anne then rejects Robert's suggestion that the deaths of those killed in the war served some purpose when she states, "It's fine for the living, this system by which everything leads to something else. But the dead stay dead and we're constantly betraying them; they don't lead to anything" (49). To avoid this betrayal, one must evoke those particular people who, like casualties of war, elude purposeful, theoretical, and idealized frameworks of comprehension. In this spirit, Beauvoir remarks that she made none of her female characters "feminist heroines," because she sought to represent, not the exceptions of her sex, but women as she saw them (1987, 278).

The male characters' blindness toward the notion that the impasse between intellectual theories and political practice must be reconciled with particular human lives mirrors the failure of Hegel's dialectic to describe the role of woman as involved in the struggle for recognition. Just as acknowledging woman is able to demystify Hegel's dialectical struggles for recognition, Anne's position outside of the theoretical dialectic between theory and practice renders her able to diagnose the problem in a way that the men who are struggling with it are unable to see. In *Force of Circumstance*, Beauvoir explains that she self-consciously placed Anne in the roles of narrator and witness to the relationship between Robert and Henri (1987, 273). Beauvoir writes, "Anne, being profoundly involved in the conflicts I was recounting while remaining outside them, envisaged them from an entirely different point of view than either Dubreuilh or Henri" (276). As witness, Anne situates a public, seemingly dialectical struggle in terms of personal contexts. Her viewpoint is an embodiment of the idea that the struggle between theory and political practice inevitably takes place upon a field of personal, private relationships. Man to man dialectics and dialectics of ideas that apply only to the public, masculine sphere overlay and obscure the womanly realm of personal relationships—just as in *The Mandarins*, Henri and Robert's theoretical problems overlay and obscure the particular lives of individuals who are suffering in postwar Europe. Nadine enacts this critique of male intellectuals when she fumes at Henri, "How can anyone love an intellectual! You have a set of scales where your heart should be and a little brain at the tip of your pecker. And fundamentally . . . you're all just a bunch of fascists. . . . You never treat people as equals; you deal with them according to the dictates of your little consciences. Your generosity is simply imperialism, and your impartiality, conceit" (1999b, 172). Woman, in particular, is adversely affected by the dangers of theoretical and political abstractions. The conflation of woman with an abstract category, especially one that is defined by man, masks her very particularity as a being who "incarnates no stable concept" (1989, 143) and, hence, enables sexist oppression. Volange makes the unique relationship between woman and abstraction explicit when he drunkenly tells Henri, "Women are part of your humanism. . . . You screw them just like any other man" (1999b, 391). Volange's words recognize the irony of humanism: in fighting for the abstract freedom of all human beings the particular situations of certain social groups are rendered invisible and thus their political needs are obscured as well.

Sartre's discussion of the third party in the *Critique of Dialectical Reason* (1978) also focuses on the role of an invisible third in relation to the dialectic.[12] Sartre situates his discussion of the third within his personal experience of watching two manual laborers working on opposing sides of the same fence from his hotel while on holiday. On his view, only a third party can give meaning to the reciprocity of two dialectical terms. Sartre claims that "it is only the third party in fact who can, through mediation, show *the equivalence* of the goods exchanged and consequently of the successive acts" (1978, 108). This reciprocity is actualized by the third party, because only an observer would be capable of putting the two terms in objective comparison. Because the third party is able to situate dialectical relations within a given social context, it is capable of disclosing the interactions between individuals and the ways in which the surrounding society and history shape those individuals. Sartre makes this point clear when he claims, "A binary formation, as the immediate relation of man to man, is the necessary ground of any ternary relation; but conversely, a ternary relation, as the mediation of man amongst men, is the basis on which reciprocity becomes aware of itself as a reciprocal connection" (109). In sum, for Sartre the third party, like the female characters of *The Mandarins*, situates various dialectical struggles within their social and historical contexts and points to that which defines or eludes the boundaries of those struggles.

The conclusion of *The Mandarins* implies that the philosophical problem of reconciling intellectual, political, and personal commitments has been temporarily resolved by the male character's movement toward the personal sphere and the particular human lives that constitute it. When Henri's allegiance to his intellectual commitments is tested because he must choose between lying and saving the life of his lover, Josette, Henri lies. However, Henri remains unconvinced that he has made the right choice. He wonders whether losing *L'Espoir* is the price that he has to pay for "trying to hold on to a private life when political action requires a man's whole being" (Beauvoir 1999b, 512). Even though Robert refuses to tell Henri what he would have done in his place, his refusal on account of the fact that he would have to be told "everything in detail" (518) in order to make a meaningful decision reinforces the existentialist idea that there are no moral or political absolutes. Since old French humanist values cannot even retain their worth in the face of changing political and historical situations, good intellectual decisions must be made by taking the particularity of a situation into account. Robert says, "You can't lead a proper life in a society which isn't proper. Whichever way you turn, you're always caught" (518). Henri appears to recognize the importance of taking particularity into account when he decides to remain in a romantic relationship with Nadine. Thus, after the failure of their intellectual and political bonds, Robert and Henri finally end up in a familial bond, which is largely responsible for the promising air surrounding the male characters at the end of the novel. As a result, the conclusion to the novel is a disruption of Hegelian gender roles in regard to men. However, although the male characters find the personal sphere, the female characters do not move to the political or theoretical spheres. Thus, the women are unable to partake in the hopefulness that results from a reconciliation of the intellectual, political, and personal realms.

Political Trinities and the Movement of History

Just as Hegel's master-slave dialectic can be interpreted as a paradigmatic account of both personal relationships and of the relationships that move history, the critical trinities of *The Mandarins* offer an image of relationality that is at once personal and historical. Paralleling the way in which Anne, as third-party witness, provides the milieu within which Robert and Henri's friendship unfolds and the way in which the private sphere is the milieu that situates the tension between intellectual commitments and political practice, in *The Mandarins* French socialism serves as the milieu within which the political dialectic of American capitalism and Soviet communism unfolds. Thus, socialism, like woman and like the French nation, plays the role of a third party that stands outside of a dialectical struggle and gives contextualized meaning to the opposition between its two terms. Because of their unique external position, the socialists must assert themselves, not by choosing a side of the struggle to align themselves with, but rather by assuming an attitude toward the entire struggle itself.

Although the political struggles that history is based upon often appear to be dialectical in nature, upon a closer inspection they often depend on the exclusion of an invisible third term. Robert gives symbolic voice to history's tendency to exclude the people who are subsumed by these seemingly dialectical relations when he laments the fact that French socialism never even had an opportunity to contend with communism or capitalism: "The game was between Russia and the United States from the start. We were completely out of it . . . we were trapped" (Beauvoir 1999b, 514). Robert's words are reminders that political struggles are not merely based upon positive assertions and binary oppositions; they also exist through the erasure of certain social groups and certain political ideas. To conceptualize the movement of history as involving three distinct terms is to pose the question of who has been excluded and why. The asking of this question is a way to give voice to the silenced third party that serves as the ground upon which historical struggles are fought. In this light, *The Mandarins* can be read on all of its levels as a description of the field upon which dialectical struggles take place. In the novel, this field has many faces: France, socialism, personal relationships, woman, the Jew. Likewise, in contemporary politics, the question of the invisible third party is just as pertinent as it was when *The Mandarins* was first published fifty years ago. For example, the Third World provides a physical and symbolic milieu for developed nations to play out their struggles by serving as a space where factories, war, and environmental pollution are deposited. In addition, the US "War on Terror" is currently being fought between rich American men and rich Middle Eastern men upon fields of civilians (many of whom are women, people of color, and impoverished) who neither understand their justifications nor support them. Because the particularity of the existences of these civilians finds no expression within contemporary political discourse and media representations, their experience is one of erasure. Similarly, Anne feels the erasure of herself and of France most vividly when she observes a discussion that her American friends have about World War II: "It was their war they were talking about, a war in which we had been only the somewhat pitiful excuse. Their scruples concerning us were like those a man could feel toward a weak woman or a passive animal" (552). Anne's likening of the French people to a woman or an animal emphasizes the idea that theoretical articulations of what it means to be human often render the subjectivities and desires of particular people invisible.[13] The binary oppositions of man and woman, the United States and Soviet Union, and theory and political practice are all abstract articulations that obscure the true ontological structure of human to human relationships. In pointing this out, *The Mandarins* embodies Beauvoir's repeated claims that particular lives in all of their ambiguity exceed theoretical and political representations. In *The Prime of Life* she writes, "I had always maintained that words could not fully express the physical essence of reality" (1962b, 313). The power to oppress is gained through the production of a distorting representation that is widely distributed along with an enforced forgetting of the discrepancy between words and life. In *The Second Sex* Beauvoir claims, "Representation of the world, like the world itself, is the work of men; they describe it from their own point of view, which they confuse with absolute truth" (1989, 143). To attend to the particularity of individual lives in one's experiences and in one's writing is to remember the fields upon which dialectical struggles are fought as well as the discrepancies between abstractions and particular lives.

When the particularity of the third party's situation is considered, one is able to see that history does not progress only as a result of dialectical oppositions. In *The Ethics of Ambiguity* Beauvoir criticizes Hegel for conflating the modes of free expression available to the slave's will with those available to the master's will. Beauvoir describes the difference between the two as follows: "In these two cases the given is present in its surpassing; but in one case it is present insofar as it is accepted, in the other insofar as rejected, *and that makes a radical difference*" (1997, 84; emphasis added). She adds that Hegel's mistaken assumption that the master and slave both seek to affirm themselves "is what allows one to regard the future of the world as a continuous and harmonious development" (84). Beauvoir thinks that Hegel's formulation of the master-slave dialectic only describes positive movements that are necessarily acceptances of a given system. However, because the slave has "no other issue than a negative one," his or her very situation must be eliminated before he or she can choose positively (85). In other words, because the slave's desire is not affirmative, the slave is trying to free himself or herself from the system itself; she or he is not struggling for recognition within that system. In this respect, the third party is like the slave, because, as a witness who is outside of the dialectic, the third party is able to come to its own subjectivity, not through participation in a binary opposition, but by confronting the decision of whether to be complicit with or to revolt against the dialectical system itself. Anne's analysis of the final fight between Nadine and Lambert makes manifest the idea that those who are socially positioned differently must come to their own subjectivity differently: "[A] male, to win the dignity of adulthood, must know how to kill, must make others suffer, must suffer himself. Girls are weighed down with restrictions, boys with demands—two equally harmful disciplines" (1999b, 378). Even though the weight of demands and restrictions are equally as harmful, they nonetheless have a different character, because while Lambert is told how to participate in a given system, Nadine, like woman in Hegel's dialectic, is not allowed access to that system at all. Confined to her role as observer, Nadine cannot oppose anything. On the other hand, because Lambert is a recognized term in the political system from the start, insofar as he acts and desires he is demonstrating an acceptance of that system. In a sense, all of the characters in *The Mandarins* as well as the reader, as survivors of war and the Occupation, are third-party witnesses to the atrocities of World War II. During the Occupation, the French people literally served as the milieu upon which the war was fought. Because of the survivor's position as witness, she or he must decide whether or not to be complicit with the human constructions, both abstract and concrete, that permitted the horrors of World War II. One's decision to revolt against those human theories and actions will not enter one into a dialectical struggle for recognition, because one's position as witness makes the myopia necessary for such a relation impossible. From the perspective of an occupied witness, Hegelian optimism is nearly unthinkable. As Beauvoir writes, "Revolt is not integrated into the harmonious development of the world; it does not wish to be integrated but rather to explode at the heart of the world and to break its continuity" (1997, 84).

Even though all of the characters in *The Mandarins* are surviving witnesses to the war, the lives of the female characters, as third-party witnesses on the political, theoretical, and personal levels as well, are poignant expressions of the decision that characterizes their one opportunity for subjectivity: to be complicit or to revolt. The suicidal gestures that all of the female characters make are symbolic embodiments of the fact that woman, in particular, is faced with this decision.[14] While the male characters act in ways that manifest acceptance for the existing social and political systems (e.g., Vincent and Sézenac kill; Robert, Henri, and Lambert either affirm or refute war and human suffering through their writing), the female characters Paule, Anne, and Nadine reject the system by focusing their acts of violence on themselves. These suicide attempts are recognitions of the futility of taking a stand within the binary structure that is characterizing present social and political systems. Woman has no stake in the outcome of the discursive and political structures that use her and affect her; like France, she has been out of it from the start and loses either way. In *The Second Sex*, Beauvoir claims that the relation between man and woman is different than the relation between master and slave, because "woman also aspires to and recognizes the values that are concretely attained by the male" (1989, 65). She then qualifies this statement when she writes, "He [man] it is who opens up the future to which she [woman] reaches out. In truth women have never set up female values in opposition to male values; it is man who, desirous of maintaining masculine prerogatives, has invented that divergence" (65). If society will never change in a way that will allow women their own desires and values, then the fact that all of the female suicides in the novel fail is somewhat tragic, because it is a denial of woman's only opportunity for freedom. Beauvoir herself sees Anne's decision to go on living as a submission "to their conventions and their lies" and a betrayal of "real life" (1987, 283).

At the end of *The Mandarins*, when Anne is on the brink of suicide, she describes her reason for coming to that point as follows: "It isn't because of those men who are being murdered almost everywhere in the world, nor because of the war hanging over us: whether you're killed or whether you die doesn't make very much difference. And everyone dies, at the same age, at about forty" (1999b, 606). Anne considers suicide because she thinks that her existence does not count. On the surface it seems that Anne's problem is a human one that will manifest itself regardless of whether one is a woman or not, for mortality is an aspect of each human life. However, due to the failure of social, political, and historical conceptualizations to realize woman's experiences, she feels an existential crisis more deeply than man does. While life itself, as a movement toward death, does not recognize the existence of individual men, society affirms this existence with language and theories that correspond to a man's sense of himself as subject. Hegel's theory of dialectic, by excluding woman, is a perfect example of a widely held theory that recognizes male as subject and denies woman's individual subjectivity. In regard to woman, theories, society, and life do not recognize her individual existence. Beauvoir's theory, espoused in *The Second Sex*, that woman lives life as both subject and object is made manifest in the female characters of her novels: "The drama of woman lies in this conflict between the aspirations of every subject (ego)—who always regards the self as the essential—and the compulsions of a situation in which she is the inessential" (1989, xxxv). Elaine Marks explains the divergences between the dramas of the male characters in Beauvoir's novels and "the severe, nearly fatal bouts of anguish" (1973, 9) that the female characters experience when she writes that "all the male characters work constantly at a project which absorbs and distracts them" (9). More specifically, the characters of Anne, Paule, and Nadine consider and attempt suicide because they lack hope. Literally, Anne, Paule, and Nadine lack *L'Espoir* ("Hope"), the independent journal that Henri and Robert produce. None of the female characters in *The Mandarins* write, whereas *all* of the male characters in the novel are authors both literally and figuratively. The absence of a space where Anne, Paule, and Nadine's experiences can find expression directs them toward suicide. Toward the beginning of the novel Anne insightfully notes that for Robert, "[r]enouncing writing would be suicide" (1999b, 56). Likewise, for the female characters of *The Mandarins*, their exclusion from the philosophical and political struggles that write history means their suicides. Because woman, like France, is merely occupied by the conceptual dialectical struggles that shape human life, she becomes Anne's image of herself: "a woman waiting to die, no longer knowing why she's living" (447).

The trinities in *The Mandarins* are evocations of the personal, political, and theoretical relationships that Beauvoir witnessed in postwar France; they are not idealized pictures of these relationships. These evocations bring to light the notion that social, theoretical, and political relationships are often theorized dialectically even though these very dialectics are fundamentally dependent upon the erasure of a third party. But these erasures are not inevitabilities. No one is a "spotless victim of historical necessity" (Beauvoir 1999b, 516). Third parties are oppressed and rendered invisible because of chosen actions. Likewise, humanity will only arrive at peace and solidarity through chosen actions. The political dialectic of Soviet communism and American capitalism subsumes French socialism, the philosophical dialectic of intellectual theory and political practice perpetuates itself at the expense of particular lives, and the dialectic of love subsumes woman. The way for one to counter these erasures is to write them. When the third party writes its own experiences, the terrors of humanity come to light, as does the need for their remedy. Beauvoir exemplifies this type of writing in *The Second Sex*, where she describes her task as follows: "[F]rom a woman's point of view I shall describe the world in which women must live; and thus we shall be able to envisage the difficulties in their way as . . . they aspire to full membership in the human race" (1989, xxxv). And Beauvoir exemplifies this type of writing even more so in her literary works. A literary work, in particular, is an especially apt medium for writing the third party, because it is capable of evoking individual lives in all their specificity and ambiguity. The critical trinities of *The Mandarins* serve as reminders of the fact that there are no ideal couples, whether in terms of love relationships, political oppositions, or Hegel's dialectic: there are only particular lives. As such, they are reminders that for any solidarity or reciprocity to occur, one must assume responsibility for its construction.

In conclusion, through a juxtaposition of Beauvoir's philosophical descriptions of woman's experience in *The Second Sex* with her narrative attempts to re-create this very experience for her readers, a more coherent interpretation of her notions of personal and political relationships can be formulated than through a consideration of *The Second Sex* alone.[15] The critical trinities in *The Mandarins* give an account of the movements of personal and historical relationships that exceeds Hegel's dialectical account. By giving voice to the unmentionables that Hegel excludes from his dialectical relations, Beauvoir ends up describing a new theory of relationality that does not have opposition at its center. Instead, the triadic theory that emerges from *The Mandarins* makes a space for gifts, withdrawals, and solitude. This triadic theory also recognizes that individuals who are positioned differently socially and historically will have different avenues available to them to realize their subjectivities. Specifically, third parties who are positioned outside of various dialectics—for example, woman, intellectuals, socialists, the French people—realize themselves through the choice of whether to be complicit with or revolt against the systems that they are observing. Descriptively speaking, history progresses, not through oppositions, but through chosen erasures. The excluded third party serves as the field upon which the meanings of various oppositions congeal. When one is remembering this third party, one is also recognizing the inevitable interplay between the personal, the theoretical, and the political. This critical remembrance would disrupt the contemporary political arena, just as *The Mandarins* disrupts the notion that a war has been, or could ever be, won. Thus, the individuals of this contemporary world should foster the sorts of disruptions that give third parties voice as they live through and struggle against Scriassine's prophecy: "American imperialism, like Russian totalitarianism, requires unlimited expansion. In the end, one or the other has to win out. . . . You think you're celebrating the German defeat, but what you're actually witnessing is the beginning of World War Three" (Beauvoir 1999b, 41).[16]

Beauvoir claims that "a writer's business is not to transcribe thoughts and feelings which constantly pass through [her] mind so much as to point out those horizons which we never reach and scarcely perceive, but which nevertheless are there" (1962b, 732–3). The excluded, silenced third parties of life are these horizons. Writing the third party is a way to undertake the political work of changing the theories, politics, and people that are responsible for these erasures. Perhaps for this very reason Beauvoir was able to write *The Mandarins* in the aftermath of World War II. She confesses, "[I]n the face of the H-bomb and the hunger of millions words seemed futile; and yet I worked at *The Mandarins* with a furious doggedness" (1987, 277). But one can never be sure of the results of one's actions before one undertakes them. And one can never be sure of the social and political situations that will be available to one in the future. At the end of *The Mandarins*, Anne intimates that on her granddaughter's "inscrutable little face I again see my death" (1999b, 607–8). The future of woman as it is actualized through the relation between her present and her past is especially uncertain and ambiguous because of the enduring stability of oppression and the discursive, practical, and personal structures that support it. This uncertainty is rendered concrete with the birth of the final trinity of the novel: that of woman's past (Anne), woman's present (Nadine), and woman's future (Maria). As uncertain as woman's future is, this ambiguity is what characterizes human existence and as such is inescapable. This ambiguity allows for the possibility of freedom through the formation of concrete relationships in which the notions of responsibility and failure become present. Thus, on personal, theoretical, and political levels, subjectivites and the moral actions that stem from them are fostered by that which exposes this ambiguity rather than denies it. Following this notion, the depressingly accurate conclusion to the novel points out the ever-present horizon that is often, yet unnecessarily, masked by the practice of philosophy and by the way it theorizes itself: "Who knows? Who knows?"

Notes

1. Comments and encouragement from several people helped me to create this piece, and to those people I give many thanks. I follow Beauvoir in using the word "evocation" to describe *The Mandarins* (1987, 274), because it emphasizes that Beauvoir's novels should not be interpreted as containing the definiteness of a philosophical theory. In *Force of Circumstance*, Beauvoir explains that *The Mandarins* is not "a novel with a message" (1987, 282) and that one of the essential purposes of literature is "to make manifest the equivocal, separate, contradictory truths that no one moment represents in their totality, either inside or outside myself..." (275).

2. I cite Beauvoir's original French text in addition to the English translation, because Parshley's translation omits a large section of text at this point. The omitted portion includes a lengthy quotation from the French translation of Hegel's *Phenomenology of Mind* that highlights Hegel's description of woman's inability to possess individuality and desire, and thus to participate in the struggle for recognition.

3. Because an analysis of the validity of Beauvoir's interpretation of Hegel is not directly relevant to my claim that *The Mandarins* can be read as an answer to her criticisms of his master-slave dialectic and theory of history, such an analysis will not be undertaken here. See Lundgren-Gothlin (1996) for a detailed discussion of Beauvoir's Kojèvian interpretation of Hegel, with which I am in agreement.

4. As Elaine P. Miller rightly explains with reference to *The Second Sex*, "given the seemingly ineluctable triumph of Hegel's dialectical method" (2000, 135), the task of "endeavoring to articulate a feminine subjectivity that cannot be reduced to oppositionality (if this is at all possible), namely, a sexual difference that is not articulated in terms of conflict and resolution" is imperative to the formation of a positive feminist stance (135).

5. This impossibility is exemplified when Beauvoir writes that when she tried to see Olga Kosakievicz through Sartre's eyes, she "felt she was playing [her] own emotions false" (1987, 306). In other words, adopting a third-party perspective took Beauvoir out of the framework for comprehension implied by her own subjectivity.

6. Beauvoir's early claim that freedoms are neither unified nor opposed could be interpreted as discontinuous with the characterizations of woman in terms of oppositional struggles for recognition (1989, 65) and in reference to the Heideggerian notion of *Mitsein* (1949, 1:32) that she later presents in *The Second Sex*. Nonetheless, I find these claims consistent, because I believe many of Beauvoir's characterizations of woman in *The Second Sex* refer only to the discursive way that woman has been *defined* and categorized and not to the ontology of woman, which is the subject of her earlier claim. For discussions of whether and how Beauvoir appropriates Hegel and Heidegger's philosophies in *The Second Sex*, see Bauer (2001), Bergoffen (1997), Hutchings (2001), Lundgren-Gothlin (1996), and Miller (2000).

7. In *Force of Circumstance*, Beauvoir recounts her discovery that parts of *L'invitée* (*She Came to Stay*) recur "word for word" in *The Mandarins* (1987, 428–29).

8. For example, see Marks (1973, 77) and Barnes (1998).

9. Scriassine is also an "insider" to all three of the novel's political poles. He fled Russia for Austria, and in turn fled Austria for France, eventually becoming a naturalized French citizen. He had also been living in America for the past four years (1999b, 38). His resulting ability to assume concurrently inside and outside perspectives gives his character a prophetic air.

10. Beauvoir's choice of "L'Espoir" as the name for Henri's journal provides her with a symbolic way of representing the problem of reconciling one's theoretical, political, and personal commitments. In *The Prime of Life*, Beauvoir writes that in 1937 she and Sartre read André Malraux's *L'Espoir* with great excitement, because Malraux "was tackling themes hitherto ignored in literature, such as the relationship between individual morality and practical politics, or the possibility of maintaining humanist standards in the thick of war" (1962b, 388). She continues, "Total war was utterly to abolish the whole pattern of humane relationships which so concerned Malraux, and by which we ourselves set such great store" (388–89).

11. Elizabeth Fallaize defines the *épuration* as "the 'purge' or meting out of justice to those who had collaborated with the Germans during the war" (1990, 88).

12. Sartre's one-act play *No Exit* (1976) is in many ways a preview to his discussion of the third party in the *Critique*.

13. Butler's discussion of the relationship between representations of humanity and the recognition of particular human lives has helped me to articulate here how this relationship plays out in Beauvoir's phenomenology. See Butler (2004, 128–51).

14. Although Nadine does not make an explicit suicide attempt like Anne and Paule do, I consider her reckless motorcycle ride to be a youthful premonition of the

suicide attempts of the older female characters in the novel, because the ride is Nadine's confrontation with her exclusion from the public, masculine world. Anne says, "[T]he motorcycle remained in her [Nadine's] eyes the symbol of all the masculine pleasures of which she wasn't the source and in which, to make matters worse, she was unable to share" (Beauvoir 1999b, 369).

15. Beauvoir makes this distinction between writing as description (philosophy) and writing as re-creation of an experience (literature) in "Littérature et métaphysique" (1946). See also Holveck (1999).

16. Robert explicitly refers to Scriassine as a prophet (Beauvoir 1999b, 45).

Works Cited

Barnes, Hazel. 1998. Self-encounter in *She came to stay*. In *Simone de Beauvoir: A critical reader*, edited by Elizabeth Fallaize. New York: Routledge.

Bauer, Nancy. 2001. Being-with as being-against: Heidegger meets Hegel in *The second sex*. *Continental Philosophy Review* 34, no. 2:129–49.

Beauvoir, Simone de. 1946. Littérature et métaphysique. *Les Temps Modernes* 1, no. 7:1153–63.

———. 1949. *Le deuxième sexe*. 2 vols. La Flèche: Éditions Gallimard.

———. 1954. *Les mandarins*. 2 vols. St-Amand: Éditions Gallimard.

———. 1962a. *Pour une morale de l'ambiguïté: Suivi de Pyrrhus et Cinéas*. St-Amand: Éditions Gallimard.

———. 1962b. *The prime of life*. Translated by Peter Green. New York: Lancer Books.

———. 1987. *Force of circumstance*. Translated by Richard Howard. New York: Penguin.

———. 1989. *The second sex*. Translated by H. M. Parshley. New York: Vintage Books.

———. 1997. *The ethics of ambiguity*. Translated by Bernard Frechtman. Secaucus, N.J.: Carol Publishing Group.

———. 1999a. *She came to stay*. New York: W. W. Norton & Company.

———. 1999b. *The mandarins*. New York: W. W. Norton & Company.

Bergoffen, Debra B. 1997. *The philosophy of Simone de Beauvoir: Gendered phenomenologies, erotic generosities*. Albany: State University of New York Press.

Butler, Judith. 1998. Sex and gender in Simone de Beauvoir's *Second sex*. In *Simone de Beauvoir: A critical reader*, edited by Elizabeth Fallaize. New York: Routledge.

———. 2004. *Precarious life: The powers of mourning and violence*. New York: Verso.

Fallaize, Elizabeth. 1990. *The novels of Simone de Beauvoir*. New York: Routledge.

Hegel, G. W. F. 1977. *Phenomenology of spirit*. Translated by A. V. Miller. Oxford: Oxford University Press.

Holveck, Eleanore. 1999. *The blood of others*: A novel approach to *The ethics of ambiguity*. *Hypatia* 14, no. 4:3–17.

Hutchings, Kimberly. 2001. De Beauvoir's Hegelianism: Rethinking *The second sex*. *Radical Philosophy* 107:21–31.

Lundgren-Gothlin, Eva. 1996. *Sex and existence: Simone de Beauvoir's "The second sex."* Hanover, N.H.: Wesleyan University Press.

Marks, Elaine. 1973. *Simone de Beauvoir: Encounters with death*. New Brunswick, N.J.: Rutgers University Press.

Miller, Elaine P. 2000. The "paradoxical displacement": Beauvoir and Irigaray on Hegel's Antigone. *Journal of Speculative Philosophy* 14, no. 2:121–37.

Sartre, Jean-Paul. 1976. *No exit & The flies*. Translated by Stuart Gilbert. New York: Alfred A. Knopf.

———. 1978. *Critique of dialectical reason*. Vol. 1, *Theory of practical ensembles*. Translated by Alan Sheridan-Smith. London: NLB.

Tidd, Ursula. 1999. The self-other relation in Beauvoir's ethics and autobiography. *Hypatia*, 14, no. 4:163–74.

CHAPTER 9

Simone de Beauvoir on Achieving Subjectivity

Thomas W. Busch

In 1938, Albert Camus joined the staff of the left-wing newspaper *Alger Republicain*, and within a short time reviewed two works of fiction that crossed his desk, both of them authored by a certain Jean-Paul Sartre. While Camus found Sartre to have "remarkable fictional gifts" as well as "the toughest and most lucid mind," he warned of the dangers in constructing a philosophical novel: "[T]he philosophy need only spill over into the characters and action for it to stick out like a sore thumb, the plot to lose its authenticity, and the novel its life" (Camus 1968, 199). Camus spotted this tendency in Sartre's work. Simone de Beauvoir was determined to avoid it in her own fiction. Whereas Sartre insisted upon the "transparency" of writing in *What Is Literature?* (Sartre 1988), Beauvoir tells us that in her novels "I set great store by nuances and ambiguities. . . . Existence—others have said it and I have already repeated it more than once myself—cannot be reduced to ideas, it cannot be stated in words; it can only be evoked through the medium of the imaginary object; to achieve this, one must recapture the surge of backwash, and the contradictions of life itself" (Beauvoir 1965, 319). Beauvoir's favorite novel, *The Mandarins*, successfully withstands, I believe, any temptation to reduce character to idea, and manages to evoke richly a specific historical situation and characters struggling to make sense of their lives in that situation. Indeed, the relation of characters to their situation is tightly drawn without denying freedom. Her characters have "character," not in an essentialist sense, but as carrying the effects of their personal histories in a profound way. Her main characters are conflicted by multiple strains of past negotiations with others and happenings in their lives. For Beauvoir, these people are clearly shaped by life events. Nadine is a fine example. She is a complex person, full of the contradictions and tensions that for Beauvoir characterize life as lived. At times Nadine is aggressive, angry, defensive, and indifferent, as well as vulnerable, wounded, naïve, childlike, and caring. Her very birth into a situation where her mother was not particularly happy about a third who would break into the relationship between Robert and Anne produced a competition and love/antagonism between Nadine and Anne. Then the loving relationship with Diego that ended with his death at the hands of the Nazis devastated the young Nadine to the point of her exuding a protective cynicism about life and indifference to others. Beauvoir tells us that she originally intended "to avenge myself on Nadine" for traits that offended Beauvoir in some of her friends. However, "little by little, the circumstances which explained her unpleasant qualities began to appear to me as full of valid excuses; Nadine began to seem to me more to be pitied as a victim than to be blamed; her egoism flaked off; she became, beneath her touchy uncouthness[,] generous and capable of attachment" (Beauvoir 1965, 265). Gradually, Nadine changes; she comes to know herself more clearly, to gain some critical perspective on herself and in the process an ability to develop deeper relationships with others. But the process is mutual, for Nadine herself contributes to helping others clarify their lives and to change. Nadine is a most appropriate example of what Beauvoir wanted to evoke in her novel: "I showed some people, at grips with doubts and hopes, groping in the dark to find their way" (271). This evocation is a highly nuanced understanding of the existentialist notions of facticity and transcendence, an understanding that belies any simple repetition of Sartre's well-known views on facticity and transcendence in *Being and Nothingness.*

In *Being and Nothingness*, Sartre articulates an ontological understanding of freedom based on the distinction between being-for-itself and being-in-itself. Whereas being-in-itself is a mode of being in which a being is in deep identity with itself, being-for-itself "is a being which perpetually effects in itself a break in being" (Sartre 1956, 78). The for-itself is subjectivity in a form of nonpositional self-consciousness. The for-itself is positionally aware of objects (and in reflection, of itself as an object) while always at the same time being nonpositionally self-aware. As nonpositionally present to itself, the for-itself exists at a distance from itself, and it is this distance, in the form of *néant* (nothingness), that prevents the being of the for-itself from coinciding with itself. This *néant*, a principle of difference in the very being of the for-itself, disperses the for-itself in temporality, and guarantees its freedom. Having no deep identity, the for-itself's actions spring from its nonidentity in the form of unconditioned choices. The tradition inspiring this ontology is that of the cogito as developed by Descartes and embellished by Husserl. Sartre exploits the power of negativity of consciousness exemplified in methodic doubt and the phenomenological *epoché* to produce a very sexy picture of self-construction. Another significant inspiration at work is that of Heidegger's notion of being-in-the-world. Sartre insists that subjectivity is radically situated, and *Being and Nothingness* offers numerous and memorable examples of situatedness. However, given the cogito tradition's metaphor of "distance" and Heidegger's metaphor of "belonging," there is bound to be tension (after all, Heidegger offered his understanding of situatedness as definitive criticism of the cogito tradition). In my view, when push comes to shove in *Being and Nothingness*, situatedness gives way to the power of consciousness.

Sartre's intention in *Being and Nothingness*, it is fairly clear, is to defend freedom from determinism, and his notion of the *néant* is central to that project. Consider what he says when discussing the relationship of subjectivity to any given (situation): "[I]t is necessary that the intention by its upsurge realize a rupture with the given" (Sartre 1956, 478). Indeed, without the negation/difference of the subject vis-à-vis the object there would be no "given" to the conscious subject, which "surpasses" it in bringing into a state of objective givenness, bringing it into meaning. He goes further:

> It would be vain to imagine that consciousness can exist without a given; in that case it would be consciousness (of) itself [non-positional self consciousness] as consciousness of nothing—that is, absolute nothingness. But if consciousness exists in terms of the given, this does not mean that the given conditions consciousness; consciousness is a pure and simple negation of the given. . . . But freedom is simply the fact that [its] choice is always unconditioned. (Sartre 1956, 478–79)

Here, in defending freedom from determinism by presenting free subjectivity as "the pure and simple negation" of the given, Sartre is led to defend free subjectivity as "unconditioned" (not only undetermined). The very being of the for-itself is defined in terms of the *néant*: "Human reality is free . . . because it is perpetually wrenched away from itself and because it has been separated by a nothingness from what it is and what it will be" (Sartre 1956, 440). Sartre leaves the reader with only two alternatives: "[E]ither man is wholly determined (which is inadmissible, especially because a determined consciousness—i.e., a consciousness externally motivated—becomes itself pure exteriority and ceases to be consciousness) or else man is wholly free" (Sartre 1956, 442). One can either accept one's absolute freedom in authenticity or flee from it in a variety of forms of bad faith, as the fiction Sartre wrote based on *Being and Nothingness* clearly illustrates.

The characters in *The Mandarins* are clearly conditioned by their pasts and relationships to their various situations. They are complex, in denial in some areas of their lives, clearheaded in others, befuddled in others, and hardly fit into well-defined types of bad faith and authenticity. Events in their lives are interpreted perspectively, leaving the impression of ambiguity of meaning.

Their lives and destinies are intertwined with one another and mediated by social/historical events. It would be hard to fit all of this into *Being and Nothingness.* A more suitable framework would be Beauvoir's own previous work, *The Second Sex*, where, as opposed to Sartre's cogito approach to subjectivity, one finds a social/historical *developmental* approach. Here, she discusses "the formative years," centered around the body/self: "In girls as well as boys the body is first of all the radiation of a subjectivity, the instrument that makes possible the comprehension of the world" (Beauvoir 1989, 267). While biology is a dimension of one's body, in the concrete bodies are "produced" through "civilization" and "values." In the lengthy discussion of the social situation, Beauvoir stresses repeatedly that the "girl" and the "woman" "are shaped as in a mold by [their] situation" (562). For example, "the passivity that is the essential characteristic of the 'feminine' woman is a trait that develops in her from the earliest years. But it is wrong to assert that a biological datum is concerned; it is in fact a destiny that is imposed upon her by her teachers and by society" (262). This passivity infects qualities of body and mind by delimiting experience, thus confirming woman's "otherness" in the eyes of patriarchal society. Woman's "otherness" is an otherness from transcendence, subjectivity itself, making subjectivity (in the Sartrean sense) an *achievement* tied to social/historical conditions. Beauvoir seems to hold that the capacity of transcendence is in all humans, but that the realization of this capacity depends on developmental factors. Thus, in order for women to become subjects their situation must be altered: "The young girl's character and behavior are the outcome of her situation: if this is modified, then the adolescent girl also takes on a different aspect" (345). This understanding of the relation between freedom and situation allows for degrees of freedom and emphasizes how freedom is understood in terms of social/historical structures.

Beauvoir's emphasis on these factors is not reducible to Sartre's depiction of the relationship of freedom to situation in *Being and Nothingness* as "a pure and simple negation of the given." In responding to determinism, the story Sartre offers is that of a wholly active, self-defining giver of meaning protected from being acted upon by its situation by the abyss of the *néant.* The for-itself (subjectivity) appears to be adult; at least all of the examples of its situation are adult. There are no infants or children in *Being and Nothingness.* That is why Nadine is such a powerful and convincing example of Beauvoir's complex developmental understanding of subjectivity as contrasted with Sartre's ontologically guaranteed subjectivity.

At one point during the turbulent off-again, on-again relationship between Nadine and Lambert, the latter comes in exasperation to Anne seeking an explanation for Nadine's erratic behavior. Anne responds that "to understand Nadine, you have to go back to her childhood" (Beauvoir 1966, 375). Anne should know, since by her own admission she is at the heart of Nadine's problems. "Had

I loved her more, our relationship might have been different . . . . I hadn't wanted her . . . I've always held it against Nadine that she upset my life alone with Robert" (68–69). "[T]hat little intruder" had to compete with her mother for Robert's affections, and Nadine, sensing her mother's feelings, felt both unwanted and guilty. With Diego, Nadine found herself wanted, and self-esteem, and self-empowerment, began to emerge. Diego's death dashed this and left her feeling betrayed by existence itself. It was only gradually, in her relationship with Henri, that Nadine began again to grow. She found it difficult to believe in her worthiness: "I'm not a very lovable person . . . why should you love me?" Henri gently insists: "'Get that out of your head, I love you.' (Nadine) '. . . If only I could believe you.' (Henri) '. . . If you want to you can'" (598). Henri sensed that his persistence had an effect: "[I]t seemed that something had given way in her" (601). Henri's love for Nadine has the result of drawing Nadine out of her shell, of opening her to others. One can see this in her sacrifice of the "sun" of Italy for Henri's good. Nadine dreamed of solving her problems by escaping her situation, but she realized that Henri would not be happy without his work, that he needed to be encouraged to return to his idealism by staying in France and working again with Robert. "I ask only one thing of you," she tells Henri, "do what you want to do" (605). By the end of the novel, Nadine has grown, with great difficulty and while still in many ways wounded, to be capable of reciprocity.

Subsequent to *Being and Nothingness*, Sartre's thought became much more sensitive to situatedness and a recognition of "the force of things." A text from *Search for a Method* is a good indicator of this new appreciation:

> Every man is defined negatively by the sum total of possibles which are impossible for him; that is, by a future more or less blocked off. For the under-privileged classes, each cultural, technical, or material enrichment of society represents a diminution, an impoverishment; the future is almost entirely barred. Thus, the social possibles are lived as schematic determinations of the individual future. And the most individual possible is only the internalization and enrichment of a social possible. (Sartre 1958, 95)

(It is interesting to note Beauvoir's contention in *The Second Sex* that "individual 'possibilities' depend upon the economic and social condition" (Beauvoir 1989, 35).) Sartre readily admits, subsequent to *Being and Nothingness*, that people are conditioned: "[I]t is men themselves who make their history, but within a given environment which conditions them . . ." (Sartre 1958, 31). Conditioned, yes; determined, no. The conditioning is understood as a dialectical interchange between transcendence and situation, thus making a concrete act of freedom intelligible in terms of an exchange between a capacity to transcend and the conditions that allow for transformation. Subjectivity understood as the power of consciousness is decentered: "[S]ubjectivity is neither everything nor nothing: it represents a moment in the objective process (that in which externality is internalized)" (Sartre 1958, 33). "Concrete" subjectivity is spelled out in the *Critique of Dialectical Reason* as "praxis," a body/subjectivity both acting upon and acted upon by the world. These changes of emphasis put enormous (I would say fatal) strain upon the ontological categories of *Being and Nothingness.* The reconsideration of subjectivity as praxis, for example, as both a subject and a thing, has serious repercussions on the ontological claim of incommensurability between body as subject and body as object. All of these changes of emphasis bring Sartre's thinking closer to Beauvoir's understanding of the transcendence/situation relationship in *The Second Sex* and *The Mandarins*, and even, as demonstrated by Beauvoir scholars, her work previous to these. Surely, in the light of all of this, Beauvoir was not simply repeating in her works the positions taken in *Being and Nothingness.* A more interesting suggestion is offered by Sonia Kruks: that "a case can be made that, at certain points in his development, it was Beauvoir who led Sartre intellectually" (Kruks 2001, 30).

My own work on the changes that occurred in Sartre's philosophy (Busch 1990) led me to feature the significance in that regard of his *Saint Genet: Actor and Martyr*, for one can clearly see in this book a move away from an ontologically guaranteed subjectivity and freedom to an achieved subjectivity and freedom. In order to make sense out of Genet's life, Sartre is compelled to probe Genet's childhood and, astoundingly, is led to speak of "the making of Genet." Published in 1952, three years after the appearance of *The Second Sex*, *Saint Genet* arrives at some very Beauvoirian conclusions. There is a distinct echo between Sartre's articulation of the interpellation "It's a thief!" and Beauvoir's "It's a girl!" Both claim social/historical prescription instead of essentialism, and both introduce a notion of "destiny" into a discourse of freedom. The first part of *Saint Genet*, resembling Beauvoir's treatment of "the formative years," emphasizes the passivity and vulnerability of the child. Young Genet is "suddenly provided with a monstrous and guilty 'ego,' isolated, separated, in short changed into a bug" (Sartre 1963, 27). The philosopher of freedom goes so far as to admit that the "alienation" produced by this social condition can in some cases be definitive:

> But when children are subjected from their earliest days to great social pressure, when their Being-for-Others is the subject of a collective image accompanied by value judgments and social prohibitions, the alienation is sometimes total and definitive. This is the case of most pariahs in caste societies. They internalize the objective and external judgments which the collectivity passes on them, and they view themselves in their subjective individuality on the basis of

> an "ethnic character," a "nature," and "essence" which merely express the contempt in which *others* hold them. (Sartre 1963, 44)

In elaborating upon the effects of "internalization" in *Search for a Method*, Sartre admits that a certain form of "character" is produced by social conditioning:

> What was once both a vague comprehension of our class, of our social conditioning by way of the family group, and a blind going beyond, an awkward attempt to wrench ourselves away from all this, at last ends up inscribed in us in the form of *character*. (Sartre 1958, 101)

Genet's story is one of achieving subjectivity, of moving from an abstract capacity to transcend to the concrete ability to effectively do so. The child Genet does not grid onto the alternatives of authenticity and bad faith proposed in *Being and Nothingness*, since young Genet was not attempting to hide his freedom from himself. He was not the culprit of this story, but rather the "decent folk" who made a "monster" of the child are held liable by Sartre. Only gradually, through the act of writing, did Genet get a sense of his capacity of transcendence, of "writing" himself. The child's condition before assuming an active subjectivity was that of the mix of transcendence/immanence (a transcendence held in immanence or what Sartre would later term in his *Critique of Dialectical Reason* a "transcendence transcended")—the very terms in which Beauvoir depicts the life of the young girl in patriarchal society. The sort of alienation displayed through Genet is not the self-alienation of bad faith, but a social alienation, curable by social change. This is implied in the Genet story, but would have to be spelled out in Sartre's future works: "It is obvious," Sartre said in an interview, "that the study of the conditioning of Genet at the level of institutions and of history is inadequate—very, very inadequate" (Sartre 1974, 43). Sartre's (belated) turn to a developmental approach thrust him immediately into social and political issues.

A number of feminist scholars have convincingly pointed out that Beauvoir's philosophical views are much closer to Merleau-Ponty's than to Sartre's, raising the interesting and difficult question of sorting out the relationship between Beauvoir and Merleau-Ponty. I think that Judith Butler's criticisms of both can afford a helpful perspective on that relationship. After some originally sympathetic work on Beauvoir, Butler lowers the hammer in *Gender Trouble*: Beauvoir is a closet Cartesian "who is clearly limited by the uncritical reproduction of the Cartesian distinction between freedom and the body" (Butler 1990, 12). Beauvoir is viewed to be complicit with "the philosophical tradition that begins with Plato and continues through Descartes, Husserl, and Sartre" (12). While Merleau-Ponty's name does not appear on this list of suspects, this is compensated for in a condemnatory footnote:

> Note the extent to which phenomenological theories such as Sartre's, Merleau-Ponty's, and Beauvoir's tend to use the term *embodiment*. Drawn as it is from theological contexts, the term tends to figure "the body" as a mode of incarnation and, hence, to preserve the external and dualistic relationship between a signifying immateriality and the materiality of the body itself. (Butler 1990, 152)

One gathers that the move to an existential phenomenology, in Butler's estimation, consists in plunking a Cartesian transcendental consciousness into a bodily form (as she seems to understand the religious doctrine of incarnation to be the plunking of a divine being into a bodily form). However, as I read both Merleau-Ponty and Beauvoir, it is the body itself (as they understand it) that is the basis of a freedom or transcendence. Merleau-Ponty's first work, *The Structure of Behavior*, presented his notion of subjectivity in terms of a study of the "organism." Arguing against forms of empiricism and mechanism, he built the case that human hardwiring has a very narrow reach. Human anatomy and physiology, while serving as general conditions of possibility, require supplementation from learning, socialization processes, and a developmental narrative. There is a fundamental indetermination of the hardwiring, opening up a variety of behavioral possibilities. The social, cultural, historical codes, mores, and so on that are supplements to the weak hardwiring have, for Merleau-Ponty (and Beauvoir), only the reality of sedimentation and are thus themselves always haunted by the indeterminate. This appears in the "existentialism" of the *Phenomenology of Perception* with his claim that "existence is indeterminate in itself, by reason of its fundamental structure . . ." (Merleau-Ponty 1962, 168). Furthermore, the discourses of biology, anatomy, physiology, and psychology are themselves, in isolation, abstract, for in the functioning of the organism the phenomena isolated by these disciplines bleed (Merleau-Ponty uses the work "leak") into one another, giving rise to the notion of "ambiguity."

> It is impossible to superimpose on man a layer of behaviour which one chooses to call "natural," followed by a manufactured cultural or spiritual world. Everything is both manufactured and natural in man, as it were, in the sense that there is not a word, not a form of behaviour which does not owe something to purely biological being—and which at the same time does not elude the simplicity of animal life, and cause forms of vital behaviour to deviate from their

> pre-ordained direction, through a sort of *leakage* and through a genius for ambiguity which might serve to define man. (Merleau-Ponty 1962, 189)

Beauvoir, of course, opens *The Second Sex* with a discussion of biology, highlighting a message similar to the one made by Merleau-Ponty in *The Structure of Behavior*—that of the indetermination of the biological, to the point that "every biological fact implies transcendence" (Beauvoir 1989, 10). In this regard it is interesting to note that she quotes Merleau-Ponty—"man is not a natural species: he is an historical idea"—instead of Sartre's expression "existence precedes essence." Her general context is historical, not ontological, and this marks her approach to biological issues that are entangled with cultural/historical issues. "Biology is *not enough* to give an answer to the question that is before us: why is woman the *Other*?" (Beauvoir 1989, 33; emphasis added). Biological facts are always, she reiterates throughout the chapter, open to interpretation, and of themselves do not cause particular behaviors, but necessarily open up possibilities. Her notion of "situatedness," running throughout the book, plays a role in her thinking parallel to Merleau-Ponty's notion of ambiguity. All scientific discourses are abstract and require to be contextualized in application to actual existence. Human activity must be understood in terms of the complexity of its continuous interchanges with the environment and in terms of its own overlapping dimensions—biological, psychological, social, institutional, historical. For both Merleau-Ponty and Beauvoir, it is in the body itself that one first finds the indeterminate, an openness to multiplicity of meanings. What Merleau-Ponty's account lacks and what Beauvoir's provides is the issue of gender difference, and, again, this is apparent with Nadine, who offers not only, as we have seen, an example of the development of subjectivity, but also puts into play gender difference in the process. Rejecting her mother's comparisons to Lambert, Nadine insists that "you can't make comparisons. I'm a woman." Her struggle with her gender identity runs throughout her story. Anne remarks that "Nadine believed herself ugly, and it was in spite, more than anything, that she disdained looking feminine" (Beauvoir 1966, 371). Nadine, while repressing identity with her body, was well-aware of the effect of her body on men, and used this manipulatively, with the result that sexual activity for her was more often than not mechanical. Her ambivalence regarding her gender identity is an integral dimension of all her issues with identity, and this is reflected in all of Beauvoir's characters in the novel, underlining this concrete dimension of the ambiguity of human existence.

While it is true that Merleau-Ponty and Beauvoir work as self-described "phenomenologists," it is clearly possible to give a more generous reading of their phenomenology than that ascribed to them by Butler. Their projects contest the Cartesian legacy of phenomenology (separating themselves in significant ways from Descartes, Husserl, and Sartre). They do not oppose a body identity to a subjectivity insofar as they identify the body and subjectivity in the body's physical and biological incompleteness and opening to a social/cultural development. The notion of ambiguity is central to this strategy, for here one can see the subject being shaped (by its natural and social environment) as it gives shape to the environment. In the former case they enter territory overlapping the Foucaultian project and Butler's powerful discursive read of that project. Butler's discursive turn commits her to a social constructionism of a subject capacity that makes social determinism her antagonist, something she avoids with her notion of "resignification." Merleau-Ponty's and Beauvoir's developmental approach to a subject capacity features a notion of "transcendence," based upon the indeterminacy of the physical, biological and social. Their different entries into the cause of overcoming the legacy of Cartesianism are undeniably different, but Butler's discursive path of "resignification" has the ring of a certain poststructuralist existentialism in comparison with the phenomenological existentialism of Merleau-Ponty and Beauvoir.

The deep similarities with one another's projects have led to speculation about whether and to what extent Merleau-Ponty and Beauvoir influenced one another. There are reasons to believe that Merleau-Ponty did exert an influence on Beauvoir. She notes in her autobiography that, without directly challenging the basic features of Sartre's ontology, she already had serious reservations about the lack of weight he gave to situatedness in his understanding of freedom. Add to that her appreciation in her review (Beauvoir 1945) of the *Phenomenology of Perception* of how Merleau-Ponty's phenomenology differs from Sartre's precisely in its rejection of dualism and its emphasis on a fundamental relatedness of a bodysubject to its situation. Commentators have appropriately noted the sympathetic tone of her review and the fact that she finds his analyses "convincing." It would not be a stretch to claim that Merleau-Ponty offered to Beauvoir a phenomenological framework other than Sartre's in which her own insights into situatedness could be more adequately expressed. In *Sense and Non-Sense*, Merleau-Ponty comments on Sartre and Beauvoir. In the two essays in which he discusses Sartre's work, he expresses serious reservations. Sartre's understanding of freedom and subjectivity is too abstract. In "A Scandalous Author," he says of Sartre's understanding of freedom: "The problem is to instill that radical freedom, which is the negation of humanity as a given species and which is an appeal for a self-created humanity, into human relations and to transmute it into history" (Merleau-Ponty 1964, 16). And in "The Battle over Existentialism," he very diplomatically writes: "It is obvious that the author's primary concern in dealing with the subject and freedom is to present them uninvolved in any compromise with things and that he is putting off the study of the 'realization' of nothingness in being—which is action . . ." (Merleau-Ponty 1964, 72). On the other hand, when he comes to review Beauvoir's novel *She Came to Stay*,

Merleau-Ponty has no such reservations, stressing the complexity and nuances she introduces in her portrayal of her characters and their situatedness. Typical of his statements are: "All life is undeniably ambiguous. . . . Indeed, perhaps our actions have no *single* meaning." "It is simply that all of our actions have several meanings . . ." (Merleau-Ponty 1964, 34, 37). *She Came to Stay* expresses Beauvoir's lived experience, her sensibility, and her comprehension of life; they all belie an ontological dualism. Her comprehension of the ambiguity of life, especially the embeddedness of character in situatedness, preceded her encounter with the *Phenomenology of Perception*. If her encounter with the latter helped her to philosophically formulate her comprehension, it is also true that her phenomenology went beyond that of Merleau-Ponty in her attention to sexual difference: "This [sexual] differentiation is characteristic of existents to such an extent that it belongs in any realistic definition of existence. . . . Woman, like man, *is* her body; but her body is something other than herself" (Beauvoir 1989, 24). Perhaps we can give Beauvoir the last word in this issue of influence. When he left *Les Temps Modernes* in 1956, Merleau-Ponty accepted a position on the socialist paper *L'Express*. He would write responses to readers' questions. On one occasion, a reader expressed concern about women assuming a greater role in society and asked whether Merleau-Ponty thought that this was "normal." In his response, Merleau-Ponty refers to the "two thick volumes" that Beauvoir had addressed to this question and reiterates how woman has become "other." He says that "masculinity being the norm, as is the white and the adult in other domains, the woman, like the child and the person 'of color,' becomes a being both other and secondary. Many of her character traits, whether real or the creation of popular mythology, are in this view the result of that situation. . . . In short, the *woman* we speak of is the woman we have created" (Merleau-Ponty 1992, 22). Whereas the questioner assumes a natural justification for the role of men and women, Merleau-Ponty counters that "Perhaps one should first ask whether it is not as a result of a long history that men and women have become absolute others" (22). He ends by suggesting to the questioner that we "must begin to think in a new way" (23). This is a Merleau-Ponty with a consciousness raised beyond what is said, or rather what is not said, in the chapter on sexuality in the *Phenomenology of Perception*.

Both Merleau-Ponty and Beauvoir cut a similar path in the development of phenomenology by attempting to exorcise its Cartesianism, opening up a developmental understanding of subjectivity and the consequent enmeshing of subjectivity in social structures, ethics, and politics. At the core of this reappropriation of phenomenology is a view of the bodysubject, wherein the body is subject insofar as it is, in its biology and physiology, indeterminate and in need of supplementation by revisable cultural/historical categories. It is fair to say that in the process of working out their projects, these friends of many years learned from one another.

Works Cited

Beauvoir, Simone de. 1945. La phenomenologie de la perception de M. Merleau-Ponty. *Les Temps Modernes* 1, no. 2:363–67.

———. 1954. *She came to stay.* Translated by Y. Mayse and R. Senhouer. Cleveland: World Publishing.

———. 1965. *Force of circumstance.* Translated by R. Howard. London: André Deutsch and Weidenfeld and Nicolson.

———. 1966. *The mandarins.* Translated by L. Friedman. Cleveland: Meridian Books.

———. 1989. *The second sex.* Translated H. M. Parshley. New York: Vintage.

Busch, Thomas. 1990. *The power of consciousness and the force of circumstances in Sartre's philosophy.* Bloomington: Indiana University Press.

Butler, Judith. 1990. *Gender trouble: Feminism and the subversion of identity.* New York: Routledge.

Camus, Albert. 1968. *Lyrical and critical essays.* Translated by E. C. Kennedy. New York: Vintage.

Kruks, Sonia. 2001. *Retrieving experience: Subjectivity and recognition in feminist politics.* Ithaca, N.Y.: Cornell University Press.

Merleau-Ponty, Maurice. 1962. *Phenomenology of perception.* Translated by C. Smith. New York: Humanities Press.

———. 1963. *The structure of behavior.* Translated by A. Fisher. Boston: Beacon Press.

———. 1964. *Sense and non-sense.* Translated by H. Dreyfus and P. Dreyfus. Evanston: Northwestern University Press.

———. 1992. *Texts and dialogues: On philosophy, politics and culture.* Translated by H. Silverman and J. Barry. Atlantic Highlands, N.J.: Humanities Press.

Sartre, Jean-Paul. 1956. *Being and nothingness.* Translated by H. Barnes. New York: Philosophical Library.

———. 1958. *Search for a method.* Translated by H. Barnes. New York: Random Books.

———. 1963. *Saint Genet: Actor and martyr.* Translated by B. Frechtman. New York: Mentor.

———. 1974. Itinerary of a Thought. In *Between existentialism and Marxism.* Translated by J. Mathews. New York: William Morrow.

———. 1976. *Critique of dialectical reason.* Translated by A. S. Smith. Vol. 1. London: Humanities Press.

———. 1988. *"What is literature?" and other essays.* Cambridge, Mass.: Harvard University Press.

CHAPTER 10

When a Woman Loves a Man

Ownness and Otherness in The Mandarins

Eleanore Holveck

In his novel *Slowness*, Milan Kundera reflects on sexual ecstasy by recounting an incident in Vivant Denon's 1777 novella *Point de lendemain*. A young gentlemen, named simply by Kundera "the Chevalier," is seduced one night by Madame de T. at her husband's château. Her lover, the Marquis, assumes, incorrectly, that this is a fake seduction, a mere ruse by Madame de T. to dupe her husband, in order to screen her real affair with the Marquis himself. Using this eighteenth-century literary myth, Kundera weaves a view of sexual pleasure or ecstasy as ultimately private, anonymous, and unexpressed. Although pleasure is approached slowly, tantalizingly, through conversation as seduction, at its core sexuality is a private, immediate relationship between one man and one woman. No one else is involved, and neither one of them will ever talk or write about it.

In the end, as he leaves Madame de T.'s apartment, the Chevalier hears the Marquis and Madame de T. laughing. Has the Chevalier been used in a comic role by both of them? The joke is also on the Marquis, because the Chevalier has spent a secret night of pleasure with Madame de T., but the Marquis tells the Chevalier that she is frigid (Kundera 1996, 140). The Chevalier understands that "the night would have no sequel. No tomorrow" (147). He decides to respect Madame de T.'s request never to speak about his experience. "As if the most important thing were not the beauty of the night he had just spent, the beauty that still grips him in such intoxication that he is seeing phantoms, confusing dreams with reality, feeling himself flung out of time" (151).

One might find oneself agreeing with Kundera's defense of the privacy of sexuality, given his amusing juxtaposition of the Chevalier and Vincent, a young disciple of a Bernard-Henri Lévy–type figure, who shows up for an entomology convention at a contemporary château converted to a ritzy hotel. Vincent's view, modeled on that of the Marquis de Sade, emphasizes sexuality as political rebellion, completely public, and so totally exhausted in representation that it peters out in the real world. In the end, Vincent replaces sexual ecstasy with that of the speed of his motorcycle. "[T]he man hunched over his motorcycle can focus only on the present instant of his flight; he is caught in a fragment of time cut off from both the past and the future; he is wrenched from the continuity of time; he is outside time; in other words, he is in a state of ecstasy" (Kundera 1996, 1–2). The desires of quite a few contemporary French philosophers seem to wilt in the fumes of this motorcycle, and one is inclined to acknowledge that "the feeble intellectuals of this sophisticated, overcultivated, and ultimately perfidious country" (94) deserve the laughter that Kundera generates at their expense.

I am not so amused, however, when Kundera concludes that the "ideal of hedonism," that it is "possible to live in pleasure and for pleasure and be happy" (Kundera 1996, 143), is exemplified in Madame de T. "Yet the moral is there: Madame de T. embodies it: she lied to her husband, she lied to her lover the Marquis, she lied to the young Chevalier. It is she who is the true disciple of Epicurus. Lovable lover of pleasure. Gentle protective liar. Guardian of happiness" (141). In a world where men compete to possess one woman, a true woman, as the guardian of pure pleasure, has to lie. Kundera's woman is no longer in the clutches of the Marquis de Sade, but she still lies, presumably flat on her back.

In this paper I will discuss Simone de Beauvoir's view of a sexual relationship between a man and a woman, using her example of her affair with Nelson Algren as she wrote about it in *The Mandarins*, as well as in a few selected passages in her letters to Algren and *America Day by Day*. These texts give us a clearer picture of Beauvoir's concrete view of an authentic sexual relationship than her more abstract philosophical essays. I will argue that Beauvoir accepts the notion that sexual ecstasy is private in some sense, but she reconfigures the temporality of privacy, giving it an intersubjective expression. Privacy is an intentional reduction to the present; as such, it is the result of the free choice of each one involved to join their intentional time; it is not characterized by lying, but it actualizes the ground of truth-telling. I argue that Beauvoir's position is based on her reinterpretation of Edmund Husserl's sphere of ownness, which he developed in his notion of intersubjectivity in *The Cartesian Meditations* and reformulated in his later manuscripts.

After delineating Beauvoir's position on sexual ecstasy, I will argue that her account provides an alternative to the Kojèvian-Hegelian analysis of intersubjectivity based on master and slave, an analysis that underlies a position found in several early novels and short stories of Nelson Algren—specifically, *Somebody in Boots*, *The Neon Wilderness*, and *Never Come Morning*. I will create a debate between two different conceptions of a sexual relationship, Simone de Beauvoir's and Nelson Algren's, using texts, primarily fiction, that both of them were writing at about the time of their love affair. I will argue that, while Beauvoir and Algren agree on privacy, Algren's conception of a woman is strikingly similar to the female role in the master-slave relation that Beauvoir criticizes in *The Second Sex*. It is too bad that Nelson Algren did not seem to learn enough from the nights he spent with Madame de B.

Edmund Husserl on Intersubjectivity: The Sphere of Ownness and Inner Time

Simone de Beauvoir's description of the sexual relationship between Anne Dubreuilh and Lewis Brogan in *The Mandarins* may be illuminated by looking at Edmund Husserl's theory of intersubjectivity, beginning with his notion of the sphere of ownness in *The Cartesian Meditations*. I have argued elsewhere that Beauvoir's novel *L'invitée (She Came to Stay)* reveals the influence of *The Cartesian Meditations*, which was translated into French in 1929 (Holveck 2002, 20–26, 79–80). Beauvoir states that she read and studied the German text of the *Phenomenology of Inner Time Consciousness* in the 1930s (Beauvoir 1962, 162), and her position in *The Mandarins* emphasizes the temporality of intentionality.

Husserl's discussion of the sphere of ownness in *The Cartesian Meditations* occurs as part of his answer to a traditional question in Cartesian philosophy—namely, how can I have knowledge of an external world? Descartes, meditating alone in his room, is certain only that "I think," "I exist." His "I" will have knowledge of an external world and other persons only after a long excursion subsidized by an omniscient, omnipotent, and perfectly good God. Husserl reinterprets this Cartesian question in phenomenological terms. "Whatever exists for me, exists . . . thanks to my knowing consciousness. . . . I attain certainties . . . in my own domain of consciousness, in the nexus of motivation determining me. . . . But how can this business, going on wholly within the immanency of conscious life, acquire Objective significance?" (Husserl 1960, 82).

Husserl answers that "the whole problem is inconsistent" (Husserl 1960, 83). When I ask, "How can I have knowledge of an external world?" or "How can my perceptions, immanent to me, refer to real, transcendent objects?" "I," "my," and "me" refer to me as a human being who has a body. I have knowledge of my body, because I can see, hear, and touch myself, outside and alongside of other objects in space. In short, traditional questions about the validity of perception and the reality of the external world presuppose my body, which in turn presupposes the validity of my perceptions and the existence of objects in space outside that body. The question attempts to doubt what must be presupposed as true in order to give it meaning. Since traditional theory of knowledge founders on this inconsistency, Husserl suggests that the problem of transcendence must be clarified by the phenomenological method. Using an *epoché* that brackets all existence claims, Husserl asks more basic questions. How is my consciousness, which intends a meaningful world, embodied in a particular spatial point of view among others with different points of view? The problem of the existence of the external world becomes the problem of embodied intersubjectivity—that is, how do different embodied consciousnesses intend one and the same world?

Husserl begins his explication of otherness as embodied otherness with a discussion of the embodiment, the spatialization, of the "I." Husserl calls for an abstraction within *epoché* to the *Eigenheitssphäre* (Husserl 1973, 6), my sphere of ownness, a world of meaning that is unique to me. Husserl brackets out not only all other persons and other animals but also "all cultural predicates" and everything "*other-spiritual*" (Husserl 1960, 95; emphasis in original)—in short, all meanings that have any reference at all to an "other." What is left is unique to me. The world of ownness is the most basic level of conscious experience of the world; it is the world that I as animated body, *Leib*, can perceive by touching, seeing, and so on. The temporality of this world is my inner time, the essential intentional structure of the conscious experiences of myself as an animated body. My animated body is the center of my intentional life, the point of view of my consciousness on the world. Hence, the original sense of otherness, including the otherness of the external world, for Husserl, is an other animated body, an other embodied consciousness.

In many texts, Husserl discusses a serious problem in his analysis of the other consciousness, centering on his notions of inner time consciousness and space. The problem can be seen best by looking at a few of Husserl's manuscripts on intersubjectivity. In a text written in 1930, Husserl distinguishes between (1) each consciousness's own reduced immanent time, "so to speak, his private time" and (2) the intersubjective synthesis, "each in his immanent Present [Gegenwart] finds it in coincidence with the Present of each Other" (Husserl 1973, 66). The bridge between these two private times is empathy across space. I see the Other Now as There while I am Here. Our Nows, our Presents, are synchronized via a unification of our two different places. The places are much too far apart, however. I, as *Leib*, as animated body, am Here, embodied as conscious. The body of the Other from my point of view, however, is *Körper*, There, an object in space like any other object in space. Hence I am the only embodied subjectivity; the Other's subjectivity is appresented by empathy in a pairing relation with my animated body. Husserl's analysis might be seen as the ground of Sartre's famous discussion of *Le Regard*, the Look. At any moment I, the only consciousness embodied as *Leib*, can reduce the body of the Other to *Körper*, body as spatial object, or vice versa.

In some later manuscripts on temporality, however, Husserl develops a different position on my inner time; it is a living, streaming Present, *lebendige Gegenwart*. As Iso Kern points out in his introduction to the intersubjectivity manuscripts, Husserl writes of the Other in 1931 as a "transcendental Co-subject [Mitsubject]" and as "streaming Co-Present [Mitgegenwart]" (Kern, in Husserl 1973, xlviii). For example, in Manuscript C 3, Husserl writes, "The Coexistence [Mitsein] of Others is inseparable from me in my living self-presenting, and this Co-Present of Others is fundamental for the worldly present [Gegenwart] which in its turn is the presupposition for the meaning of all worldly temporality with worldly coexistence (Space) and temporal order" (Kern, quoting Husserl's Manuscript C3 in Husserl 1973, xlix).

In the intersubjectivity manuscripts from 1931 on, Husserl sometimes stresses that the temporality of the Other, the primordial ownness of the Other, is copresent, coprimordial. "My primordiality carries in itself another, his primordiality, and this one again, etc.... The coexistence of transcendental subjects, the coexistence of their immanent temporality, the coexistence of their primordiality, is no empty (precisely seen as unthinkable) being-together [Zusammensein], but rather a being-for-another [ein Füreinandersein]" (Husserl 1973, 191). Again, Husserl writes, "This innerness [Innerlichkeit] of *being-for-one-another* as an intentional *being-in-one-another* [Ineinanderseins] is *the 'metaphysical' original fact* ['metaphysische' Urtatsache], it is an absolute in-one-another [Ineinander des Absoluten]" (Husserl 1973, 366; emphasis in original). Hence, the spatial external world, and its intersubjective character that guarantees all intersubjective truth, presupposes that two primordial spheres, my own and that of the other, are unified. My inner time intentionally includes the temporality of others; each Present intends the Other as Copresent. Synchronization is not achieved via empathy across space but via intentionality. We are intentionally *Ineinandersein*, being in one another. This is the origin, the metaphysical fact that grounds all truth, which is intersubjective.

Anne Dubreuilh and Lewis Brogan in *The Mandarins*: The Sphere of Ownness-Otherness

Now I will discuss how Simone de Beauvoir's characterization of the relationship between Anne Dubreuilh and Lewis Brogan illuminates and furthers Husserl's discussion of intersubjectivity. Beauvoir's position reconfigures Husserl's notion of the sphere of ownness, revealing the relation between ownness and otherness on the level of embodied consciousness. The relation between Anne and Lewis may be viewed as the result of an *epoché* to the sphere of ownness. This sphere is the setting for the I and the other to find each other, to recapture each other on the level of embodied consciousness. The core relation, which I might call ownness-otherness, is the result of the free choice of each to find the other, to be embodied with the other here and now. The choice breaks down when the weight of past social, political, and economic worlds intrudes and when either I or the other make a choice no longer to be with the other.

In *America Day by Day*, Beauvoir describes her first trip to New York City in terms that are quite familiar to anyone with knowledge of Husserl's *epoché*. As she boards the plane in Paris, she thinks, "I feel I'm leaving my life behind" (Beauvoir 1999, 3). The first time Beauvoir walks down Broadway, she exclaims, "My eyes have no memory. . . . Cut off from the past and the future, a pure presence—a presence so pure, so tenuous that it doubts itself. All the world seems in limbo" (7). Beauvoir's French states Husserl's *epoché* clearly as she describes a presence, "Si pure, si ténue qu'elle doubte d'elle-même et que le monde aussi est en suspens" (Beauvoir [1947] 1997, 17). She reflects that on previous travels in Europe and Africa, she

> still felt that Paris was the heart of the world. . . . [But now] Paris has lost its hegemony. I've landed not only in a foreign country but in another world—an autonomous, separate world. I touch this world; it's here. It will be given to me. . . . In a flash I'm freed from the cares of that tedious enterprise I call my life. I'm just the charmed consciousness through which the sovereign Object will reveal itself. (Beauvoir 1999, 13–14)

Notice that the world is reduced to what she can see and touch; she herself is reduced to a streaming, intentional temporality, what Husserl calls one's own inner time. She comments, "I am traveling incognito, like a phantom. Will I manage to reincarnate myself?" (Beauvoir 1999, 7). She answers her own question, "If I want to decode New York, I must meet New Yorkers" (10). Beauvoir, as the disinterested onlooker of the *epoché*, reveals her inner time, an embodied pure temporal intentionality. But New York is constituted by layers of meanings for those who live there; since she does not yet know anyone, she is left with a world reduced to what she can experience by walking around, looking, touching. New York will be meaningful when she participates in the meanings others give it.

Right after she meets and spends a night with Nelson Algren, Beauvoir boards a train for the West Coast; her description of her sleeping compartment echoes themes from Husserl's sphere of ownness.

> This sleeping berth [couchette] . . . it's a whole dwelling [toute une demeure] reduced to the dimensions of a bed. There are childhood memories associated with this pleasure. I remember . . . that dark compartment where I loved to hide under my father's desk. Psychoanalysts see in that a desire to return to the maternal womb, but this language is too symbolic and does not clarify anything. My berth is not the recollection of lost happiness. . . . [I]t is refuge, solitude, separation. . . . [E]ach person achieves an absolute solitude. . . . [N]o appeal from the outside world can penetrate here. My life is no longer . . . tied to anyone or anything; it is closed in on itself in the silence of death. . . . I am not situated at any particular spot in the universe: I'm just passing through [rien qu'un passage]. I have no more ties to earth. (Beauvoir 1999, 103–4; [1947] 1997, 148–49)

It is interesting that this description of a *couchette*, with its similarity to Husserl's sphere of ownness, is Beauvoir's description of falling asleep, akin to death. In order to sleep one must deliberately block out all reference to others; in Beauvoir's world of ownness, I reduce myself to solitude, and others assume an imaginary existence for me. A world that is completely my own is equivalent to the death of my consciousness, or, at best, sleep.

This description immediately follows Beauvoir's first brief meeting with Nelson Algren. Reduced to a sphere of ownness by travel that cuts her off from her entire meaningful world, she is now reduced to her own streaming present consciousness. She is ready to meet another on this level. It is no accident that on this train journey Beauvoir read Algren's collection of short stories, *The Neon Wilderness* (Beauvoir 1998, 12). In her world of ownness, Beauvoir was ready to admit an other, whose world was Chicago. Apparently Beauvoir frequently described her relation to Nelson Algren as an immediate relation to an other on the level of incarnate consciousness. For example, Sylvie Le Bon de Beauvoir in her preface to Beauvoir's letters to Algren describes Beauvoir's relation to Algren as "a meeting with someone totally 'other.' . . . [W]hen the reassuring familiarity of the world has vanished, all that remains is the nakedness of pure presence" (Le Bon de Beauvoir, in Beauvoir 1998, 6–7).

To turn to *The Mandarins*: while references to phenomenological *epoché* are not quite so explicit, the private world that Anne and Lewis create with each other is exemplified in Lewis's Chicago apartment where they eventually find each other; this apartment is the situation for the sphere of ownness-otherness. When Anne first meets Lewis, she hesitates before knocking on his door, because "the life of the poor is an intimate thing [c'est intime]" (Beauvoir 1956, 325; 1954, 11). She likes his apartment, including the signs of his life in his simple room, "the Mexican blanket and then Van Gogh's yellow chair, the books, the phonograph, the typewriter" (Beauvoir 1956, 325); she is tempted to stay there, but she wants to tour Chicago. Anne thinks to herself that she hardly knows him, but she "felt the reassuring presence next to me of a body which could be warm or cold, a living body" (328). To look at his shoes, which he had obviously shined himself, was "to become a part of his intimate life" (328). But Anne turns away from Lewis's good-bye kiss and begins touring New Orleans, Florida, Virginia, and Canada.

Back in New York, Anne finally calls Lewis and asks if he has time for her to come back to Chicago. He answers "I have all my time. . . . My time is all mine" (Beauvoir 1956, 332). Even though Anne and Lewis agree to spend their time together, to merge their times, they waste an entire day milling around Chicago, because they cannot express their true intentions. Lewis should have said, "Come and rest a bit at my place [Venez vous reposer chez moi]" (Beauvoir 336; 1954, 28). *Se reposer* carries the connotation to settle in one place, e.g., as a flying bird alights on a branch.

Anne's relation to Lewis has three stages, as does Kundera's analysis of Madame de T.'s relation to the Chevalier in Denon's novella. First, Madame de T. and the Chevalier walk in the parklike garden of her husband's château. Madame de T. permits the Chevalier to kiss her, but "she transforms a kiss into an act of resistance" (Kundera 1996, 31). The first day that they meet, Lewis and Anne walk around Chicago; in the end she turns her lips away from his kiss. In the second stage, Madame de T. and the Chevalier reach the door of the château, but they walk back into the garden. Madame de T. scolds the Chevalier for not telling her about his mistress, the Comtesse. Madame de T. "gives him a short course in . . . her practical philosophy of love and its need to be freed from the tyranny of moral rules and protected by discretion, of all virtues the supreme virtue" (35). At the end of stage two, Denon's couple make love in an outdoor pavilion. Finally, in stage three, Madame de T. and the Chevalier make love, not in a secret chamber of the château, walled with mirrors which "multiply their reflections in such a way that suddenly an endless procession of couples are embracing all around them" (Kundera 1996, 38), but in a room next door, "a grotto deep in darkness and all tufted in cushions; only there do they make love, lengthily and slowly, until the break of day" (38).

Anne's and Lewis's love has a second and third stage, also, but their stages are not examples of a mistress of "the art of conversation" (Kundera 1996, 31) educating a younger man in the prolongation of arousal and the necessity for secrecy; nor are they examples of a Don Juan taking his time to seduce a woman. Rather, in the second stage, Anne and Lewis are silent about their intentions; they cannot express their free choice to settle down together in one place.

Anne and Lewis make silent, slow progress from public places to private ones. At the beginning of Anne's second visit, Lewis kisses Anne at the airport, and she is "disconcerted by that public kiss" (Beauvoir 1956, 333). He wants to visit the zoo, and she replies curtly that she did not come here "to exhibit myself to your animals" (334). Rather, she suggests that they find "some quiet place, where . . . we'll look at each other" (334). Anne's French clearly distinguishes (1) "me donner en spectacle à vos bêtes," i.e., making myself a spectacle for animals to look at and (2) finding "un endroit tranquille où. . . . nous nous regarderons l'un l'autre" (Beauvoir 1954, 27), i.e., a quiet place, spot, or point where we can look at each other, the one and the other both looking together. These two expressions clearly distinguish, in Husserl's terms, two relations between I and the other. First, Husserl's analysis in *The Cartesian Meditations* posits the "I," the self, as one animated body among all the other ones; I can allow myself to be viewed as one animal, one *Körper*, who is a spectacle There, for any other animal, *Leib*, who has a Here. Rather, secondly, Anne wants to find an *endroit*, a spot, a point, where the I and the other can look at each other as embodied consciousnesses together. Beauvoir uses *endroit*; Husserl wrote of one's body as the point of view of one's consciousness in the world, the *Nullpunkt* of consciousness (Husserl 1969, 158). Of course, Husserl took this point from Leibniz, a philosopher that Beauvoir studied. Beauvoir suggests that it is possible for two people to share the same point, if they intend to, if they freely choose to unite their times, to spend their time at the same spot.

It takes Anne and Lewis some time to freely choose to find this spot. Anne rents a hotel room where she naps and wonders if she is dreaming that Lewis wants to join her there (Beauvoir 1956, 337). This interlude repeats Beauvoir's recounting of her own experience in the *couchette* in *America Day by Day*, but now Anne does not just sleep; she dreams about Lewis's joining her there. Later, still roaming around Chicago, Anne and Lewis try to talk seriously, but Lewis's friends keep interrupting, until, finally, Lewis kisses Anne in a cab—thank heavens a streetcar didn't come first!—and soon they end up in Lewis's apartment.

Unlike Vivant's couple, Anne and Lewis do not progress from seductive conversation to silence; they progress from everyday, idle talk to real, intimate communication in Lewis's apartment, where they declare that they have "found" each other, and they "rediscover [retrouver]" each other (Beauvoir 1956, 338–40; 1954, 38). Anne says, waiting for Lewis, "c'etait réconfortant de me sentir chez moi, dans ce lit étranger; l'homme que j'avais choisie et qui m'avait choisie allait se coucher à mon côte" (Beauvoir 1954, 38). I would translate this "it was reviving to feel myself at home in this strange bed; the man whom I had chosen and who had chosen me was going to lay himself down by me." Anne uses two expressions from Marcel Proust. *Retrouver* is to recapture, to recover, to regain the past. Lewis is about to sleep *à côte* to Anne. In French history *Du côté de chez Swann* was a different path from *Le côté de Guermantes*; Swann was the aristocracy's pet Jew, kept for amusement, but he was never really one of them. This French past must be retrieved, recaptured.

Anne is choosing to lie with Lewis who chooses to lie with her in this place. She will lie next to Lewis, who is the son of a "Hungarian Jewish mother" (Beauvoir 1956, 326). In the joint diary that Simone de Beauvoir and Nelson Algren kept of their time together, they use the English "found each other" (Drew 1989, 192, 391).

The end of the second stage occurs as Anne and Lewis make love for the first time. Anne describes herself as passive in this scene; her body is brought back from the dead by Lewis's caresses. His desire transforms her; she is "as nourishing as bread" (Beauvoir 1956, 341). Anne, from the beginning of the novel, has described herself as dead to sensation, to physical pleasure, because she is mourning, in her body, those murdered in the Holocaust, especially Diego. In her first monologue in the book, Anne thinks that at the Christmas party, "We were dancing, we were kissing each other . . . and there were many, oh, so many, who weren't there" (32). She remembers Diego's face as he devoured Kant or Hegel. She recalls the day Diego stole money from his father and invited Nadine and her to eat all the food they wanted, a welcome respite from the scarcity of war; Anne remembers kissing Diego and Nadine good night (32–33). She is especially dismayed that Diego has "[n]o tombstone, no date of death" (32). If consciousness has no spot, no point of view placing it, it disappears. Anne cannot even mourn Diego properly, because he has no grave, not even a small point where he has been. It is as if he has never existed at all. It is Lewis who helps Anne to recover her place. Because Anne, who has been dead for so long, needs to be revived by Lewis's living love, she is passive when they first make love. This is the end of their stage two.

Stage three occurs a few days later when Anne and Lewis have been completely honest with each other. Each one declares love openly for the other; each is active and passive together. Lewis is the first to tell Anne he loves her (Beauvoir 1956, 345); Anne tells Lewis how much her marriage and her life in Paris mean to her, yet she delays her return to Paris to be with Lewis (349). Then Anne and Lewis make love in a different way. Now Anne is "a totally new woman. . . . I felt my life leaving me, my old life with its worries, its weariness, its worn-out memories" (350). Lewis and Anne create a new time together: "The past, the future, everything that was separating us died at the foot of our bed. Nothing separated us any longer . . . Lewis, complete, was in my arms, and I in his. We wanted nothing else; we had everything forever. Both together we said, 'What happiness!'" (350). The translation takes away some of the unity between Anne and Lewis. "Lewis était tout entier dans mes bras, moi dans les siens, nous ne désirons rien d'autre" (Beauvoir 1954, 55) might be translated "Lewis was entirely in my arms and I in his; we lacked nothing of the other," i.e., we were entirely united, *Ineinander der Absoluten.*

This physical unity is attained through a merging of intentional temporality. "I spent two weeks in Chicago. For two weeks we lived without a future . . . ;

from our past we drew stories and told them to each other. . . . He knew neither my country, my language, my friends, nor my worries, only my voice, my eyes, my skin" (Beauvoir 1956, 350). Here is Beauvoir's reinterpretation of Husserl's sphere of ownness as ownness-otherness. Two consciousnesses embody each other in a *Nullpunkt*, a point they create by freely choosing to merge their intentional time. In this place each intends to be totally with the other. I choose freely to feel as the other freely chooses to feel here and now. Beauvoir never read Husserl's manuscripts on intersubjectivity—at best she had secondhand knowledge of them from Merleau-Ponty—but her original philosophical reflections on inner time enabled her to create in Anne and Lewis an almost perfect exemplification of Husserl's words: "My primordiality carries in itself another, his primordiality. . . . The coexistence of transcendental subjects, the coexistence of their immanent temporality. . . . is no empty being-together, but rather a being-for-one-another. . . . [This] intentional *being-in-one-another* is *the 'metaphysical' original fact*, it is an absolute in-one-another" (Husserl 1973, 191, 366; emphasis in original).

I am emphasizing the relationship of Beauvoir's theory of intersubjectivity to Husserl's, because she, like him, grounds the otherness of the world in the consciousness of the other. Being is always meaningful, the intended meaning of some consciousness, and so there is no world without someone's intention. Having an intersubjective world is possible only if two consciousnesses intend the same meaning. The ground of this structure of intersubjective intentionality is a Present and a Co-Present who intend to include each other at the same point of view. Beauvoir describes this grounding in the sexual experience that expresses the love between Anne and Lewis, because sexual orgasm is a reduction to a present sensation of pleasure; if we both choose to be our pleasure here and now, together, ownness and otherness merge intentionally. Of course, the love between Anne and Lewis may be viewed at different levels of constituted meanings in Husserl's sense, as Beauvoir developed in *The Second Sex*: psychologically, socially, politically, economically, historically, and so on. But sexual love can be the metaphysical ground of all common worlds; all being, beginning with perceived being, is grounded intersubjectively as the I and the other choose to be, intentionally, at the same point. This cointentionality incarnates and grounds all higher-level intersubjective meanings.

Madame de B. does not seduce men with her rhythmic art of conversation based on lies. She speaks the truth to her lover; she declares her intentions; they create togetherness without mirrors in their own time as they lie in their place of choice. Milan Kundera obviously wastes too much time mooning over women from his past. Ecstasy is not "feeling himself flung out of time" (Kundera 1996, 2); it is in an entirely new intentional intersubjective time that a man and a woman who love each other must freely create. A true Véra might remind Kundera of what his mother really used to say: "Milanku, you have been feeling yourself so much, you have lost all sense of time" (90–91).

Alas, however, to create a new intersubjective time, to share all their time, would mean that Anne and Lewis would have to completely restructure their entire past lives; they would have to turn all of their pasts into "stories" they tell each other (Beauvoir 1956, 350). Anne in Paris and Lewis in Chicago find that they cannot share time; "even the clocks laughed at us" (362). The weight of the past, with its already constituted social, cultural, political, and economic structures, soon puts pressure on the love between them. Lewis resents Anne's commitment to her past ties to her husband and her life in Paris. Anne, in her circle of Parisian intellectuals, begins to side with the Soviet Union and socialism against the capitalist United States (409).

Anne and Lewis reject oppression, but they have different perspectives. When they are vacationing in Mexico, for example, on Anne's return visit to the United States, Lewis becomes angry as they view the ruins of Chichen Itza, "[T]hink of those millions of miserable creatures turned into beasts of burden by the warriors and the priests. And why? Out of stupid vanity" (Beauvoir 1956, 454–55). Anne, who does not find her past here as she does in the Acropolis or Forum, seems more dismayed at the "dead beauty," the "sterility" of the ruins, than at the slavery that built them (455). In these scenes in Mexico, Anne seems to be the vacationing bourgeois tourist appreciating the aesthetic beauty of peasant life as opposed to Lewis, who rages helplessly against evidence of past oppression. For a short time, they paper over their differences. Anne covets an old cape from a peasant woman in Chichicastenango's marketplace, "antique embroidery in which a vivid blue blended tenderly with dull reds and golds" (458), an indication that blue skies do not come unmixed with royal gold mingled with the blood of the oppressed; Lewis talks the woman into trading the old cape for a new one (460). Anne will have a fashionable blouse to display in Paris, while Lewis thinks of the real woman who needs a serviceable cape. In his turn, Lewis pouts and refuses to seriously engage in conversations with intellectual friends.

The major cause of Anne's and Lewis's breakup occurs during and following this trip to Mexico. Lewis begs Anne to marry him and stay with him, but she replies, "[A]t my age, you can't throw your whole life overboard" (Beauvoir 1956, 461). Later, however, Anne seriously considers relocating to the United States; she waits for Lewis's appeal to her. "He had promised to write me first, in a week. If he still called to me in his letter, if his expressions of regret had the sound of a call [l'accent d'un appel (Beauvoir 1954, 359)], I would find the strength to give up my old security; I would answer, 'Yes, I'll come, I'll come to stay with you as long as you want to keep me'" (Beauvoir 1956, 527). Lewis writes no such thing, however, and Anne concludes that he really prefers to continue to live alone, to keep the security of his past. In short, Anne and Lewis consciously choose not to merge their times in one joint enterprise, not to create a new time in one place together.

Nelson Algren's Sphere of Ownness

In *The Mandarins* the relationship between Anne and Lewis is told completely from Anne's point of view. It is only fair to present the other's side of the story, and the easiest way is through the man who was his model, Nelson Algren. At least one Algren scholar, Daniel M. Simon, conjectures that Algren wrote his major philosophical reflections on literature, composed during 1950–53 but published only in 1996 as *Nonconformity: Writing on Writing*, because "he felt he had to best Sartre in some kind of imagined battle for Simone's heart" (Simon, in Algren [1950–53] 1998, 88). I would emphasize, rather, that *The Mandarins* represents Beauvoir's own reflections on the value of literature after the Holocaust and Hiroshima and on the kind of literature that she herself wanted to continue writing; her views would have encouraged Algren's questioning of his own social role at a time when one of his finest novels, *The Man with the Golden Arm*, was trivialized by Hollywood after being stolen from him. In the 1961 afterword to *Chicago: City on the Make* (1951), Algren adds his own definition of literature to Sartre's. "'What is Literature?' Jean-Paul Sartre once asked in a small volume bearing that title. I submit that literature is made upon any occasion that a challenge is put to the legal apparatus by conscience in touch with humanity. Now we all know" (Algren [1951] 2001, 81). In another work Algren phrases it more simply: "Any challenge to laws made by people on top, in the interest of people below . . . is literature" (Algren 1963, 152).

In an interview in 1955 for the *Paris Review*, Algren comments that he preferred to live among

> the people underneath . . . rather . . . than with the business classes. . . . [Y]ou write out of—well, I wouldn't call it indignation, but a kind of *irritability* that these people on top should be so contented, so absolutely unaware of other people, and so sure that their values are the right ones. I mean, there's a certain satisfaction in recording the people underneath, whose values are as sound as theirs, and a lot funnier, and a lot truer in a way. There's a certain satisfaction in kind of scooping up a shovelful of these people and dumping them in somebody's parlor. (Algren [1947] 1986, 300)

Algren's commitment to accurately depicting lives at the lower depths, based on their own words, which he recorded as he lived with them, seems motivated by three claims. (1) A study of outcasts reveals the empty core of meaninglessness at the heart of a life based on the pursuit of wealth built upon the oppression of others. "From the penthouse suspended silently so high above the winding traffic's iron lamentation, forty straight-down stories into those long, low, night-blue bars aglow below street-level, a lonely guilt pervades us all. . . . [T]he spiritual desolation of men and women made incapable of using themselves for anything more satisfying than the promotion of chewing gum . . . or some detergent ever-urgent" (Algren [1950–53] 1998, 45). (2) The most abject of the poor are at least honest; they are the only innocents. (3) Only after seeing the bankruptcy of the empty pursuit of wealth is there any hope for creating a truly human world.

Algren claims that a Martian trying to decipher human beings would have no understanding of humanity at all until he experienced

> the lives of those who live out their hand to mouth hours without friendship or love. They belong to no particular street in no particular city. They pass from furnished room to furnished room, and belong not even to their own time; not even to themselves. They are the ones who are displaced in time, and again displaced in the heart. . . .
>
> Not until he walked the unswept streets in the hundred-storied evening and saw the legend in the first-floor-front—ROOM FOR TRANSIENT—did he begin to understand. . . .
>
> Not until he saw them sleeping in the all-night restaurants and the all-night movies and the night-blue bars of the whiskey wilderness did he understand at last that he was on the ancient unswept street where most of humanity has always lived.
>
> . . . Who one really is depends on what world he belongs to. The secret multitudes who belong to no world, no way of life, no particular time and place, are the truly displaced persons: displaced from their true selves. (Algren [1950–53] 1998, 35–36)

This quotation is strikingly compatible with Simone de Beauvoir's position on intersubjective time that I have developed above; Algren places it in a social-political-economic context. Outcasts are homeless; they have no place to call their own. They are displaced in time and in the heart. They have no meaningful life, no human time, no time with others. Outcasts represent the futility of a way of life where everyone is "on the make," an attitude that has historically characterized the city of Chicago. "You remember we began by saying No man is an island, but . . . changed it to I'm getting mine" (Algren 1963, 157).

In his 1963–64 conversations with H. E. F. Donohue, Algren gives a sketch of what a truly human life would be like. The ultimate purpose of human life is "to live it. . . . You're alive. That's its only purpose. . . . Life's meaning simply comes in within your senses . . . just sight and sound and smell" (Donohue and Algren [1963–64] 2001, 326). Algren attributes this kind of love of life to Simone de Beauvoir. "Existentialism, to her, was not a philosophical complex of Hegel, Kierkegaard, Kafka, and Kant, but a means of living in the world with freedom and joy" (Algren 1963, 98). A free, open society for Algren would be one "wherein people are given a choice and the opportunity to realize their own possibilities rather than to have no choice except to be used by that society in return for being well clothed and well housed" (Donohue and Algren [1963–64] 2001, 254). In "a *real* society . . . each person would have enjoyed every day. He would have enjoyed the weather. He would have enjoyed food. He would have enjoyed friends. He would have had love. He would have seen the world. He would have read. He would have used his mind and his heart and his brain" (260). The basis for such a society is public spending for the social good, e.g., for health care, for the arts, and for schools (217, 262); travel would be encouraged "to try to establish human relationships with other human beings in every aspect of life" (263). Algren believes that artists, actors, and writers have an essential role in a good society: "[T]here's *no* limit to what you can do if you once interpret the human being to the rest of the race. It lasts. That's the only thing that does last" (261). Algren comments on sexual relations, also. Chicago will remain the realm of "Dingdong Daddy" (Algren 1963, 311), Algren's nickname for Hugh Hefner, "until we recognize sex as a natural urge, pleasant, beautiful, interesting and useful, to be treated, like any other important faculty, such as work or learning, by welcoming it, enjoying it" (Algren [1951] 2001, 101).

Of course, the United States where Algren lived was not the ideal world. *Somebody in Boots* is the tale of an illiterate drifter from Santa Fé during the depression, Cass McKay; "I had seen him riding shoeless on a box-car roof. I had seen his face framed between the bars of the El Paso County Jail. . . . taking charity in a Salvation Army pew. . . . A walker in search of something to belong to in order to belong to himself" (Algren [1935] 1965, 8). This first novel is criticized for being overwritten and a Marxist morality tale, but I do not know of another work which so captures the experience of being hopelessly unemployed and homeless.

There is no *Grapes of Wrath* nobility among Algren's dispossessed. There is no love for self or any other. At fifteen, Cass McKay knew "long cold nights when you walked unlit streets, hungry, ill, alone. When the wind cut so that you gasped with pain, and so tired you were you scarce could stand. . . . and the hate that is yellow and springs from shame rose within you and made numb your heart till you could think of nothing save how sweet it would be just to kill for the simple pleasure of killing. . . . you knew then that to vent your own pain you must see another man suffer too" (Algren [1935] 1965, 19–20). A particularly violent scene occurs in a jail when the inmates, with the obvious collusion of the guards, nearly beat to death a Mexican who has been thrown in with them (136–41). Vagrants riding in a boxcar at first accept a Black woman sharecropper who is traveling to get a better job, but soon one of the men jokingly suggests that she marry him, and the joke leads to gang rape. "All moved slowly, in silence, toward the black woman. . . . They were all of them men; they were men without women" (94).

The imagery of displacement is used effectively throughout the short stories in *The Neon Wilderness*. In "Please Don't Talk About Me When I'm Gone," the narrator, Rose, comments that when the police wagon picked her up after she killed her companion (an example of battered-woman syndrome, but try telling that to the judge), the "crowd moved back a little to make room for me. . . . I was thinkin', my whole life it's the first time anyone made room for me. And now just look what for" (Algren [1947] 1986, 147).

In "Design for Departure," a powerful tale of drug addiction, the child Mary learns to pretend to be dead as her only defense against her drunken, violent mother and stepfather. "She thought of death as a warm and windless place, like thinking of a room with a key all her own. A cornerless room, that was quiet all night long" (Algren [1947] 1986, 241). When Mary gets a job wrapping bacon at the stockyards, she finally rents her own room, but "when life goes by in rented moments. . . . each hour must be purchased with the sweat of fear and every meal must be eaten with privation, like a false friend, sitting on the other side of the table counting each forkful" (243). Mary dreams of a room that she could really call her own. "And when she was tired she made up a lie, all to herself, about a doorless room which she'd never have to leave at all. A little windless windowless room in which she lay quietly and white, half awake and strangely dreaming, safe from human voices" (243–44). Eventually drug addiction becomes the lullaby that puts Mary in this room of her dreams: "Veronal. Allonal. Luminal. Veronal" (257).

In these quotations from Algren's book that Beauvoir was reading in her *couchette* as she traveled to California, Algren develops his own notion of the sphere of ownness. Mary has no childhood memory of a safe place under a desk in her father's library; her safe place is an imaginary room where she can sleep and dream; it is like death, where she will be safe from the threat of others. The homeless, for Algren, are "displaced in time and again displaced in the heart" (Algren [1950–53] 1998, 36); they have no *Innerlichkeit*, no inner time of their own, in Beauvoir's adaptation of Husserl's sense, because their lives go by only "in rented moments," purchased by hours of mind-numbing labor. The actions of the poor are not free choices but "co-incidents," in the words of a drug-addicted petty thief, who is trying to explain away his role in a robbery, in the police precinct lineup in "The Captain Has Bad Dreams." "It's all a silly coincident" (Algren [1947] 1986, 34). The class that creates values in Algren's world is at the top. The intentions of the powerful, like the single light shining on each one testifying at the lineup, make the usual suspects into spectacles for the amusement of the audience, like animals in a zoo. The Captain is sickened and disgusted with his role as the minor functionary who has to execute the values of the upper classes—who, of course, in their penthouses, have no direct experience of what happens underneath the El. The Captain mimics the humor of the petty criminals, but he has bad dreams, because he senses that they are less guilty than he.

Homelessness and lack of light are used effectively in a sustained way in the relationship between the aspiring boxer Bruno Lefty Bicek and his girl, Steffi Rostenkowski, in *Never Come Morning*, the novel of Algren's that Beauvoir arranged to have translated and published in France. At three, Lefty took shelter under the shadow of the El at the Division Street Station. "As a child he had learned that the safest place to play was beneath the El. For the streets belonged to streetcars and walks to people who lived in houses and not behind stores or above poolrooms. Nobody but pigeons owned the littered places under the steep Division street steps" (Algren [1941] 1996, 29).

It is under the El in an old warehouse that serves as headquarters for Lefty's gang, where the teenage Lefty, too scared and too embarrassed to admit that he really loves Steffi, allows his entire gang to share her. Badly injured by the gang rape, Steffi is taken in by the neighborhood pimp, and, ultimately, her world is reduced to her room in the whorehouse. "[I]t seemed to Steffi R. that she had been nowhere else all her life. She ceased to remember the outside world. . . . The world was a room. . . . Like an inside room in some exclusive madhouse. The city itself was a sealed up room" (Algren [1941] 1996, 208–9). Steffi's brothel room is comparable to Lefty's cell in prison; he is ultimately executed for killing a stranger, a Greek, who tried to line up with the gang at Steffi's rape.

Both Lefty and Steffi are overcome with guilt about their choices in regard to each other: Steffi, because she didn't have the power to fight off Lefty when they first had sex, and Lefty "because of what he had made of Steffi R. He had snuck off with a bottle in his hand while the one human he loved had been turned into a loveless thing" (Algren [1941] 1996, 133). Hence these two lost teens long for a loving relationship and feel guilty because they could not create one; they somehow understand fundamental human values in a society that lacks all sense of them. In her room in the brothel, "Steffi thought nostalgically of places where beds like hers were never rented and sheets were changed twice a week: Polish homes, set amidst gasworks, churches, grammar schools, taverns and factories. Men and women who worked by day in order to sleep together by night. If it wasn't for that they labored, what then was their labor for, she wondered. To sleep together. In a place of their own" (211).

At least some of Algren's poor manage to create a place where a man and a woman can live and love together. In "Stickman's Laughter," the former boxer Banty Longobardi comes home on payday planning to atone for past bouts of gambling by paying his back rent and taking his wife to the movies; he "wanted her by his side, to take care of him now. 'What is life without a wife?' he hummed idly" (Algren [1947] 1986, 67). But his wife is visiting her mother, and he cannot go there. "Her people didn't trust wops. They said things in Polish about Dagos" (68). So Banty succumbs to the lure of the local gambling establishment and, when he finally comes home drunk, penniless, and partially beaten up, he finds his wife in bed.

> When he reached the bed he had only to wait for her to take his head on her breast.
>
> That's the kind of old woman Banty had himself.
>
> "My fault," she assured him softly, like a storyteller making up stories to put a child to sleep. "I knew it was payday but I went out just the same. No supper for poor Banty. . . . Lost all his money and no supper either."
>
> She felt his tenseness lessening. Felt his tears between the shadowed valley of her breasts. And knew they were for her.
>
> . . . She held him so . . . till his breath began coming regularly and untroubled. When his hand clutched at hers in sleep she smiled a little. . . .
>
> So nothing important had been lost after all. (72)

This is Algren's view of the sphere of ownness. In a world where everyone is on the make to get his own in opposition to others, ownness is an imaginary room where one is safe at last from others, in drug-induced dreams or death; it is one's room in a brothel or a boxing ring, where one's body is an animated thing rented out to, or on display for, the entertainment of others; it is a prison cell, where the chair is no reproduction of Van Gogh's, but electric. However, sometimes a bed in a rented room can serve as a situation where two can make time for each other. Banty's wife accepts him for himself; she understands his lost dreams of being a champion, his bleak job, his addiction to gambling and alcohol, his desire for a home.

Algren's old woman is some improvement over Kundera's. Madame de T. pays no mind to the servants who sacrifice their own desires to maintain her pleasurable escapades in her husband's château; the Chevalier does not try to possess Madame de T., but he still uses her husband's room. Across the economic ocean, Algren's European descendants of servants see the man's role as bringing home the paycheck and fighting off other men, in a boxing ring or on the streets. And a good old woman shelters her old man on her breast, offering him solace. Her body is literally a bed of his own.

Banty Longobardi's old woman is an almost perfect example of the woman's role in the Kojèvian-Hegelian position that Beauvoir criticizes in book 1, part 3, chapter 9 of *The Second Sex*, "Dreams, Fears, and Idols." "[E]ach separate conscious being aspires to set himself up alone as sovereign subject. Each tries to fulfill himself by reducing the other to slavery" (Beauvoir 1989,

140). In the harsh fight against Nature to satisfy needs and the fight to death for recognition among other men, man's "dream incarnated is precisely woman. . . . She opposes him with neither the hostile silence of nature nor the hard requirement of a reciprocal relation. . . . [S]he is a conscious being and yet it seems possible to possess her in the flesh" (140–41).

For Algren, the Hegelian struggle between master and slave is created by the capitalist economy in the United States, which tolerates, even requires, inadequate wages and unemployment for the underclass. Those at the lower depths realize the lack of human meaning in a society based solely on the pursuit of wealth at all cost; they accept guilt and try to create truly human relationships between men and women. But the mythical Banty Longobardi's old woman (Algren never gives her a name!) is no solution for Simone de Beauvoir. Her answer to the struggle between the I and the other is for man to attain "an authentically moral attitude when he renounces *mere being* to assume his position as an existent; through this transformation also he renounces all possession, for possession is one way of seeking more being; but the transformation is . . . never done, it is necessary to make it without ceasing" (Beauvoir 1989, 140).

Conclusion: The Time of Simone de Beauvoir and Nelson Algren

In this chapter I have attempted to show that the philosophical difference between Simone de Beauvoir and Nelson Algren on sexuality is roughly the difference between Beauvoir's reconsideration of Husserl and Algren's agreement with Kojève's Hegel. For Beauvoir, historical, political, and economic time comprise layers of constituted meanings that are part of the human world; these levels of meaning look at human beings as animals with needs, and the needs of some go completely unrecognized. In Algren's world some animals can barely compete with others for basic food and shelter, and this is an appalling situation; the only respite a few have is the numbness of addiction, the release of death, or, for very few, a comforting mate at home. For Beauvoir, however, an authentic human being, even a poor one in a rented room, must renounce mere being as an animal, must renounce all possession, and find a place he might be entirely in some other's arms, and she in his, *Ineinandersein*, because they freely choose to be so. Beauvoir writes in *The Second Sex*, "[F]riendship and generosity, which alone permit in actuality this recognition of free beings . . . are assuredly man's highest achievement" (1989, 140). In *The Mandarins* when Anne and Lewis are completely in each other's arms, Anne exclaims, "Nothing separated us any longer. What a victory!" (350). *The Mandarins* reveals not just the mutual recognition of two free beings, but the intentional realizing, the embodying, the concrete incarnation of authentic human communication at the same point of view, because each one freely chooses to feel and to be, here, together, now.

But this victory must be continuously won anew. The transformation of mere animal being through the renouncing of all possession must be made by free choices day by day. And needs must be satisfied as a necessary precondition for the transformation. In historical, social, political, and economic time, Simone de Beauvoir and Nelson Algren were attempting to change the world in two different, but compatible, ways. Her audience consisted of left-wing intellectuals who read her novels and essays, and who supported but criticized the socialist Soviet Union against the capitalist United States. Algren expressed the lives of those who lived beneath Chicago's El "on the ancient unswept street where most of humanity has always lived" (Algren [1950–53] 1998, 36). Algren tended to mock intellectuals, and Beauvoir, at the end of *The Mandarins*, presents a drug addict who participated in the Holocaust by denouncing Jews for money to support his habit. Both Algren and Beauvoir needed to recognize that their tasks were different and that they could neither merge their entire pasts together, nor share a completely common future.

The crisis in the relationship between Beauvoir and Algren came in the autumn of 1951. For a year Algren had claimed that he no longer loved her and was thinking of remarrying his first wife. Beauvoir told Deirdre Bair that, at the end of her visit on October 28, Algren came to her, "'his face crumbled, he fell to his knees beside the bed, he told me he loved me'" (Bair 1990, 430), and they made love. Bair's account is credible, because in the letter Beauvoir wrote to Algren on October 30, 1951, from the Hotel Lincoln in New York City, she writes that she was shattered when, at the end of the visit, "You said you do no longer evict me from your heart" (Beauvoir 1998, 435). She is frightened, because she was learning to accept that he no longer loved her, but now she "can be hurt again and again if you decide again to evict me" (435). She will accept it if he really loves his former wife, and he has to accept that she cannot give up her life in Paris. "You would never have accepted to come and live in France for keeps, and you had not in U.S.A. the tie that above all ties me to Paris" (435). She loves him, "Just because you are who you are.... I'll have to keep you in my heart for ever" (436). And she begs him, "Keep me in your heart until we meet again. Let us meet within not too long a time" (435). Beauvoir's use of the word *heart*, which Algren also uses, is Husserl's *Innerlichkeit*, which becomes *Ineinandersein*. It is clear from Beauvoir's letters dated November 9 and after that Algren's answer was no. He needed his old woman. In an unpublished manuscript, "The Man in the Hotel Mirror," Algren later acknowledged his responsibility for the break (Drew 1989, 250–51).

I submit that in her letter of October 30, 1951, Simone de Beauvoir gives us a new image in the Cartesian tradition of philosophy. Instead of a man, alone in a room, meditating about what he can know for certain, Beauvoir gives us a woman, alone in a hotel room, choosing to love a man and begging him to continue to choose to love her. Her free choice requires the cochoice of an other to join her. The free choice to merge our times in one place is the ground of all truth; it is not certain at all, because it depends on the free choice of others. This philosopher in *her* room writes, Let us keep each other in our hearts for all time, and let us try to find a point to meet, in some place, from time to time.

Works Cited

Algren, Nelson. [1935] 1965. *Somebody in boots*. New York: Berkley.

———. [1941] 1996. *Never come morning*. New York: Seven Stories Press.

———. [1947] 1986. *The neon wilderness*. New York: Seven Stories Press. (This book includes the 1955 interview of Algren by Alston Anderson and Terry Southern, reprinted from the *Paris Review*, 1955.)

———. [1950–53] 1998. *Nonconformity: Writing on writing*. Notes by Daniel Simon and C. S. O'Brian. Trade paperback edition. New York: Seven Stories Press.

———. [1951] 2001. *Chicago: City on the make*. Annotated by David Schmittgens and Bill Savage. Chicago: University of Chicago Press.

———. 1963. *Who lost an American?* New York: Macmillan.

Bair, Deirdre. 1990. *Simone de Beauvoir: A biography*. New York: Summit.

Beauvoir, Simone de. [1947] 1997. *L'Amerique au jour le jour*. Paris: Gallimard.

———. 1954. *Les mandarins II*. Paris: Gallimard.

———. 1956. *The mandarins*. Translated by Leonard M. Friedman. Washington, D.C.: Regnery Gateway.

———. 1962. *The prime of life*. Translated by Peter Green. Cleveland: World.

———. 1989. *The second sex*. Translated and edited by H. M. Parshley. New York: Vintage.

———. 1998. *A transatlantic love affair: Letters to Nelson Algren*. Compiled and annotated by Sylvie Le Bon de Beauvoir. New York: New Press.

———. 1999. *America day by day*. Translated by Carol Cosman. Berkeley and Los Angeles: University of California Press.

Donohue, H. E. F., and Nelson Algren. [1963–64] 2001. *Conversations with Nelson Algren*. Chicago: University of Chicago Press.

Drew, Bettina. 1989. *Nelson Algren: A life on the wild side*. New York: G. P. Putnam's Sons.

Holveck, Eleanore. 2002. *Simone de Beauvoir's philosophy of lived experience: Literature and metaphysics*. Lanham, Md.: Rowman & Littlefield.

Husserl, Edmund. 1960. *Cartesian meditations*. Translated by Dorion Cairns. The Hague: Martinus Nijhoff.

———. 1969. *Ideen: Zweites buch*. The Hague: Martinus Nijhoff.

———. 1973. *Zur Phänomenologie der Intersubjektivität: Texte aus dem Nachlass. Vol. 3, 1929–1935*. Herausgegeben von Iso Kern. The Hague: Martinus Nijhoff. (My translation.)

Kundera, Milan. 1996. *Slowness*. Translated by Linda Asher. New York: Harper Collins.

Chapter 11

Salon-Haunters

The Impasse Facing French Intellectuals

Peg Brand

Artists as well as philosophers may take particular interest in the unique theory of aesthetics espoused by Simone de Beauvoir. Operating below the surface of her more familiar and contentious theories of gender difference, sexuality, and oppression, a unified philosophy of art can be constructed by unearthing shards of evidence that fit together into a cohesive whole. At least three sources function as prime sites for excavation: her award-winning 1954 novel, *The Mandarins*; her densely written 1947 philosophical treatise, *The Ethics of Ambiguity*; and her landmark treatise on gender construction, *The Second Sex* ([1952] 1989).

One of Beauvoir's clearest statements of aesthetic purpose praises the creation of particular types of artwork as a means of helping people face "the truth," for example, the horror of Nazi atrocities. Such works of art, when created correctly, function ethically as guides to self-awareness, proper behavior, and ultimately, the achievement of genuine freedom. When created incorrectly, they serve to glorify their maker and may lead others to unethical ends. The impasse facing French intellectuals is the choice between the two. Beauvoir explores this choice in traditional essay form in *The Ethics* and *The Second Sex*, and also more imaginatively through the fictional characters Henri and Robert in *The Mandarins.* She pits the "comfortable, carefree, esthete's life" ([1954] 1991, 564) of those she derisively calls "salon-haunters" (535) against the difficult life of the humanist intent on helping the world. For Beauvoir, all intellectuals—artists and writers alike—face an impasse that will set them on a freely chosen path toward inaction or action, i.e., toward culture or politics.

This chapter will reconstruct Beauvoir's theory of art through the novel's fictional characters who exemplify the internal struggle intellectuals undergo when facing the impasse: choices of creativity and purpose of life. Within Beauvoir's ethical theory, artists and writers have the potential to play an invaluable role in the improvement of society and the nurturing of individual freedom. While she shows little patience or sympathy for those intellectuals who do not choose the proper course, we can also imagine how strongly she felt the force of this impasse herself and attempted to find a compromise position between the two. This essay will attempt to exhume Beauvoir's "compromise" theory of art from her various writings. Section 1 will address the nature of the impasse for (French) intellectuals and the ways it is constructed out of the past. Section 2 will explore the types of creative productivity Beauvoir advocates while choosing, within the present moment, to move beyond the impasse. Section 3 will explore the artist's problem of self-doubt that is embedded within the process of choosing and that is inevitably encountered by artists as they face the future.

Out of the Past, An Intellectual Impasse

> *[Scriassine to Anne:] French intellectuals are facing an impasse. It's their turn now... Their art, their philosophies can continue to have meaning only within the framework of a certain kind of civilization. And if they want to save that civilization, they'll have no time or energy left over to give to art or philosophy.*
>
> —*The Mandarins*

This quote, from the first chapter of *The Mandarins*, defines the impasse of French intellectuals who stand on the brink of the future while being firmly rooted in the past. The image provided is of an amorphous French civilization forced to confront the momentous decision of defining its future. Beauvoir stages the problem to reveal the valuable role that historical context plays, revealing her main thesis that all intellectuals—replete with past values and principles and a history of prior actions and choices—face an impasse.

In the words of Scriassine (a writer within the novel who fled Russia and Austria to become a naturalized French citizen), Beauvoir initially poses the impasse as an exclusive either/or situation in which compromise is not an option. Against the backdrop of French civilization and its rich cultural achievements and, most importantly, situated squarely within the turmoil of post–World War II transitioning, the impasse for French intellectuals is staged as a choice between political activity that is meaningful to the worthy goal of improving society and the contrasting activity of art, literature, and philosophy devoid of political purpose. On this strict dichotomy, the latter has no aim other than the delight and pleasure taken in the pure aesthetic activity of the enterprise. Beauvoir invokes the classic, historical distinction between the aesthetic response to art (aestheticism: art for its own sake) and its nonaesthetic counterpart. In light of the aftermath of World War II and the spreading knowledge of the Holocaust, the psychological and political rebuilding of France is cast as the necessity of "saving" one's civilization. The urgency of this task elevates it to a level of importance above all others. It is a situation that forces a choice between ethical action, i.e., some form of *doing* in terms of political activity, and unethical inaction, considered here to be synonymous with aesthetics (and presumed to be apolitical).[1]

Scriassine pictures French intellectuals on the brink of their cultural future as if the French are the *only* ones facing such an impasse after World War II. He is engaged in conversation with Anne Dubreuilh, whom he has just met; she is a psychoanalyst and the wife of Robert Dubreuilh, sixty-year-old noted writer and political activist. Assessing other writers in the room, Scriassine ultimately focuses on the contrast of his own work (rooted as it is in the sociohistorical context of Russia and his recent travels to America) and that of Robert, whose work was already well known before the war and who has most recently been immersed in the pressing political activity of the French Resistance. Robert has been keeping a journal for three years, which Anne is urging him to publish. She wants him to continue writing in addition to engaging in political activity, believing he can do both at once. In contrast, Scriassine's initial remarks to Anne express deep skepticism:

> "To be able to continue taking an interest in things cultural in the face of Stalin and Hitler, you have to have one hell of a humanistic tradition behind you. But, of course," he went on, "in the country of Diderot, Victor Hugo, Jaures, it's easy to believe that culture and politics go hand in hand. Paris has thought of itself as Athens. But Athens no longer exists; it's dead." (Beauvoir [1954] 1991, 39)

Scriassine represents the viewpoint that motivates Beauvoir's theory of art—namely, the strict dichotomy between aesthetics (culture) and politics. He challenges Anne (and, indirectly, other writers in the room) to explain how an author might engage in meaningful political activity while still remaining a good author, or even a writer at all. That the two are incompatible is apparent from his remarks; if France sets about saving its cherished civilization, it will (ironically) have no time left for cultural production. If France is intent on maintaining an interest in "things cultural" under the belief that culture and politics are mutually compatible, it is self-deceived, much like the long-lost intellectuals of ancient Greece. Why is Scriassine so pessimistic, and how does Anne defend her husband against this negativity?

As the narrator of the novel, Anne is Robert's prime spokesperson and defender. Her immediate reaction is what might be considered "the compromise position" in that she responds, "This isn't the first time Robert's been active in politics. . . . And it never stopped him before from writing" (Beauvoir [1954] 1991, 39). Scriassine actually agrees, noting Robert's past successes, but he continues to hold fast to his prediction for the future:

> "The remarkable thing in all of Dubreuilh's works," said Scriassine, "is that he was able to reconcile high, esthetic standards with revolutionary inspiration. And in his own life, he attained an analogous equilibrium: he was organizing vigilance committees at the same time he was writing novels. But it's precisely that beautiful equilibrium that's now becoming impossible." (39–40)

Anne grapples with the harshness of his claim, presenting a rather weak defense—"You can count on Robert to devise some new kind of equilibrium"—but Scriassine is undaunted in his conviction: "He's bound to sacrifice his esthetic standards" (40). He reasons as follows:

> [R]ight now we're at the edge of a new era in which, for different reasons, humanity will have to grapple with all sorts of difficult problems, leaving us no time for the luxury of expressing ourselves artistically . . . among other things, art and literature will become nothing more than peripheral divertissements. (40)

Thus, for Scriassine, the arts become a luxury for which political imperatives allow no time. The war, he explains to Anne, was no ordinary war; it was "the liquidation of a society, and even of a world" by which—ultimately—the earth will be "ruled by either Russia or the United States," succumbing to either totalitarianism or imperialism (Beauvoir [1954] 1991, 40). In a paternalistic mode of advocating for the future success of France, he encourages writers like Robert to direct their energies exclusively toward political activities, in order to avoid the inevitability of either US or Russian domination. The model is his own written work—a treatise on Austria under the Nazis. At one point, he defends the political nature of his writing by saying, "Don't you think I dreamed of writing other kinds of books too? But it was out of the question" (39). Clearly, his own work reflected the lack of options he felt due to the pressure of the political weight upon him. Thus Beauvoir uses the character of Scriassine to set the parameters of both debates—political and aesthetic—that serve as the foundation of the novel. Anne is used as the foil to Scriassine, introducing the compromise position between the two political extremes. She advocates good literature that also gives rise to worthwhile political action.

Living within the Present: Aestheticism or Humanism?

> *[Scriassine to Anne:] To make something good of the future, you have to look the present in the face.*
>
> —*The Mandarins*

Beauvoir condemns artists who live the "comfortable, carefree esthete's life" in pursuit of literary success at any cost (Beauvoir [1954] 1991, 564). Avoiding their social responsibilities, these so-called salon-haunters produce artworks that stray far from the path of humanistic concern and improvement. While Anne is introduced to a room full of writers, she analyzes their transparent character and blatant intent to be a literary success:

> I had my doubts about their futures; you can't tell at first sight whether someone has or hasn't any talent, but you can tell quickly enough whether he has real reasons for wanting to be a writer. All those salon-haunters wrote only because it's difficult to do otherwise when you're bent on leading a literary life. But none of them really enjoyed the tête-à-tête with blank paper; they wanted success in its most abstract form, and, after all, that isn't the best way of achieving it. I found them as disagreeable as their ambition. (535)

Anne worries that even Robert, a writer of beautiful prose, might be mistaken for a "pure esthete" who is interested *only* in words and "things" for their own sake, and she insists that he truly is a humanist—a writer who delves deeply into personal relations and emotions, and who works toward the bigger goal of the betterment of humankind. It was Beauvoir's belief that such writing can affect other people by bringing about more individual freedom and ethical behavior on their part, resulting in the overall improvement of society. As the character Henri, also a writer, contends, "If you spend the best of your days trying to communicate with others, it's because others count . . ." (Beauvoir [1954] 1991, 385). Let us examine why Beauvoir believes in a theory of art predicated on social responsibility and how she suggests artists engage in such a valuable form of creativity.

Beauvoir takes the opportunity on numerous occasions to flesh out what she means by humanistic writing. Recall Anne's comment that a writer with a conscience, such as Robert, concerns himself with people's problems; he makes them his own and seeks a solution. Seeing it as his role to help "decide what can and what should be the role of an intellectual today," Robert adamantly advocates against silence and inaction ([1954] 1991, 434). "History isn't rosy. But since you can't escape it, you've got to seek the best way of living in it. In my opinion, abstention isn't the answer" (585). In assessing the role of literature, Robert asks, "Why do I write?"

> Because man doesn't live by bread alone and because I believe in the need for that added element. I write in order to capture all the things action ignores—the truths of the moment, the individual, the immediate. (435)

One of Beauvoir's main points in aesthetics is that writing and making art are vital to living an ethical life; these are the duties of creative intellectuals; there is no other choice. An American, Philip, says to Anne at one point, "Action—it's the obsession of every French writer!" ([1954] 1991, 563). Action, i.e., some sort of *doing*—provided it is of the right sort—is imperative. Beauvoir is very clear about this in *The Mandarins*, particularly as she tracks an array of characters to document the difficult transition from a world of war to one of peace. Scriassine prophesies that no one can live life as he did before the war. Everything has changed. Henri is another good example of an author struggling with the impasse of what to do after the war. Best friend to Robert, he attempts to return to writing but to stay out of the political fray, in spite of Robert's persuasion to the contrary. Henri relates to another colleague, Lambert, that he is indeed no longer the person he was before the war; he can no longer—in good conscience—write the same type of books he wrote before the war. But Lambert, caught up in the jubilation of the postwar moment, encourages him to write something light:

> You ought to show us the pleasant things on earth. And you could also make it a little more livable by writing beautiful books. It seems to me that that is what literature should do. (149)

But Henri's response is "Literature isn't necessarily pleasant," to which Lambert replies, "But it is! . . . Even things that are sad become pleasant when they're done artistically." He adds his reasons for believing so: "After all . . . we fought in the Resistance to defend the individual, to defend his right to be himself and to be happy. It's time now to reap what we sowed" (149). However, like Robert, Henri feels the weight of social responsibility calling him to action and away from writing that is pleasant and beautiful:

> The trouble is that there are several hundred million individuals for whom that right still doesn't exist. . . . I think it's precisely because we began to take notice of them that we can no longer stop. (149–50)

Thus human suffering necessitates intervention. Henri tries to write a novel about himself, but admits to having "nothing in common with the person he had been in 1935" ([1954] 1991, 150). Previously he had been selfish, thoughtless, stubbornly insistent on individualism, and politically indifferent (150). His apparent conversion to political awareness is in jeopardy more than once in the novel, however, e.g., when he wants to move to Italy to live a peaceful and idyllic life in the country.

Moreover, sometimes the main characters switch roles. When Robert becomes discouraged by his lack of success in politics, pronouncing "the impotence of French intellectuals" and the uselessness of writing literature, Henri is the one who bolsters his ego and encourages a return to the fight ([1954] 1991, 514, 517). Toward the end of the novel, they switch roles again; Henri asks, "[W]hat possible influence could we exert? None," while Robert responds, "Nevertheless there are still certain things we could do . . . there's a point on which we could organize some resistance" (574). Henri tries one more time to free his life from politics but again is unsuccessful and ends up writing an article on behalf of oppressed persons: exposing the injustices perpetrated upon them, citing the guilty government parties involved, and divulging information on those who abstained from preventing the atrocities. He condemns "the newspaper which remained silent and the millions of citizens who accepted that silence" (576). Somewhat content with his published essay, he concludes "Now, at least, there are a few thousand who know" and, shortly thereafter, agrees to be part of a committee to work more actively on a solution to the problem (576). He self-consciously and wryly acknowledges his predictable return to politics and political writing: "It's the same old story: every time you do something decent, it leads to new duties" (578).

The final page of the novel is illustrative as well. Anne contemplates suicide, depressed over a lost love in America (recall Beauvoir's dedication of the novel to Nelson Algren, with whom she recently had had an affair in the US). Her final thoughts are a fitting close to a life of observation, where she has watched her husband and her friend, Henri, move in and out of active political life. After reaffirming her own existence—"I am here . . . I am alive. Once more, I've jumped feet first into life"—she summarizes the dictum Beauvoir has intimated throughout: "Either one founders in apathy, or the earth becomes repeopled" ([1954] 1991, 610). Denying the possibility of apathy and indifference, Anne (and Beauvoir) insists on the urgency of people and their concerns. As Anne concludes, "[S]ince my heart continues to beat, it will have to beat for something, for someone" (610). Being useful to something or someone is the bottom line. Being apathetic, distanced, or aloof from others is less than ethical and an abnegation of one's social responsibilities.

That is the "why" of Beauvoir's humanistic theory of art—why artists should paint, why authors should write. How does she propose they go about it? What are her suggestions for the type of art that should be created? What qualifies as substantive, legitimate, and valuable creativity? As Nadine—the young female character and romantic interest of Henri—states when speaking of a controversial play Henri has written, "People damned well need to have their memories refreshed" ([1954] 1991, 370). Within the novel, Nadine most clearly expresses the philosophy of art that Beauvoir also revealed in her two nonfiction works, *The Ethics of Ambiguity* and *The Second Sex*.

Originating in the "tragic ambiguity" of the human condition, Beauvoir's brand of existentialism offers a "philosophy of ambiguity" replete with a well-developed ethics that encourages us to face the truths of the past in order to be more fully equipped—in terms of knowledge—to deal with the future. In *The Ethics of Ambiguity* Beauvoir writes of the bonds we share with others:

> In spite of so many stubborn lies, at every moment, at every opportunity, the truth comes to light, the truth of life and death, of my solitude and my bond with the world, of my freedom and my servitude and my significance and the sovereign importance of each man and all men. There was Stalingrad and there was Buchenwald, and neither of the two wipes out the other. Since we do not succeed in fleeing it, let us therefore try to look the truth in the face. ([1948] 1996, 9)

This is the crux of Nadine's claim within *The Mandarins* that people need to have their memories refreshed; Scriassine likewise says to Anne, "To make something good of the future, you have to look the present in the face."[2] Artworks are one means of accomplishing such a task. They freeze the past in the present, and provide a continuing means of communication into the future. Beauvoir clarifies in *The Ethics*:

> It is existence which they [artists] are trying to pin down and make eternal. The word, the stroke, the very marble indicate the object insofar as it is an absence. Only, in the work of art the lack of being returns to the positive. ([1948] 1996, 69)

As Anne proclaims in the novel, bringing attention to the longevity of art: "As for me, I value books greatly, too much perhaps. When I was an adolescent, I preferred books to the world of reality, and something of that has remained with me—a slight taste for eternity ([1954] 1991, 55).

Correctly crafted works of art lend a timelessness to truth and its import, and turn the negative human source of tragic ambiguity into something positive and life-fulfilling. In *The Ethics*, Beauvoir analyzes the experiential and enduring nature of art:

> One of art's roles is to fix this passionate assertion of existence in a more durable way . . . in telling a story, in depicting it, one makes

> it exist in its particularity with its beginning and its end, its glory or its shame; and this is the way it actually must be lived. ([1948] 1996, 127)

What does this entail on a practical level? Beauvoir's theory requires French intellectuals to shun the life of the aesthete, i.e., aestheticism. In *The Ethics*, she creates a vivid image of the Italian aesthete who is "occupied in caressing the marbles and bronzes of Florence," yet who is under the delusion that he remains above, or apart from, the political fray ([1948] 1996, 76). She also condemns her fellow countrymen during World War II who erroneously believed they remained neutral and apolitical: "[T]hose French intellectuals who, in the name of history, poetry, or art, sought to rise above the drama of the age, were willy-nilly its actors; more or less explicitly, they were playing the occupier's game" (76). Rather, she encourages active participation, active *doing* that brings positive results: "Let the 'enlightened elites' strive to change the situation of the child, the illiterate, the primitive crushed beneath his superstitions; that is one of their most urgent tasks" (138).

In *The Second Sex*, she even zeros in on particular styles of writing, advocating social motivation over aesthetic description, particularly for women who write. She bemoans the fact that past women writers—even those of note such as Willa Cather, Edith Wharton, Dorothy Parker, and Katherine Mansfield—have tended to "take inventory without trying to discover meanings"; they have excelled "in the observation of facts, " thereby succeeding only as "excellent reporters" (Beauvoir [1952] 1989, 710). Often writing extensively about nature (seen as "a kingdom and a place of exile"), they are "interested in things rather than in the relations of things" (710). Even the writings of Brontë and Woolf, whose works extend beyond description into more serious realms, suffer in comparison to male writers. Writing in the 1940s, Beauvoir suggests that women have not yet learned to write, because they have not yet learned to live.

> No woman wrote *The Trial, Moby Dick, Ulysses*, or *The Seven Pillars of Wisdom*. Women do not contest the human situation, because they have hardly begun to assume it. This explains why their works for the most part lack metaphysical resonances and also anger; they do not take the world incidentally, they do not ask it questions, they do not expose its contradictions: they take it as it is too seriously. (711)

Given that her assessment of women writers is couched in the numerous gender inequities explored in *The Second Sex*, women fall short of the sort of experiences and thought processes men have experienced and exploited for centuries. Summarizing her view on the arts, she says women are deemed less capable because of their prior lack of opportunities and continuing shortage of freedom.

> Art, literature, philosophy, are attempts to found the world anew on a human liberty: that of the individual creator; to entertain such a pretension, one must first unequivocally assume the status of a being who has liberty. The restrictions that education and custom impose on woman now limit her grasp on the universe . . . what woman needs first of all is to undertake, in anguish and pride, her apprenticeship in abandonment and transcendence: that is, in liberty. ([1952] 1989, 711)

Once that is accomplished, women can attain artistic heights equal to that of the greatest male writers. Beauvoir invokes the sentiment of the writer Marie Bashkirtsev, who said, "Without that liberty you cannot become a true artist" (712).

It is interesting to note that the few women that Beauvoir thought capable of artistically expressing themselves at high levels were those independent women who were actresses, dancers, and singers. In discussing their work, she adds another dimension to the characteristics by which great artists/writers/intellectuals excel. Not only must women be fully free to exercise their options, but they must also be free of narcissistic self-obsession in order to concentrate fully on the task at hand. In the last chapter of *The Second Sex*, Beauvoir outlines the hardships of being an independent woman, often caused by lack of passion and depth. She fails to exhibit "a taste for adventure and for experience for its own sake . . . a disinterested curiosity." She does not "lose herself in her projects" ([1952] 1989, 702). American women, in particular, "are not passionately concerned with the *content* of their tasks" but are rather distracted by their individual accomplishments. They chart their meager progress without striving for a larger goal (702). "Woman similarly has a tendency to attach too much importance to minor setbacks and modest successes; she is turn by turn discouraged or puffed up with vanity" (702). When success occurs, "They are forever looking back to see how far they have come, and that interrupts their progress" (702). What is required instead is no easy task:

> What woman essentially lacks today for doing great things is forgetfulness of herself; but to forget oneself it is first of all necessary to be firmly assured that now and for the future one has found oneself. Newly come into the world of men, poorly seconded by them, woman is still too busily occupied to search for herself. (702)

Thus we learn to unpack the mystery of "metaphysical resonances," a requirement for women writers in addition to justified anger. Women are encouraged to think beyond themselves, particularly beyond their own physicality and accomplishments, and to move their thoughts onto another plane. As Beauvoir notes in praising certain actresses, "A great actress will aim higher yet: she will go beyond the given by the way she expresses it; she will be truly an artist, a creator, who gives meaning to her life by lending meaning to the world" (703).

This explanation of the status of women's personal freedom, transcendence over tragic ambiguity, and conquering of natural narcissistic tendencies serves to demonstrate that when facing an impasse, no one can choose a path, much less an ethical path, if she is not fully free. This is undeniably the cornerstone of Beauvoir's existentialist ethics and her analysis of the oppression of women.

But it is also essential to the ethics of that choice that it be predicated upon a concern for others, and not be selfish or myopic. It must be rooted in humanism. Beauvoir advocates a passion for the task at hand and a deep investigation into its intricacies; these can bring one to a level of concern that focuses outside oneself. To make something good of the future, you have to look the present—including oneself—in the face. For women, particularly when Beauvoir was writing in the 1940s, this was a new experience, an unprecedented challenge. When a woman looks the present in the face, she must see herself fully free and sincerely committed to the welfare of others. Doing so will enliven a passionate humanism that rejects the comfortable, carefree life of the aesthete.

It is rather ironic that in *The Mandarins* Beauvoir puts the words of such lofty goals in the mouth of Paula, yet another female character, who was previously weak and dependent, and new to the task of writing: "I don't want to be taken for a society woman who writes for housewives" ([1952] 1989, 536). Beauvoir thus reveals her own worry that her writing might be judged as an example of aestheticism—lighthearted and pleasant—and not humanism. Is it not altogether fitting that she won the highest literary prize in France, the Prix Goncourt, for the novel that voices this concern?

Facing the Future: Artistic Self-Doubt

> *Now I see the impasse. Robert believes completely in certain ideas, and before the war we were positive that one day they would be realized. His whole life has been devoted to enriching them and preparing for their birth. But suppose they're never born? Suppose the revolution takes a different tack, turns against the humanism Robert has always defended? What can he do?*
>
> —Anne, in *The Mandarins*

Anne's realization of this dilemma for her husband clearly indicates not only how an impasse functions within one's personal history and past beliefs but also how internal questioning affects the conviction and confidence with which the actual choice is made. Devoting his life to humanism predisposes

Robert to a promising future, yet Anne imagines her husband at the threshold, looking forward, contemplating the political effectiveness of his actions in two opposing ways: as a man helping to build a future hostile to his values—an undesirable option, given his value system—and as a man insistent on his old values and ideals, yet totally ineffectual. Foreseeing the possibility of artistic and/or political failure, the process of choosing is, in advance, naturally affected by self-doubt and worry.

Beauvoir utilizes a different vocabulary than that of "impasse" when she has Robert utter the words, "We're at the crossroads" ([1954] 1991, 44) and "We're at a critical moment of history right now" (47). He dismisses the urgency of finishing his memoirs and rejects Anne's insistence that "First and foremost, you're a writer" by responding, "You know that's not true. . . . For me, the revolution comes first" (46). His determination is underscored when she suggests the compromise position "you can best serve the revolution by writing your books." In response he proclaims, "[F]irst we have to win the political battle" (47). To Anne, it is as if Scriassine's dire predictions—that Robert can no longer maintain "that beautiful equilibrium"—have come true. She abhors Robert's lack of interest in future literary work, particularly in light of a successful twenty-year history of writing. When he adds resolutely that "one book more or less on earth isn't as important as all that" (46) and "[t]here are a lot of things that have to be prevented before one can afford to amuse oneself writing books that no one might ever read" (47), Anne can only reply, "But a world without literature and art would be horribly sad" (47). She is at a loss to explain his shift in thinking.

Desperate to understand, she sets out to discover the essence of what she believes makes his work so successful, aesthetically and politically. Anne's musings allow the reader a deeper glimpse into Beauvoir's compromise theory of art.

> I reread all his novels. And I soon realized I had completely misunderstood them the first time. Dubreuilh gave the impression of writing capriciously, for his own pleasure, completely without motivation. And yet on closing the book, you felt yourself overwhelmed with anger, disgust, revolt; you wanted things to change. To read certain passages from his works, you would take him for a pure esthete; he has a feel for words, and he's interested in things for themselves, in rain and clear skies, in the games of love and chance, in everything. Only he doesn't stop there; suddenly you find yourself thrown in among people, and all their problems become your concern. That's why I'm so determined for him to continue writing; I know through my own experience what he can bring to his readers. There's no gap between his political ideas and his poetic emotions. ([1954] 1991, 56)

Her concluding statement summarizes Beauvoir's theory of ethical, valuable art. Upon further reflection, Anne comes to the conclusion that Robert must never stop writing (and that she must inevitably and unceasingly play a role encouraging him in his endeavor): "[A]fter all, writing is the thing he loves most in the world; it's his joy, his necessity; it's he, himself. Renouncing writing would be suicide for him" (56).

Anne defines Robert as a writer; his written work is his essence. But the humanistic goal of procuring and enhancing individual freedom while striving for improved conditions for society contains the seeds of potential failure that, on Beauvoir's aesthetic theory, can undermine even the best intellectual efforts. As we have seen, Anne (a psychoanalyst, not a writer, who is still interesting to consider as part of the discussion of lack of confidence) feels useless at the end of the novel and contemplates suicide. Paula, a woman too much in love with Henri (who has deserted her for a much younger Nadine), undergoes much improvement as she takes up writing but worries that she might be writing only for housewives. It is not surprising to see the female characters undergo serious self-doubt, since Beauvoir clearly highlighted woman's potential lack of confidence and feelings of inferiority in *The Second Sex* ([1952] 1989, 685, 699–701).

It is surprising, though, to see Beauvoir's two main characters—both male—also vacillate between moments of confidence and self-doubt. She suggests that even under the best of circumstances in which men "naturally" enjoy a position of social and cultural privilege, they too struggle with the erosion of artistic confidence and require support from their colleagues. Recall the shifting roles occupied by Robert and Henri throughout the novel; each attempted to carve out an individual creative niche while at the same time serving broader human interests. Each faltered and sometimes failed, and each questioned the entire enterprise. When they intermittently asked "What is the role of the intellectual today?" or "What use does literature serve?" they were searching for reasons to continue, as was Beauvoir herself. In light of the possibility of artistic failure (which differs from political failure, which is considered a failure to motivate others toward certain ideological goals and action), the two authors routinely struggled with the temptation to abandon writing. Clearly the worst form of artistic failure was the lack of readers; recall Henri's sense of satisfaction that at least a few thousand had read his article. Voiced even more stridently is the diatribe of a taciturn character named Lewis (Anne's American lover), who impatiently expresses his thoughts to Anne:

> Why does one write? For whom does one write? If you begin asking that, you stop writing! You write, that's all. And people read you. You write for the people who read you. It's writers nobody reads who ask themselves questions like that! ([1954] 1991, 480)

Beauvoir's words, "You write, that's all," can mislead one into thinking that facing the impasse is simplistic and easily negotiable. On the contrary, there is nothing simple about the artistic enterprise at all, whether for writers, artists, dancers, actors, or anyone else: male or female. Beauvoir, of course, knew this all too well.

Perhaps the most potent threat to Beauvoir's compromise position that aesthetics can successfully function alongside politics is embodied in Henri's thought, "You don't prevent a war with words" ([1954] 1991, 602). It is a revealing admission that, on the surface, appears to be about the potential failure of the written word on the printed page. Although it can be interpreted in that way, it reveals an even deeper level of pessimism about the enterprise of humanism itself as an ideology. For Henri thinks these words to himself while he is at home, in the quiet and safety of his study, knowing that Robert is out in public, speaking (words) at a political gathering. Beauvoir's description captures both the admiration and jealousy of Henri for his friend: "Henri pictured the hall filled with people, their faces upturned toward Dubreuilh, Dubreuilh bent toward them, throwing out words. There was no room in them for fear, for anguish; together, they were hoping" (602). Henri regrets the fact that he is not there, not actively engaged. "Dubreuilh was speaking out against the war, and Henri suddenly wished he were in his place. . . . Doing something, even though it were only speaking, was better than sitting by himself in a corner with that dark weight on his heart" (602). Thus, in spite of a lingering hope in the power of literature, one can never fully rely on the written or spoken word to prevent disaster. More cynically, one might not even be able to rely on the power of political speech as a worthwhile and successful motivating action. Each has a potential for failure and each requires strength of character that can withstand the nagging self-doubt that can cause not only the abandonment of one's project but, ultimately, the adoption of an avoidance tactic: taking refuge in indifference.

Henri's hesitation to commit to politics and political writing finally evolves into a mature dedication after he has a long discussion with Robert in which Dubreuilh declares, "There's one thing that you must realize . . . and that is that acceptance is always a matter of choice, love always a matter of preference" ([1954] 1991, 584). Henri interprets this to mean that life is about choosing, not about resignation, viz., accepting the *less* desirable choice. He notes the importance of "humanity," which is preferable to all else, in spite of its flaws. He comments on how appropriately the advice pertains to books and works of art, more so than to politics: "The books you want to write are never written, and you can amuse yourself by seeing a defeat in every masterpiece. And yet, we don't dream of a superterrestrial art; the works we prefer command our absolute love" (588).

This is Beauvoir's way of saying that an artist or writer is always beleaguered by self-doubt, can always see the possibility of failure within the work of art in terms of the effect it may have on an audience. However, the ultimate goal of serving humanity overrides this concern and inspires the artist to continue in her pursuit. As she states in *The Ethics*,

> Thus, we can set up point number one: the good of an individual or a group of individuals requires that it be taken as an absolute end of our action; but we are not authorized to decide upon this end *a priori*. . . . To put it positively, the precept will be to treat the other . . . as a freedom so that his end may be freedom. ([1948] 1996, 142)

Within the novel, Robert is seen by Anne as the link between the past, present, and future. She characterizes him as a leader who inspires others but who is still human, complete with doubts and failings. His goal is to enhance the freedom of others and, like other writers and artists, his attempts are valiant insofar as he tries as best he can, within his limitations. Anne lovingly describes him as a bridge between generations as she summarizes the high quality of his work:

> What exactly did he stand for to them? He was both a great writer and a man who was part of the vigilance committees, the anti-fascist meetings; an intellectual dedicated to the revolution without repudiating himself as an intellectual. For the old, he stood for the pre-war era; for the young, the present and its promises. He effected the unity of the past and of the future. And no doubt he was a thousand other things to them besides: each loved him in his own way. (Beauvoir [1954] 1991, 222)

Conclusion

This essay unearths a cohesive theory of the arts promoted by Beauvoir through three of her best-known literary sources. I cast it as a compromise theory in that it seeks to combine aspects of two opposing modes of creative choice, initially posed by Scriassine: the choice between culture (the "pure esthete" or the salon-haunter) and politics. Cast in historical terms within the subdiscipline of aesthetics, this is the well-known choice between aestheticism and humanism. Anne is the main promoter of the compromise theory of art. Robert and Henri are the primary creators of art, beleaguered with self-doubt, who face the impasse. Clearly, there is much more to the novel than what has been excavated at this point. Along with Beauvoir's *The Ethics of Ambiguity* and

The Second Sex, it is rich with suggestion, even provocation. For writers and artists, these are particularly inviting texts. They may contain seeds of truth that need to be faced by artists themselves, as they struggle with the impasse of their own future creativity.

Notes

1. The philosophical subdiscipline of aesthetics is known for historically characterizing works of art as interesting apolitical artifacts. This began with the eighteenth-century British empiricists, followed with Kant, and continued into the twentieth century with the aesthetic attitude theorists. The standard recommendation was the adoption of an aesthetic stance of "disinterestedness" toward the work of art: a stance that excluded ethical, religious, economic, or political interest. For a more thorough discussion of Beauvoir's theory of art in light of this historical trend, see Brand 2001–2.

2. It is interesting to note the number of times Beauvoir uses this phrase. For instance, Scriassine uses it again in discussing the seemingly narrow range of political choices open to the French: "You've got to look things squarely in the face" (Beauvoir [1954] 1991, 409). Henri describes friends who have suffered at the hands of the Stalinist regime as "throwing their memories in your face" (410). And Anne reflects, "Happy is he . . . who can look the truth of his life full in the face and rejoice in it; happy is he who can read it on friendly faces" (222).

Works Cited

Beauvoir, Simone de. [1948] 1996. *The ethics of ambiguity.* Translated by Bernard Frechtman. New York: Citadel Press.

———[1952] 1989. *The second sex.* Edited and translated by H. M. Parshley. New York: Vintage.

———. [1954] 1991. *The mandarins.* Translated by Leonard M. Friedman. New York: Norton and Co.

Brand, Peg. 2001–2. The aesthetic attitude in *The ethics of ambiguity. Simone de Beauvoir Studies* 18 (2001–2):45–48.

Contributors

Peg Brand is an artist and Assiociate Professor of Philosophy and Women's Studies at Indiana University–Purdue University Indianapolis. She specializes in feminist art criticism, art theory, and gender studies. She has edited *Beauty Matters* (2000), coedited *Feminism and Tradition in Aesthetics* with Carolyn Korsmeyer (1995), and most recently coedited a special issue of *Hypatia: A Journal of Feminist Philosophy* entitled "Women, Art, and Aesthetics" with Mary Devereaux (2003). She is currently working on a book manuscript with accompanying original illustrations entitled *Beauty Below the Surface: Feminist Visual Parodies.*

Thomas W. Busch is Professor of Philosophy at Villanova University. He specializes in existential and body politics with particular expertise in Sartre, Merleau-Ponty, and Ricoeur. He is the author of *The Power of Consciousness and the Force of Circumstances in Sartre's Philosophy* (1990) and *Circulating Being: From Embodiment to Incorporation; Essays on Late Existentialism* (1999). He is editor of *Participant Perspective: A Gabriel Marcel Reader* (1987) and coeditor, with Shaun Gallagher, of *Merleau-Ponty, Hermeneutics and Postmodernism* (1992).

Eleanore Holveck is Associate Professor of Philosophy at Duquesne University, where she specializes in the existentialism of Beauvoir and Sartre, Kantian ethics, phenomenology, and philosophy of literature. She is the author of *Simone de Beauvoir's Philosophy of Lived Experience: Between Literature and Metaphysics* (2002). Other publications include "Simone de Beauvoir's Desire to Express *la joie d'exister*," in *Philosophies of Desire*, ed. Hugh Silverman (2000); "The Birth of American Existentialism: Hazel E. Barnes, A Singular

Universal," *Philosophy Today* (1998); "Can a Woman Be a Philosopher? Reflections of a Beauvoirian Housemaid," in *Feminist Interpretations of Simone de Beauvoir*, ed. Margaret Simons (1995); and "*La ceremonie des adieux*: Simone de Beauvoir's Philosophical Interpretation of Death," *Simone de Beauvoir Studies* (1989).

Sonia Kruks is the Robert S. Danforth Professor of Politics at Oberlin College. She teaches political theory, including the history of political theory, contemporary European theory, and feminist theory, and she has served as director of the Women's Studies Program. She is the author of *Retrieving Experience: Subjectivity and Recognition in Feminist Politics* (2001), *Situation and Human Existence: Freedom, Subjectivity, and Society* (1990), and *The Political Philosophy of Merleau-Ponty* (1981). She is currently working on a book on Simone de Beauvoir's political thought.

William L. McBride is the Arthur G. Hansen Distinguished Professor of Philosophy at Purdue University and is currently the secretary general of FISP (Fédération Internationale des Sociétés de Philosophie). He specializes in social, political, and legal philosophy, and in nineteenth- and twentieth-century continental European philosophy, with a particular emphasis on Marx and Sartre. Among his books are *Fundamental Change in Law and Society: Hart and Sartre on Revolution* (1970), *The Philosophy of Marx* (1977), *Social Theory at a Crossroads* (1980), *Demokrati og Autoritet* (with response by Robert A. Dahl) (1980), *Sartre's Political Theory* (1991), *Social and Political Philosophy* (1994), *Philosophical Reflections on the Changes in Eastern Europe* (1999), and *From Yugoslav Praxis to Global Pathos: Anti-Hegemonic Post-Post-Marxist Essays* (2001).

Jen McWeeny is Instructor of Philosophy at John Carroll University, where she teaches epistemology and modern philosophy. Currently a doctoral candidate at the University of Oregon, McWeeny also holds an M.A. in French literature from the University of Oregon and an M.A. in comparative philosophy from the University of Hawai'i at Manoa. Her research interests are in the areas of emotion theory, epistemology, and phenomenology. She has published an introduction entitled "Martha C. Nussbaum" in *A Passion for Wisdom*, ed. Sybol Cook, Ellen Feder, and Karmen McKendryk (2004).

Shannon M. Mussett is Assistant Professor of Philosophy at Utah Valley State College, where she specializes in feminist philosophy, existentialism, and German idealism. Her publications include two introductions for *Simone de Beauvoir: Philosophical Writings*, ed. Margaret A. Simons (2004 and forthcoming), as well as an article on Hegel and Africa in *Tensional Landscapes*, ed. Gary Backhaus and John Murungi (2003), which is reprinted in the *APA Newsletter on Race* (2003). She is currently working on the dynamics of mediation in Beauvoir's writings, particularly in its relationship to the philosophies of Hegel and Lévi-Strauss.

Sally J. Scholz is Associate Professor of Philosophy at Villanova University. She specializes in social and political philosophy and feminist theory. In addition to a number of articles on Beauvoir, she has published on oppression, solidarity, and violence. Her books include *On de Beauvoir* (2000), *On Rousseau* (2001) and, co-edited (with Judith Presler), *Peacemaking: Lessons from the Past, Visions for the Future* (2000). She is currently completing a book on ethics and politics in solidarity. Scholz is the editor of the *American Philosophical Association Newsletter on Feminism and Philosophy.*

Ursula Tidd teaches in the Department of French Studies at the University of Manchester, UK, where she specializes in women's writing, especially that of Simone de Beauvoir, feminist and queer theory, and Holocaust studies. Her recent publications include "Le deuxième sexe, la conscience noire et la conscience lesbienne," in *Cinquantenaire du deuxième sexe*, ed. Christine Delphy and Sylvie Chaperon (2002); "Gendering Depersonalization: Simone de Beauvoir's 'Monologue' and R. D. Laing," *French Studies* (2002); "Simone de Beauvoir: The Subject in Question," *Nottingham French Studies* (2003); "For the Time Being: The Representation of Temporality in Simone de Beauvoir's Autobiography," in *The Existential Phenomenology of Simone de Beauvoir*, ed. Lester Embree and Wendy O'Brien (2001); and *Simone de Beauvoir*, an introduction to Beauvoir's thought (2004).

Karen Vintges is Senior Lecturer in Political and Social Philosophy at the Department of Philosophy of the University of Amsterdam. She specializes in social-political philosophy, feminist theory, and the philosophies of Beauvoir and Foucault. Among her publications are *Philosophy as Passion: The Thinking of Simone de Beauvoir* (1996 [originally in Dutch, 1992]); *Feminism and the Final Foucault* (1994), and several books in Dutch. Other selected publications include "Simone de Beauvoir: A Feminist Thinker for Our Times," *Hypatia* (1999) and "The Second Sex and Philosophy," in *Feminist Interpretations of Simone de Beauvoir*, ed. Margaret Simons (1995). She is both founder and editor of the journal *Krises.*

Gail Weiss is director of the Human Sciences graduate program and Associate Professor of Philosophy at George Washington University. Her areas of specialization are phenomenology and existentialism, feminist theory, and philosophy of literature. She is the author of *Body Images: Embodiment as Intercorporeality* (1999) and coeditor of *Thinking the Limits of the Body* (2003) and *Perspectives on Embodiment: The Intersections of Nature and Culture* (1999). She has published articles on Beauvoir in *Simone de Beauvoir Studies*, *Man and World*, and the *Journal of the British Society for Phenomenology* and is currently working on a manuscript entitled "Beauvoir's Ambiguities: Philosophy, Literature, Feminism."

Index